Getting Help from the Bible

Getting Help from the Bible

CHARLES M. CROWE

HARPER & BROTHERS
PUBLISHERS NEW YORK

GETTING HELP FROM THE BIBLE

Printed in the United States of America

FIRST EDITION

E-G

Library of Congress catalog card number: 57-7348

To the Memory of

Maud Davis McElvaney

and Estelle McElvaney

who found help from the
Bible to fight a good
fight and keep the faith

CONTENTS

PREFACE

THE PURPOSE OF this book is to help everyday people get help from the Bible for everyday problems. It is a book intended primarily for those who need to give or to receive help with the realities of life—a need never-ending and often acute.

This is not a book about the Bible itself. It is a book about life and living. It is not even Bible-centered. It is person-centered. There are many excellent volumes which shed light on the Scriptures and make the Bible more understandable. Some of them are listed in the back as an aid to further study. These chapters, however, lay no claim to being scholarly expositions of biblical truth. Their aim, rather, is to discuss, in as vivid, inspirational, and practical way as possible, some of the great biblical affirmations about life situations and questions. They are for people who honestly seek to catch some glimpse of the perspective of the word of God on the common ways of life.

In trying to fulfill this objective, I have illustrated the chapters with much human interest material drawn from historical, literary, and contemporary sources and authorities in order to help make the themes meaningful and relevant to the current scene. Also, I have drawn from both Old Testament and New Testament sources, allowing, without too much explanation, for differences between earlier and later writers in the Bible record. In choosing biblical material I have made an effort to select passages which have general acceptance and which are in keeping with the total message and spirit of the Bible. The Bible references are intended to be suggestive rather than a complete documentation of the subjects discussed. They are a starting point for further study of the Bible by the interested reader.

What we are trying to do here is to discover the will and mind of God for us through the writings of the Book. We want to see our full potential as the children of God, which is the perspective of the Bible. To be sure, there are many religionists and modern sophisticates who have outgrown the idea of authority in the Bible. For them the fact that the Bible says thus-and-so has lost its appeal. Actually, the Bible should never be thought of as a collection of divine rules and authoritative texts handed down from on high to make life easy or to frighten us into being good. And yet, in spite of those who sometimes misuse it at these points, the Bible does record man's struggle for a way of life under the providence of God which brings joy, peace, and triumph even in the face of defeat and disaster. The fact remains that the Bible has been a deep well of the water of life for uncounted millions. It is so today. I am concerned more with catching something of the over-all spirit and focus of the Bible than in meticulous, detailed documentation. It is my hope that many busy, perplexed, questioning people may find in these pages suggestions from the Book of Books, illuminated from the modern scene, which will help them in the living of these days. For, as my teacher Harry Emerson Fosdick put it, "The Bible is a searchlight, not so much intended to be looked at as to be thrown upon a shadowed spot."

I am greatly indebted to Dr. Edward P. Blair, Professor of New Testament Interpretation at Garrett Biblical Institute, for reading the manuscript and for many helpful suggestions. He is not to be held responsible, however, for any viewpoints or interpretations herein! My gratitude is due also to my secretary, Mrs. Mildred Lapp, for her careful work in preparing the manuscript for publication.

CHARLES M. CROWE

Wilmette, Illinois

Getting Help from the Bible

1 GETTING HELP FROM THE BIBLE

THE MEN WHO gave us the King James Version of the Bible met for that purpose originally at Hampton Court, outside London along the Thames. This former royal residence is noted for its beautiful gardens. One of the features of these gardens is a complicated maze made of high boxwood hedge. The path through the maze twists and turns in a baffling manner. There are many dead ends, and it is easy to get hopelessly lost. It is considered the most famous maze in the world.

Many visitors become so involved in the intricate paths that they cannot find their way out. However, there is a simple key to the maze by means of which no one need take a wrong turn. This key is found in Baedeker's guide book. The secret is "to turn to the right the first and second time that we have an option, and thereafter to the left." It is as simple as that! [1]

Most of us do not have to go to Hampton Court to get lost in a maze. For life itself is a path with many twists and turns. Dead ends are familiar to all of us. There are times when we do not know which way to go. We need help in times of decision and temptation. We need help in everyday problems. We need help in the baffling questions of existence and destiny. We need help in meeting the puzzling aspects of living with people in home and office and society.

There is a key to the maze of life and living. It is the Bible. It shows us the way to take. It warns us against the wrong turns. It gives direction, purpose, meaning, and strength to life as nothing else can. Uncounted millions have found help in its pages.

The Bible is the oldest printed book.

The very first book printed by Gutenberg, the inventor of movable type, was the Bible. It was completed in 1456, after six years of work. This Bible came in two massive folio volumes, sixteen inches tall, bound in solid oak boards covered with thick leather. It weighed twenty-eight pounds. There are only forty-six complete copies of this Gutenberg Bible known to exist today. The last one sold brought $600,000. The Gutenberg Bible is not only the oldest but also is said to be the most beautiful book ever printed.

Since Gutenberg's time the Bible has come to be the most widely read and circulated of all books. It is also the book most often banned, censored, burned, mutilated, and destroyed. It is the book most feared by tyrants. It is the most widely translated of all books, appearing in 1,118 different languages spoken by more than nine-tenths of the world's population. It is the only book that has been written on every material and by every method known. Its words have been cut in "stone, wood, bronze, silver, lead and iron, scratched on clay tablets and seals, and inscribed with stylus, quill, steel and brush, on leather, bark papyrus, linen, vellum, wax, parchment and paper."

Because of this universal availability of the Bible, it has been of more help to more people in more ways than any other book. This is because its message has been written in the hearts and affairs of men. We cannot ignore it because it is old or pass it by because it is difficult to understand. It is the most influential single volume in history. The many newer translations and the numerous excellent commentaries and helps make it a much less formidable book than in the time of Gutenberg. The oldest printed book is still the world's best seller year after year. This is no accident nor the result of clever promotion. It is because men find in it a way of life that inspires, redeems, and enlightens the human spirit.

What is the Bible?

The Bible is the highest and finest record of the revelation to man of the nature, mind, and will of God. It is likewise the record of the life and message of Jesus Christ, the divine Son of God and the Saviour of men. It is the matchless story of man's search for God in history and of God's concern for man. It is a book about religion. It is the one supreme source book of moral values and spiritual insights. It needs to be read with these things always in mind. Otherwise we are likely to get into difficulties.

Above the main door of the library at the University of Colorado these words are carved in stone: "Enter Here the Timeless Fellowship of the Human Spirit." However, a small card tacked on the door itself says: "Please use the side door." [2] This is a parable of much of our use of the Bible. The Book is plainly marked. It invites men to consider the majesty, righteousness, and fatherhood of God and the divine worth and brotherhood of man. It is the supreme library of divine truth with wide-open doors. Yet many people insist on coming in at some side door! We misunderstand the Bible when we become sidetracked by side issues. Incidental doctrine may be one of these side issues. Pseudo-science is another. Obscure history and secondary ritual are others, as are magic and materialism. A hard and fast literalism is a popular side door. These side entrances turn away many puzzled people who seek to know the truth but who are repelled by superstition or fanaticism.

There is plenty of plain, understandable, essential spiritual food in the Bible to supply every human need. Why worry around with fanciful interpretations of the dreams and visions of the Book? Why treat it as a good-luck charm or as a secret key to health and wealth? Why look for rules of thumb and debate about ecclesiastical lines of authority and ceremony? Rather, we need to look for the love of God and the saving spirit of Christ. When we do this, we find the Bible has for us a message of life and light, of peace and power, of truth and triumph.

Regardless of our opinion about Jonah and the whale, or its equivalent, we can still thrill to the voice of the prophets as they speak the voice of the most high God: "Let justice roll down as waters, and righteousness as a mighty stream" (Amos 5:24, ARV). No matter how we may interpret the Genesis story of Creation, we can exult with the psalmist as he shouts with joy: "If I take the wings of the morning, and dwell in the uttermost parts of the sea; even there shall thy hand lead me, and thy right hand shall hold me" (Ps. 139:9–10). Whatever our idea of the birth, person, and miracles of Jesus and the miracle stories of the Old Testament, we can all find the inner peace and calm of the offer of the Master: "Let not your heart be troubled, neither let it be afraid" (John 14:27). Even if we cannot understand difficult passages, we can submit our wills and consciences to the charge of St. Paul: "Watch ye, stand fast in the faith, quit you like men, be strong" (I Cor. 16:13).

Richard G. Moulton said: "Whatever other uses we may wish to make of the Bible, our first and paramount duty is to read it." Our second duty certainly is to read it intelligently. To do this we must try to understand it. The word Bible comes from the Greek *biblia*, meaning "papyrus scrolls." The Bible is a library of sixty-six books, written on two continents, in three languages, by a hundred authors, scattered over a thousand years. In the Bible there is biography, history, poetry, drama, letters, and stories. We need to ask four questions of each book. First, who wrote it? Second, when was it written? Third, to whom was it written? Fourth, for what purpose was it written? To try to read the Bible straight through is an unfruitful experience for most people. The average person in seeking help from the Bible will find rich treasures in the Psalms, in some of the prophets such as Isaiah, Micah, and Jeremiah, in the Four Gospels, and in the letters of Paul. If we search these books particularly with an open mind and a reverent heart, we will find something of the greatness of God, the love of the Saviour, and the signposts of life abundant and eternal.

The Bible is the most important book in human history.

Free men in a free nation need to be grateful for the open Bible in which anyone may find the way of life. We are likely to take the Bible too much for granted. We need to know that it is only as men do get help from its pages that life can be free, clean, and significant.

In the *Dictionary of Foreign Words*, put out by the Russian State Publishing House, in Moscow, there appears this Communist definition of the Bible: "A collection of fantastic legends without any scientific support . . . full of dark hints, historical mistakes and contradictions."

Back in October, 1941, the announced program for the Nazi National Church Reich included this statement among the instructions: "Remove from all altars the crucifix, the Bible and the Holy Pictures. On the altar will be our holy book—*Mein Kampf*—and on its left a sword." Another Nazi textbook about the same time, *Bolshevism in the Bible*, by Hans Hauptmann, stated on page 78: "The teaching of mercy and love of one's neighbor is foreign to the German race, and the Sermon on the Mount is an ethic for cowards and idiots."

Ecclesiastical as well as political tyrants hate the open Bible. Thirty years after the death of John Wycliffe, the translator of the Bible into

English, an enactment of law in England provided that any who read the Bible in English should "forfeit lant, catel, lif, and goods from their heyers forever." [3]

Edicts like these are possible only when the Bible remains dusty and unused among the people. Or when it is forcibly kept from them. For the Holy Bible, the complete, undoctored, ordinary Bible, is the original charter of human freedom and the master blueprint of human decency. When the Bible is widely read the causes of liberty and goodness are secure.

J. Richard Green, in his *Short History of the English People,* said: "No greater moral change ever passed over a nation than passed over England during the years of the reign of Queen Elizabeth. England became the people of a book, and that book was the Bible. It was read in the churches, and it was read at home, and everywhere its words, as they fell on ears which custom had not deadened to their force and beauty, kindled a startling enthusiasm. . . . Elizabeth might silence or tune the pulpits, but it was impossible for her to silence or tune the great preachers of justice and mercy who spoke from the Book which the Lord again opened to the people. . . . The whole temper of the nation was changed. . . . A new moral and religious impulse spread through every class." [4]

The Bible is always man's surest defense against tyranny. The choicest values of democratic government, public education, the Christian home, and public and private integrity are based upon a wide reading of the Bible. The Bible should be central in our faith in this fateful hour of the world's life.

Thomas Marshall showed deep insight when he said: "If I were to have my way, I would take the torch out of the hand of the Statue of Liberty in New York harbor and in its place put the open Bible." Years later another great American, Woodrow Wilson, expressed the same idea in these words: "America was born a Christian nation. America was born to exemplify that devotion to the elements of righteousness which are derived from Holy Scripture. . . . I ask of every man and woman that from this time on they well realize that part of the destiny of America lies in their daily perusal of this great Book—that if they would see America free and pure, they would make their own spirits free and pure by the baptism of the Holy Scripture."

The Bible, therefore, is much more than a crutch to help men with their personal problems. It is concerned with those issues that make for a more just and brotherly society. Yet it cannot build a better world until it makes better men. Only as it helps us to become more like the children of God can we advance the cause of the Kingdom of God on earth.

Why read the Bible?

An old story tells of a time when England woke up one day to find that the English Bible was gone. All traces of its influence had been wiped out. The results were unbelievable. Much great literature was hardly readable. Everyday speech lost many of its choicest words and phrases. Music, art, and architecture suffered the loss of their most beautiful expressions.

Most of all, however, the removal of the Bible was noticeable in the lives of the people and in the temper of the time. Life became vulgar and mean. Men became irresponsible. Values became blurred. "Something fine, high, and fair" had gone out of society.

Something like this has taken place in America. For to neglect the Bible is to lose it. The Bible is largely unread. The great mass of our young people grow up in ignorance of its contents and meaning. We are no longer the people of a Book. The evidence is all about us. Law often loses its authority. High moral idealism has lost its appeal to many. Literature frequently is filthy. For many brilliant writers life is a disease and religion a dope.

We are a literate people. But we often overlook the Christian values that give literacy meaning and purpose. For instance, we read every month in America more than nine million pulp magazines of love and adventure; nearly eight million true confessions magazines; over three million detective story magazines; nearly eleven million movie magazines; and more than twenty-five million comic books. Fifty-five million a month! [5] No wonder secular things hold sway! No wonder gambling syndicates take over without protest! No wonder narcotic rings prey upon our youth!

All of this is to say that those who have lost the Bible must find it again. Nothing can take its place. We are lost if we do not have the sense of God, the moral fiber, and the guidance for living that the Bible alone can bring to the human heart. As Joseph Fort Newton put it: "There is a spirit in the Bible which, if it gets into men, makes them tall of soul, tender of heart, just, gentle, patient, faithful in life and fearless in death." [6] This is reason enough to read the Bible these days. For it is these things that modern man, bewildered and afraid, desperately needs and deeply craves. It is this kind of help we can get from the Bible.

How can the Bible help us?

To get help from the Bible we will let its basic message speak to our deepest needs. Charlton Heston was cast in the role of Moses in Cecil B. DeMille's motion picture *The Ten Commandments.* But even on location he found it difficult to get into the Old Testament mood. For instance, the original Moses climbed Mount Sinai on foot. Whereas, for the movie shots, Heston was taken up the mountain three times a day by helicopter!

So it is that our times are strangely different from Bible times. How is it that the words of the Bible after two thousand years can have authority for us in an atomic and helicopter age? The answer lies in the fact that the needs of the human heart are much the same today as in those days. The deepest of these needs is the need of God. And in the Bible we find the supreme record of man's encounter with God in history.

We must remember that the Bible is no mere abstract, detached philosophy of life. As Bernhard W. Anderson put it in *Rediscovering the Bible:* "Situated strategically at the crossroads of the ancient world, Palestine was the very storm center of life. The Bible, therefore, does not come from a sheltered valley of Shangri-la; its message was forged out of circumstances in which people felt the maximum of tension and suffering. This book speaks out of the immediate and concrete realities of history, where men doubted and believed, hated and loved, despaired and hoped. Its message comes from the depth of life and speaks to the depth within us. It finds us where we are living." [7] Whoever we are and wherever we live the Bible has a message for each one of us.

Restive and unsure, we find in the Bible our only real security. "He that dwelleth in the secret place of the most High shall abide under the shadow of the Almighty" (Ps. 91:1).

Burdened with the heavy weight of sin, we find forgiveness, release, and redemption in the pages of the Book: "By grace are ye saved through faith; and that not of yourselves: it is the gift of God" (Eph. 2:8).

Saddened and sorrowful with the pain and suffering of life, we find inner peace and comfort in the word of God: "Peace I leave with you, my peace I give unto you" (John 14:27).

Strongly tempted with the lusts of the flesh and the lure of gold, we find both warning and strength from the Bible: "Take unto you the whole armour of God, that ye may be able to withstand in the evil day, and having done all, to stand" (Eph. 6:13).

Often barren of soul and cynical of mind, we hear above the clamoring voices of the age the wise and sure voice of the Master: "I am the way, the truth, and the life" (John 14:6).

Weak and weary, worried and anxious of spirit, we learn here the calm assurance of the nearness and love of God: "The Lord is my helper, and I will not fear what man shall do unto me" (Heb. 13:6).

Deeply concerned with the fate of our troubled nation and world, we discover the key to our problem in the Bible: "Righteousness exalteth a nation: but sin is a reproach to any people" (Prov. 14:34).

So it is. We will never get lost in the maze of life or the maze of the Scriptures so long as we keep in view and are guided by the eternal, clearly visible signposts of righteousness, love, and faith. These confront our minds and consciences with the claims of a righteous and loving God, humbling us with penitence, exalting life with vision and power from above.

How can we know that there is a God?
Does God exist in a cruel and evil world?
Where can we find God today?

2 WHEN WE WONDER WHERE GOD IS

MOST OF US do not think much of ordinary ground. It is the exclusive ground or the oil-ground or the gold-ground or the fertile-ground that seems valuable. However, in recent years, this idea has been exploded. Ordinary ground has been made to yield minerals, chemicals, and medicines of tremendous value. Even rocky ground has come into its own. Harrison Brown tells us, for instance, that "one hundred tons of average igneous rock contain, in addition to other useful elements, 8 tons of aluminum, 5 tons of iron, 1200 pounds of titanium, 180 pounds of manganese, 70 pounds of chromium, 40 pounds of nickel, 30 pounds of vanadium, 20 pounds of copper, 10 pounds of tungsten, and 4 pounds of lead." [1] Brown predicts that before long a sizable amount of these materials can be taken out with profit.

The ground we stand on is valuable ground! God made it that way. Let no one despise it. Desert ground can be irrigated. Barren ground can be fertilized. Hard ground can be cultivated. Rocky ground can be mined. Rented ground can be as productive as if we owned it. The back-yard plot of a city tenement can be made a garden spot of beauty. A piece of wasteland may hide uranium.

If this is true in fact it is also true in figure. Its truth in the world of nature is symbolic of its truth in the realm of the spirit. Moses found this to be so. He was tending the flock of his father-in-law Jethro. He had led them to the back side of the desert. There was the sacred mountain. It must have seemed an unlikely place to find God. But the record says that the Angel of the Lord appeared to Moses in the flame of fire in a nearby bush. Moses went closer and saw that the bush was not consumed. And God called to him. When Moses answered, God said to him: "Put off thy shoes from off thy feet, for the place whereon thou standest is holy ground" (Exod. 3:1–5). This was the holy place but to Moses it no doubt looked like ordinary earth.

Centuries later in the time of Jesus there were many who insisted on certain signs that would come to announce the end of the world and the coming of the Kingdom. These signs were thought of as unusual portents or catastrophes of nature. The Pharisees thought they might trip up Jesus by asking him when the Kingdom should come. But the Master calmly replied: "The kingdom of God is not coming with signs to be observed; nor will they say, 'Lo, here it is!' or 'There!' for behold, the kingdom of God is in the midst of you" (Luke 17:20–21 RSV). That is to say, wherever he was, there was the Kingdom. God was already in their midst and they knew it not.

Thus the Bible speaks both of the holiness of God who is found in certain sacred places and of the ever-present reality of the Spirit and Kingdom of God. We find that the divine presence is not altogether reserved for some sacred mountain, ark, or temple. Nor in some dimly viewed utopia of the future. God is wherever we are. And we find God where we are now or we are likely not to find him at all. We do not need a sign or a burning bush to tell us that God is here. The Kingdom of God exists wherever men are confronted with God, and respond to God. And that may take place anywhere. This message of the Bible helps us discover on our own patch of ground the hidden treasures of the spirit. As man's search for God is recorded in the Bible we find that man does not need angelic messengers and priestly ceremonies to find him. Rather, men find that the "awful and august God" is actually seeking us and that he dwells in the humble and contrite heart. Hosea and Amos were among those who sensed vividly the nearness and availability of God long before New Testament times.

We can find God wherever we are.

I Kings 18, 19 is the story of the prophet Elijah who pitted his faith in God against the prophets of Baal, and proved his point by calling down fire from heaven to consume the sacrifice on Mount Carmel. This miracle converted the early Israelites. However, the prophet was to learn later at Horeb that the Lord is not to be found in the wind and the fire. This experience is an example of the earlier expression of our faith that the exalted God is also present among men and suggests the fuller development of that faith into the spiritual presence of God in the hearts of his people.

The cynics who question the nearness of God in our kind of world need to take another look. We literally are surrounded by evidences of his presence. This is one of the glorious testimonies of the Bible. "The earth is full of the goodness of the Lord" (Ps. 33:5 ff.). Jesus declared, as we have seen, that the Kingdom is in our midst. And Paul, in his address to the men of Athens, told them that they were merely superstitious in worshiping an Unknown God. "God that made the world and all things therein, seeing that he is Lord of heaven and earth, dwelleth not in temples made with hands; Neither is worshipped with men's hands, as though he needed any thing, seeing he giveth to all life, and breath, and all things; And hath made of one blood all nations of men for to dwell on all the face of the earth, and hath determined the times before appointed, and the bounds of their habitation; That they should seek the Lord, if haply they might feel after him, and find him, though he be not far from every one of us: For in him we live, and move, and have our being" (Acts 17:24–28a). To be sure, God is a great God, infinite, holy, and majestic, as Old Testament writers declared. But likewise he dwells within the heart. Here is one of the most helpful facets of our faith. "For thus saith the high and lofty One that inhabiteth eternity, whose name is Holy; I dwell in the high and holy place, with him also that is of a contrite and humble spirit" (Isa. 57:15).

This is a biblical truth that has been confirmed rather than dimmed with the passing of the centuries. In fact, the findings of modern science only serve to underline the fact. For we can hope to understand the intricate wonder-world in which we live only as we see in it the light of a creative God of law and order and power. God is truth. And in every new truth we can find God. God makes provision for our needs in wonderful ways we are just now finding out. For instance, in laboratories the world over scientists are experimenting with a dark green substance said to be every bit as important as atomic energy. It is a powder made from billions of single-celled plants called algae. This is an elemental form of life found everywhere. It is edible and contains protein, fat, starch, vitamins, and every other food needed to sustain life. It exists in seas and lakes and ponds and can be raised in vast quantities anywhere. It may be the source of food for uncounted billions in the future.

Who put the algae in the oceans? Who put the uranium in the hills? Who arranged the delicate balance of oxygen in the air? Who gives the spark of life to all living things? Who gives the bird its song? From whence comes a mother's love? The voice of conscience? The persistence of the moral law? Why do men sacrifice for the causes of justice, freedom, and righteousness?

There is one basic answer to these questions and a thousand others like them. "Every good gift and every perfect gift is from above, and cometh down from the Father of lights, with whom there is no variableness, neither shadow of turning" (James 1:17). Our God is not an absentee God. He does not hide from us. He is where we are. The materials for our own growth and salvation are all about us. The solutions to our problems are waiting for us to use them. Our personal happiness and well-being are always within our own grasp because they depend upon our capacity to find God where we are.

Our difficulty is not that God is not present among us. Our trouble is that he has become obscured with the passing years and we do not have the eyes of the spirit to see him. The great creative power of the universe of nature and man is our God and our Father. He knows us better than we know ourselves. He confronts us on every hand. He searches us out even as we seek him. He surrounds us with his all-pervading presence. "O Lord, thou hast searched me, and known me. Thou knowest my downsitting and mine uprising, thou understandest my thought afar off. Thou compassest my path and my lying down, and art acquainted with all my ways. For there is not a word in my tongue, but, lo, O Lord, thou knowest it altogether. Thou hast beset me behind and before, and laid thine hand upon me. . . . Whither shall I go from thy spirit? or whither shall I flee from thy presence? If I ascend up into heaven, thou art there: if I make my bed in hell, behold, thou art there. If I take the wings of the morning, and dwell in the uttermost parts of the sea; Even there shall thy hand lead me, and thy right hand shall hold me. If I say, Surely the darkness shall cover me; even the night shall be light about me" (Ps. 139:1–11).

The Herndon Hall Hotel in the North London suburb of Herndon is an old building erected in 1652. The lounge is a gloomy room paneled in dark veneer. On the ceiling of the room was an old painting, partly hidden by dirt and grime. In January, 1954, the manager of the hotel had the picture cleaned by an artist. As the scum was scraped off, it proved to be a finely detailed picture that swirled with gods, cherubs, and figures representing four continents. It turned out to be a painting by a Venetian master, Giovanni Battista Tiepolo, originally hung in the Bishop's palace at Wurzburg, Germany. The hotel promptly sold it for ten thousand pounds! Research showed that David Garrick had hung the picture in the Herndon room, originally his home, in 1756. For nearly two hundred years countless numbers of people had sat in the presence of a masterpiece without knowing it was there!

It is often so with us. We look with unseeing eyes every day on the masterpieces of God. And yet endlessly speculate as to his existence and where he may be found! Our fighting, lusting, hating, commercialized world covers with grime the things of God. But we can see what we have the eyes to see. And with the help of the Bible we can cut through the soot and discover that the very ground we stand on is holy ground. There is no leaf or flower, or hospital or court of justice, or home or shop or human soul in which we may not find evidences of the presence of the eternal God. He is not confined to the Temple, nor is he to be found in lifeless idols. "And what agreement hath the temple of God with idols? for ye are the temple of the living God; as God hath said, I will dwell in them, and walk in them; and I will be their God, and they shall be my people. Wherefore come out from among them, and be ye separate, saith the Lord, and touch not the unclean thing; and I will receive you, and will be a Father unto you, and ye shall be my sons and daughters, saith the Lord Almighty" (II Cor. 6:16–18).

It is the Apostle also who sums up for us the tremendous assurance of the never-failing presence of God now and forever. "For I am persuaded, that neither death, nor life, nor angels, nor principalities, nor powers, nor things present, nor things to come, Nor height, nor depth, nor any other creature, shall be able to separate us from the love of God, which is in Christ Jesus our Lord" (Rom. 8:38–39).

We can serve God whatever we do.

Through the long years a sharp difference has often been drawn between secular pursuits and the service of God. Some men and some religious groups have seen religion as a separate and distinct area or compartment of life. Thus the service of God often becomes either a monastic dedication or merely a token thing. The counting of beads. The lighting of candles. The refusal to eat certain meats on certain days. The payment of dues to the church. The attendance upon some special service or mass of the church. These routine religious duties oftentimes substitute for the true service of God.

The Old Testament prophets and seers spoke strongly against the religious customs of the Jews in this regard. They put an ethical content into ritualistic religion. "Wherewith shall I come before the Lord, and bow myself before the high God? shall I come before him with burnt offerings, with calves of a year old? Will the Lord be pleased with thousands of rams, or with ten thousands of rivers of oil? shall I give my firstborn for my transgression, the fruit of my body for the sin of my soul? He hath shewed thee, O man, what is good; and what doth the Lord require of thee, but to do justly, and to love mercy, and to walk humbly with thy God?" (Mic. 6:6–8). And in the New Testament we find Jesus resisting the same traditions in condemning the hypocrites who were careful about their ritual observances but who missed the spirit of true religion. "Woe unto you, scribes and Pharisees, hypocrites! for ye pay tithe of mint and anise and cummin, and have omitted the weightier matters of the law, judgment, mercy, and faith: these ought ye to have done, and not to leave the other undone" (Matt. 23:23). We also hear him saying: "A good man out of the good treasure of his heart bringeth forth that which is good; and an evil man out of the evil treasure of his heart bringeth forth that which is evil: for of the abundance of the heart his mouth speaketh. And why call ye me, Lord, Lord, and do not the things which I say?" (Luke 6:45, 46). "Not every one that saith unto me, Lord, Lord, shall enter into the kingdom of heaven; but he that doeth the will of my Father which is in heaven. Many will say to me in that day, Lord, Lord, have we not prophesied in thy name? and in thy name have cast out devils? and in thy name done many wonderful works? And then will I profess unto them, I never knew you: depart from me, ye that work iniquity" (Matt. 7:21–23).

And Paul speaks out against the same practices in protesting against Jewish ritual practices. "For the kingdom of God is not meat and drink; but righteousness, and peace, and joy in the Holy Ghost" (Rom. 14:13–23).

Thus the Bible tries to bridge the gap between the sacred and the secular. In the life and teaching of the carpenter Jesus we find that true religion encompasses all of life. If, in the truest sense, the place we stand on is holy ground, and if the Kingdom is in our midst, then any useful, creative, honorable work may be blessed of God and may be done as in his service.

Just outside the walls of the Augustinian monastery of Altbrunn in Austria is a small garden plot. During the 1850's and '60's it was filled each spring with hundreds of pea plants in addition to flowers. Working patiently among these pea plants year after year was a young monk. With fine forceps he opened the white and violet blossoms of the peas, and took a camel's-hair brush and dusted the stigma with pollen from another pea plant. Finally he wrapped the treated blossom in a little paper bag. The monk's name was Gregor Y. Johann Mendel. The work he so industriously carried on was later to show the whole world how all living characteristics are passed along from parent of offspring. For here it was that Gregor Mendel in a quiet secluded garden at his own back door discovered the laws of heredity.[2] It is doubtful if he served God any more effectively before the altars of the monastery chapel. He proved among other things that even a small garden spot is holy ground.

We need to be reminded, therefore, that a garden is as likely a place to serve God as a monastery. We are not shut out from the service of God because we can not do heroic things for him. We do not have to make pilgrimages to shrines or bow before images to demonstrate our devotion to his truth and our awareness of his loving care. Even in plain and restricted places we are surrounded by opportunities to serve God and our fellow men. The extent of our service usually is limited only by the extent of our desire to serve.

The call of God to men to serve him comes in many ways. Sometimes it comes suddenly and in a vision. Like the experience of Isaiah who spoke of a time when king Uzziah died and God appeared to him in great glory. He felt unclean in the majestic presence. But his lips were touched and his sin was forgiven. It was then that he heard "the voice of the Lord, saying, Whom shall I send, and who will go for us? Then said I, Here am I; send me" (Isa. 6:1–8). Paul had a somewhat similar experience on the Damascus road. However, for the most part, such dramatic events are rare, both in the Bible and in the lives of people today. Wherever there is human need, suffering, ignorance, and oppression we find God calling to men to serve him.

Christians need to come alive to the wonderful possibilities that exist right where they live. As Edward Wagenknecht put it: "Perhaps the truth is that there are no commonplace experiences but only commonplace people. To commonplace people the coming of Christ itself may be commonplace. . . . On the other hand, everything that happens to the extraordinary person is extraordinary. Thoreau traveled extensively in Concord. Jane Austen's was the limited village experience of an English spinster, yet she became one of the great novelists of the world." [3]

No Christian need be a commonplace person. We may give to routine duties a sacramental quality. The pain of the world comes to life in the need of a neighbor. Good causes come daily to every doorstep. The work of every hand may be done as an offering unto God. It is this that glorifies the commonplace and gives wings to weary feet.

The story of Pentecost (Acts 2) may well be seen as a demonstration of the reality of the unseen God in human lives. People of many races and tongues heard and understood one another because they were brought under the spell of the divine Spirit. In his speech at the time, Peter interpreted the predictions of miraculous events made by Joel to show that these were being spiritually fulfilled through Jesus. Pentecost dramatically showed the power of the Spirit of God at work among men. But we do not need to wait for miraculous phenomena to discover it.

We can come to God whenever we will.

God is accessible to any of his children at any time. And we may come to him just as we are. This is the message of the Bible, especially the New Testament. For the gulf between man and the most high God is bridged by Jesus Christ. But ecclesiastical tyrants have denied it. In Bible times, in the early church, and even today there are those who put the priest or ceremonial rites between man and God. But the way to salvation and the things of the spirit are not subject to the whims of the professional ecclesiastics.

"Ho, every one that thirsteth, come ye to the waters, and he that hath no money; come ye, buy, and eat; yea, come, buy wine and milk without money and without price. Wherefore do ye spend money for that which is not bread? and your labour for that which satisfieth not? hearken diligently unto me, and eat ye that which is good, and let your soul delight itself in fatness. Incline your ear, and come unto me: hear, and your soul shall live" (Isa. 55:1–3a). The voice of the prophet becomes a living experience in the New Testament. "God is a Spirit: and they that worship him must worship him in spirit and in truth" (John 4:24). "Where two or three are gathered together in my name, there am I in the midst of them" (Matt. 18:20). In other words the reality of God does not depend upon nationality, symbols, or rituals but upon the penitent and seeking human heart.

It is not given only to the chosen few or to the wise and saintly to find God. The sinner, the cynic, and the troubled of spirit may also come to him and find in him new life and salvation for the soul. All that is needed, said the Master, is the simple, trustful spirit of a child. Our possession of the things of God depends on our capacity to receive them. They are here for us all. And they are the reward of those who seek God. For such the presence of God is already in their midst.

One time the disciples rebuked those who tried to bring young children to Jesus. But the Master did not like this. He declared that the eagerness and openness of the children were like the Kingdom. "Let the children come to me, do not hinder them; for to such belongs the kingdom of God. Truly, I say to you, whoever does not receive the kingdom of God like a child shall not enter it" (Mark 10:13–15, RSV). The Kingdom, that is, was not for the proud and the self-righteous, the religious experts, and those who had a sense of national superiority over others. Rather, it was available any time to those who had a sense of dependence and a willing receptivity for it, just as children have. No one has a corner on the religion of Jesus.

We like to think that the great truths and the great discoveries are reserved for the experts and the professionals. This is not so. Amateurs make discoveries, too. Take radio, for instance. E. F. McDonald, Jr., president of the Zenith Radio Corporation, said one time: "Youthful amateurs who did not know there were rules about how things should be done, tried unorthodox stunts and made nearly every basic discovery in the development that has given America the finest in radio. What the industry's engineers and laboratories have done is to refine discoveries of amateurs." Marconi was an amateur playing with a toy when he developed the world's first practical equipment for sending and receiving radio signals. Lee DeForest was an experimenting amateur when he invented the audion tube which opened the door to broadcasting. Edwin H. Armstrong was a college student when he invented the regenerative circuit. His father would not even give his son money to patent it. Later the youngster sold the invention to Westinghouse for $350,000. The nation's pioneer commercial broadcasting station, KDKA, Pittsburgh, began as an amateur station built by a young amateur, Frank Conrad. Philo Farnsworth, the father of television, was a schoolboy of sixteen in Rigby, Idaho, when he diagrammed the principles of television on the blackboard. His explanation was so accurate and clear that the teacher's testimony years later stood up in court.[4]

It is certainly so also in the discovery of the laws and truth of God. They may seem past finding out. Yet they are as available to the amateur as to the professional. Indeed, it is often only as we bypass our intellectual hurdles that we find God. It becomes necessary sometimes for us to ignore our doubts and the limitations set by the experts. We must experiment with our faith on our own. Then we will find that it is not theological doctrine or ecclesiastical forms that keep us from God. These are the excuses we offer. Rather it is such things as anger and selfishness, prejudice and pride that shut him out. "Draw nigh to God, and he will draw nigh to you. Cleanse your hands, ye sinners; and purify your hearts, ye doubleminded" (James 4:8, ARV). He is ready and waiting for us whenever we choose to come. Indeed, his claims are all about us. Most of the great spirits of the Bible were not professional ecclesiastics. Burning bushes are everywhere.

Lillian Lauferty tells of a time in her life when it seemed as if God had deserted her. The doctor had told her she would lose the use of her arm in a month. Her mind was bitter with resentment and frustration. As she was out walking near her home trying to get hold of herself, she suddenly came upon a blooming forsythia bush just as the sun lighted its beauty from behind the dark clouds. "I looked at it," she said, "and I knew that God was in this place. And I heard a voice saying, 'I am the resurrection and the life.' "[5]

In many a forsythia bush beside the way we, too, may hear the voice of God claiming us for his own. And if we want to, we may find him there. For the ground we stand on is holy ground, too. "I waited patiently for the Lord; and he inclined unto me, and heard my cry" (Ps. 40:1). This has been the faithful testimony of uncounted multitudes.

Additional biblical references: Ps. 8; Ps. 139:23, 24; Heb. 4:13, 16; Heb. 10:19–25.

Is life worth living?
How can we get off dead center?
What is the use trying anyway?

3 WHEN LIFE BECOMES ORDINARY

WHEN GENERAL CHARLES DEGAULLE visited the United States he was taken to the top of the seventy-story RCA Building in New York. It was a clear day and the view was breathtaking for fifty miles in all directions. The General surveyed the scene with interest. Then a companion asked him what he thought of the view. General DeGaulle replied with a question: "Where's Coney Island?"

It is not as crass an answer as we might think. For it is true to life as it is. Some of the views we have are visions of beauty and grandeur. But as a rule they do not last long. They are rudely interrupted by our interest in purely ordinary affairs. The magnificence of life easily becomes dwarfed by its more minute things. The far look too often becomes a quick glance. We cannot see the distant horizon for looking for Coney Island.

The experience of the shepherds after the birth of Jesus is typical of us all. These plain people had seen a wondrous thing. They had heard the songs of angels. They had followed a star. They had knelt in adoration before the manger of the Christ Child. But now the great experience was past. "And the shepherds returned" (Luke 2:20). These four simple words are packed with meaning. For the shepherds returned from a shining experience to the demands of commonplace and humdrum things. So do we all. It is true they returned "glorifying and praising God." But there was work to do. And the big question was, What then?

The Bible offers real help as we try to answer this question for ourselves. In itself it is the record of great ideas, significant people, and unusual experiences. But in between the Ten Commandments, the 23rd Psalm, the birth at Bethlehem, the Sermon on the Mount, and the Resurrection story there is a vast record of everyday activities and counsel. The life and death of Jesus thrill us. But we forget his many hidden years as a carpenter in Nazareth. The Old Testament is replete with the names of average people woven into the great events in the history of the Hebrew people. And Paul the great missionary must have had many dreary days of routine affairs and discouraging experiences. In it all we will find that the real tests of faith come when we leave our high moments of spiritual exaltation and return to the ordinary chores of everyday.

When life turns ordinary we need to remember that it is easy to lose track of the important things.

When the Israelites moved into the land of Canaan from the desert areas to the southeast, they gave up their nomadic existence for the life of the cities. There they quickly took for granted the good things that were theirs. But the writer of Deuteronomy reminds them that others had built this civilization and God's goodness had led them to it. He warns them not to forget this heritage and whence it came. God commands them to teach the love of God to their children and to bind it on their hands and post it on their gates. "And it shall be, when the Lord thy God shall have brought thee into the land which he sware unto thy Fathers, . . . to give thee great and goodly cities, which thou buildest not, And houses full of all good things, which thou filledst not, and wells digged, which thou diggedst not, vineyards and olive trees, which thou plantedst not; when thou shalt have eaten and be full; Then beware lest thou forget the Lord, which brought thee forth out of the land of Egypt, from the house of bondage" (6:10–12).

It is so with us all. When things go along easily with us, we are apt to forget the really significant factors that contribute to our well-being. We all receive far more from God's hands than we acknowledge. We, too, need to beware lest we forget him.

Arthur Mayer, in his book *Merely Colossal,* tells of a strange experience in connection with a publicity stunt for a movie he was promoting. He engaged a stunt man who could stay buried for twenty-four hours without suffocating. After much newspaper talk about burying a man alive, Mayer finally had him duly buried the evening of the appointed day. The spot where he was interred was carefully marked with lime so it could easily be found. But during the night a heavy storm came up and washed away all traces of the lime. And they could not tell where the man was buried. It took thirty men digging frantically in the vicinity for twelve hours to locate him. When they found him the stunt man was in good condition. But he demanded overtime pay for the extra hours he was lost! [1]

Not many of us mislay people like that. But we do lose track of other important things. Moments of high inspiration. The dedication of life to God in earlier years. The upward pull of the spirit. The resolutions for prayer and service. The holy dreams and aspirations of our better hours. These things move us deeply at the time. We are sure they will last forever. Then they become buried under a mass of routine demands and daily responsibilities. At first we carefully mark where they are, so we can find them again. But storms come without warning. And all trace of them is gone. They are hidden from our sight by a thin layer of cynicism or sensuality or indifference or preoccupation.

Most of us do not set out to bury our Christian faith for keeps. We just neglect it temporarily. We neglect to pray. We quit going to church. We let our intellects smother our emotions. We take on a few questionable habits just to be smart or sociable. We listen to the idle talk of pagan-minded sophisticates. But we need also to listen to the wise words of John Stuart Mill: "Capacity for the nobler feeling is in most natures a very tender plant. . . . Men lose their high aspirations . . . because they have not time or opportunity for indulging them; and they addict themselves to inferior pleasures, not because they deliberately prefer them, but because they are either the only ones to which they have access, or the only ones which they are any longer capable of enjoying." [2]

The Bible warns us, therefore, to set a watch over the deep things of the spirit lest they be misplaced and lost. Hear again God's words in Deuteronomy, given as a warning against losing the blessings of heaven: "Take heed to yourselves, that your heart be not deceived, and ye turn aside, and serve other gods, and worship them" (11:16). Hear the words of Jesus to the sleeping disciples in Gethsemane: "Why sleep ye? rise and pray, lest ye enter into temptation" (Luke 22:46). Hear the words of Paul: "Watch ye, stand fast in the faith, quit you like men, be strong" (I Cor. 16:13). Hear the words of Hebrews: "Therefore we ought to give the more earnest heed to the things which we have heard, lest at any time we should let them slip" (2:1).

Then there is the pathetic story of the ten lepers who were cleansed at the instruction of Jesus. But after things returned to normal for them, only one came back to thank Jesus and to glorify God. Then said Jesus, "Were not ten cleansed? Where are the nine? Was no one found to return and give praise to God except this foreigner?" (Luke 17:17–18, RSV). It is so often so with us. When an emergency exists, we seek divine help. When things are at even keel, we forget even to be grateful for the benefits that are ours. Too many of us are too busy to give thanks to God. Too many are too busy to watch for his presence. And the shining light fades away and the songs of angels die in the distance. In such innocent ways inner emptiness comes to many lives today.

When life becomes ordinary the lost vision is never far away.

One summer day in 1952 a lapidary in a jewelry shop on 47th Street in New York found to his dismay that he had lost a one-and-one-half carat diamond which he had been mounting. It could be found nowhere. As required by the company, he began paying for the missing gem out of his salary. For several months he had paid sixty dollars a week toward the price of the missing diamond. Then one day in March, 1953, a telephone repairman by the name of Jim Loughran was working on a telephone near the jeweler's workbench. In the bell box of the telephone lay the gleaming long-lost diamond! It had shot from the vise on the bench through the tiny cable opening of the box. There it lay for months just a few feet away from where the lapidary who had lost it worked every day.[3]

Life is like that! Our glittering hopes for life and our precious faiths in God and goodness slip out of our hands. We do not know where they go. They seem to be lost. And sometimes we pay dearly for their loss in heartache, unhappiness, and bitter regrets. But the chances are they are not far away. It is hard to kill the soul. The strong, clean, bright faiths that give value and beauty to life may often be overlooked. They may gather dust in complacent living. They may be pushed beneath the surface by a desire to conform to some accepted pattern. They may take a back seat when stubborn self-will is in the driver's seat. But they are still around somewhere! Waiting to be rediscovered! Waiting to be polished up again! Waiting to be set in their proper mounting!

On one occasion an inquiring scribe came to Jesus and asked him which were the two greatest commandments. The Master replied that they were to love God and to love your neighbor. The scribe agreed with this. "And when Jesus saw that he answered discreetly, he said unto him, Thou art not far from the kingdom of God" (Mark 12:28–34). This is the case with many of us. We may believe with our minds but our hearts are not in it. Yet there is more to us than people sometimes think. The most ordinary people doing the most ordinary things may be close to the Kingdom! In fact, it is not far away from any of us. We have more faith than we sometimes like to admit. We can be more loving and understanding and generous than we allow ourselves to be. We like to appear "hard-boiled" and tough-minded. But most of us are not as skeptical or as selfish as we seem to be. There are good and redeemable qualities in us all. Why do we want to hide the goodness and the love and the faith that are in us? Why are we content to live so near the Kingdom and yet not in it? Why do we insist on living by some cheap and low standard when we might live like the children of God? If we believe in God, why don't we act like it? Too many of us are like the old woman who said to Muriel Lester: "God never made a better woman than I am, but I just can't live up to it." And it is here that the Bible comes to our aid.

The Bible reminds us that we are more important than we think. In the first chapter of Genesis it is said that man was made in the image of God to have dominion "over every living thing that moveth upon the earth" (1:28). The psalmist exalts the same idea: "When I consider thy heavens, the work of thy fingers, the moon and the stars, which thou hast ordained; What is man, that thou art mindful of him? . . . thou hast made him a little lower than the angels, and hast crowned him with glory and honor" (8:3–5). All that is something to live up to!

Paul gives us an unbeatable formula for the recovery of lost radiance: "Be not conformed to this world: but be ye transformed by the renewing of your mind, that ye may prove what is that good, and acceptable, and perfect, will of God" (Rom. 12:2). The Bible tells us that God believes in us. When we receive the Spirit, "We are the children of God" (Rom. 8:16). It says that God has the power to transform life and make it shine again. "As many as received him, to them gave he power to become the sons of God, even to them that believe on his name" (John 1:12). The Bible declares that all who will may find for themselves the hidden springs of the spirit they may have lost for a time. "And let him that is athirst come. And whosoever will, let him take the water of life freely" (Rev. 22:17).

When life seems ordinary we need to know that most of living is made up of ordinary things.

Duncan Hines, the eating expert, says he is not going to do a book on the eating places of Europe. He has, however, one piece of advice for Americans traveling abroad. He suggests that the diner in a restaurant merely ask the headwaiter what each dish listed on the menu means. Said he: "It might have twenty-two letters and turn out to be gull. . . . If you're not sure of the cooking, order ham and eggs. And if the yolk doesn't stand up above the white like the morning sun, those eggs are no good." [4]

It is good advice for the business of living as well as the business of eating. For the tempo and glitter of modern life give many people the idea that things are not worth much unless they are exciting and exotic. This goes for ideas and clothes and pleasures and books as well as food. We are tempted to live for the thrills. And when the thrills are few and far between, we create artificial thrills to keep us going. We must beware lest we be disillusioned by the twenty-two letter words and attractions. They so often turn out to be indigestible gull. Good, plain, everyday ham and eggs provide, after all, the real, dependable nourishment we need.

Few of us have very many mountaintop experiences. In fact, it is impossible to be keyed up all the time. The ordinary days far outnumber the extraordinary times. We must, therefore, make our peace with them. They will not be boring or self-defeating if we see in them the very stuff and substance of living. Indeed, most of the important work of the world is done by ordinary people in the ordinary routine of ordinary days.

The Bible recognizes the truth of this idea. The prophet Micah, as we have seen, spoke sharply against the idea that religious duties consist of burnt offerings and sacrifices: "What doth the Lord require of thee, but to do justly, and to love mercy, and to walk humbly with thy God?" (6:8). Jesus told the people that betrayal and hatred could not harm those who were faithful. Therefore: "In your patience possess ye your souls" (Luke 21:19). "Let us run with patience the race that is set before us" (Heb. 12:1). This, in spite of all afflictions and problems. Not the proud or the aggressive, but the meek "shall inherit the earth" (Ps. 37:11, Matt. 5:5). In fact, one of the great, distinctive ideas of the Bible is its declaration of the love of God for ordinary people and the sympathy and concern of Jesus for the plain, genuine person, who is faithful to God and to the trusts of life.

We see this in the parable of the talents. It is the story of a man who gave his three servants five, two, and one talents before going on a journey. Upon his return he asked for an accounting. To the five- and the two-talent men who had used their money to good advantage, he said: "Well done, good and faithful servant; thou hast been faithful over a few things, I will make thee ruler over many things." But to the one-talent man who had hid his small possession he gave only a stinging rebuke (Matt. 25:14–30). The point is, of course, that God expects us to use well whatever we have, however everyday our abilities or routine our responsibilities. When we do so he sees to it that life is lifted to higher levels.

The trouble is the ordinary virtue and the commonplace loyalties often seem to suffer in comparison with the bright temptations and the wicked lures. We are often inclined to let down the bars and give up the fight. In a word, we get tired of being good! We are weary of keeping up a brave front. Yet it is our own fault if goodness becomes a dull and commonplace thing. The Bible would have us know that it is the ordinary virtues that hold life together and make it livable. "Whatsoever things are true, whatsoever things are honest, whatsoever things are just, whatsoever things are pure, whatsoever things are lovely, whatsoever things are of good report; if there be any virtue, and if there be any praise, think on these things" (Phil. 4:8). By "think" Paul means commit your life to those things which are of God. In many quarters today such ordinary things as truth and honesty and purity may seem fairly stuffy and "old-hat." But they remain the solid foundations of the universe and of human happiness. We had better not get tired of them! And we try to outsmart them at the risk of reducing life from the ordinary to the tragic.

In John 21 is recorded the story of the seven disciples who went fishing in a boat on the sea of Tiberias. It was after the death of Jesus. They had thought he was to change the world. But nothing happened and they were returning to their ordinary pursuits. They had caught nothing, however, and were discouraged. Then they heard a voice from the unseen Master telling them to cast their net on the right side of the ship. They followed his bidding and made a big catch. It is a story that emphasizes the great truth that even in our everyday tasks we find Christ near. And as we listen to him we will find that our labors are not in vain.

When life gets ordinary we must realize that the big moments do not come unless we prepare for them.

In Johannesburg, South Africa, a man by the name of Maurice Hirsch made his living recapping auto tires. It would be hard to find a more commonplace job than that. However, during the years he studied art and the paintings of the masters. One day in 1954 he was poking around an auction store in the city where he lived. He came across a painting that looked interesting to him. He bought it for $375. He showed it to art collectors in Johannesburg. But they did not think much of it. Then Hirsch sent detailed photographs of his picture to the Belgian historian, Leo Van Puyvelde. This expert declared that the painting was *L'Erection de la Croix*, a "genuine work by Anthony Van Dyck, where the creative power of the painter expresses itself masterfully." He estimated the value at $30,000.[5]

This unusual find by Hirsch is the sort of thing every art collector dreams of. Yet the local experts in Johannesburg passed it up. It remained for a tire recapper to recognize its possible value. He did so only because he had prepared himself for just such a discovery during long years of study on the side while making a living at ordinary tasks.

This is no new or novel notion. No great achievement or vision or discovery or insight comes like a bolt out of the blue or like manna from heaven. Said Paderewski: "Before I was a genius I was a drudge." Said Michelangelo: "If people knew how hard I work to get my mastery it wouldn't seem so wonderful after all." Said Alexander Hamilton: "All of the genius I have is merely the fruit of labor." Said Wilfred Funk, editor and publisher: "I have never discovered a genius who spoke of talent. Or even of inspiration. Only brutal work."[6]

Not many of us aspire to be geniuses. But most of us hold some ambition or dream or hope. The trouble is we do not like the drudgery it takes to bring these plans into realization. We want to skip the tough grind of the ordinary days and reap the rewards in a hurry.

We want to start at the top instead of at the bottom. We like the glory but the discipline is hard to take.

This thing is especially true in the realm of the spirit. The high experiences of faith and the lofty visions of the soul come only to those who are prepared to receive them. The deep assurances of the presence and power of God in life do not come overnight. We spend years preparing ourselves for a trade or profession. Yet we think we ought to have offhand all the answers to the profound issues of religious faith and godly living. We go to church a few times a year and consider ourselves authorities on religion.

The Bible warns us that we find God only as we give attention to godly things. It is the pure in heart and the clean of hand that shall stand in his presence (Ps. 24:3, 4). And Paul says that God will give eternal life to those who "by patient continuance in well doing seek for glory and honor and immortality" (Rom. 2:7). But we are not to be discouraged even during the bleak and barren days. "Let us not be weary in well doing: for in due season we shall reap, if we faint not" (Gal. 6:9). Though our days may seem ordinary, we may prepare our souls to know and to keep company with the most high God.

No life is ordinary when it walks with him. The Israelites, having escaped the bondage of Egypt, were wandering in the wilderness of Sinai. They needed someone to guide them through the unknown country. A Midianite named Hobab came along. He knew the region like a book. The Israelites appealed to him to join their party and lead them to the land of promise and enjoy the fruits thereof. But Hobab turned a deaf ear to this proposition. Then the leaders changed their appeal. They told him they needed him badly because he knew the country well. This won over Hobab and he led them to their destination (Num. 10:25–34). It is a simple story of a simple man who was lifted out of obscurity and his own routine rut by giving himself to a needy cause. Even the knowledge and abilities of ordinary people may be used of God when we respond to some challenging need.

Additional biblical references: Ps. 103; Matt. 11:28–30; Rom. 8:31–39.

What is going to become of us?
What am I going to do now?
How can I take things more calmly?

4 WHEN FEAR HAUNTS OUR DAYS

JOHN MUIR WAS one of America's greatest naturalists. From 1838 to 1914 he covered most of the American wilderness alone, on foot, and unarmed. He carried only a sackful of stale bread and tea. He neither hunted nor was hunted nor harmed by any animal. Edwin Way Teale, in his book *The Wilderness World of John Muir,* said of this remarkable man: "He was unafraid of danger, of hardship, of wilderness, of being alone, of facing death. He was unafraid of public opinion. He was unafraid of work and poverty and hunger. He knew them all and he remained unafraid." [1]

This should be said of any man of faith. We who walk the ways of life as the children of God have the right to know no fear. We may be lonely and footsore. We may see the world as an unfriendly wilderness. We may know poverty and hunger and work and danger and death. But we may walk without real fear for we know that life is good and that our pilgrimage is in the hands of God now and forever.

The plain truth is, however, that most of us are tormented with a thousand fears. To be sure, some fears are important. Normal fears can be an aid to our safety, comfort, knowledge, and health. But there are other fears that keep us in hot water and undercut our efficiency, our happiness, and our mental and physical well-being. Fear of growing old. Fear of illness. Fear of loss of income. Fear of what other people think. Fear of the future. Fear of death. These and other fears, often nameless, paralyze us. They keep us under a cloud. They are enemies of the spirit and the flesh.

These things should not be! We can and must break the fear *habit* before it destroys us. The way out is not to fight fear head on. It is to build a new and positive set of habits and attitudes that work better than fear does.

The Bible helps us to do this. For in the Bible we find an attitude toward the Creator, the universe, and human life which puts us beyond the reach of deadly fear. Isaiah puts the word of God, addressed to the people of Israel, forcefully in these words: "Fear thou not; for I am with thee: be not dismayed; for I am thy God: I will strengthen thee; yea, I will help thee; yea, I will uphold thee with the right hand of my righteousness" (Isa. 41:10). Likewise, Jesus gave his followers similar basic, wise counsel. "Be not anxious for your life. . . . Which of you by being anxious can add a cubit unto the measure of his life?" (Luke 12:22, 25, ARV).

The Bible is full of such assurances. They form the bases for positive techniques by which we may break the fear habit. They are keyed to the upward rather than the inward look.

We must cultivate the habit of accepting change.

We like things to stay the same. We get to love the ruts we are in. And some of them are good ruts! The familiar scenery. The usual routine. The dependable landmarks. The security of job and family and home. The same age, the same friends, the same ideas. These are the things we become attached to. They make us feel comfortable. We are afraid of change. And when change is forced upon us, we become fearful and confused. We are like the woman who left this note for the milkman when she changed her order for milk: "Dear Milkman: We don't want milk every day. We want milk like this. Today we want milk. Tomorrow we don't. And the next day will be just like the day after tomorrow." [2]

Our natural fear of change is offset only as we come to understand that life itself is the story of change. Nothing in God's world is permanent. He made it that way. And nothing we can do can alter the fact. Human existence is a fluid thing. Time itself stands still for no man, rich or powerful though he may be. "My days are swifter than a weaver's shuttle" (Job 7:6). History is the record of the ebb and flow of the human tide. "For a thousand years in thy sight are but as yesterday when it is past, and as a watch in the night. Thou carriest them away as with a flood; they are as a sleep: in the morning they are like grass which groweth up. In the morning it flourisheth, and groweth up; in the evening it is cut down, and withereth" (Ps. 90:4–6). And nature herself tells the constant story of the restless universe. "While the earth remaineth, seedtime and harvest, and cold and heat, and summer and winter, and day and night shall not cease" (Gen. 8:22).

Lincoln Barnett gives a picture of all living things in his description of the rain forest. "Even the stoutest log of glass-hard wood may be converted in a few years by the voracious jaws of the white ants into a spongy shell scarred with the claw marks of every perching bird. And while the termites and fungi tunnel the tissues of fallen trees, bacteria are at work, rapidly transforming wood into humus, and humus into nitrogen compounds, carbon dioxide and mineral matter. So, in time, all living things from the tallest tree to the smallest bird —gauzy leaf and woody limb, spent flower and errant seed, beetle corpse and butterfly wing—return to the earth in death, dissolved in the gentle dripping of the filtered rain." [3] Why, then, should we be exempt?

We break the fear habit when we come to accept change as a normal, natural part of being alive on God's earth. In spite of our best calculations, our destinies are not in our hands. Fear does not stop change. It only adds to its intensity. To live in constant fear of change is to betray our faith in God and in his world. For change brings opportunity as well as danger. It means life as well as death. It makes living interesting and varied. It makes possible a better world. Without change life would be dull and monotonous. It is uncertainty and surprise that lend adventure to our days. We ought to be thankful we do not know what is going to happen next! To expect everything to remain as it is, is to live in constant dread. To try to re-create the past or to freeze the present or to stave off the future is folly unbecoming the child of God.

When changes do come we overcome our fear of them by the simple process of making the best of the situation. Even though it may be a second-best. This is the wisdom of common sense. It is also the wisdom of the Bible. Take the case of Rehoboam after he became the ruler of Judah. In the fifth year of his reign Shishak, king of Egypt, invaded Jerusalem and took away the gold shields and other treasures of the king's house. But Rehoboam was not to be undone by this disastrous change of circumstances. For the record says that he made in their stead shields of brass which were carried by the guards when the king went to worship (I Kings 14:21–28). So it is. Many a soul lives in fear of all kinds of invaders that will make off with his treasures. But the man of faith is equal to the occasion. When the shields of gold are gone, by whatever circumstance, he makes in their stead shields of brass and bravely carries on.

Our modern passion for security is an illusion. We are so afraid of insecurity we become victims of our own fears. Like the White Knight in *Through the Looking Glass* we try to protect ourselves against everything. The White Knight had a sandwich box which would come in handy if there were any sandwiches. He also had a beehive and a mousetrap on his horse. Alice wondered what the mousetrap was for as there would hardly be any mice on the horse's back. "Not very likely, perhaps," said the knight; "but if they *do* come, I don't choose to have them running all about. . . . You see, it's as well to be provided for *everything*. That's the reason the horse has all those anklets round his feet." "But what are they for?" Alice asked in a tone of great curiosity. "To guard against the bites of sharks," the knight replied. "It's an invention of my own." [4]

So it is with so many of us. We clutter life with many weird devices and charms of our own invention to ward off every possible unforeseen trouble. We are afraid of sharks even on dry land! But in spite of the best we can do, trouble and age and disaster and illness and war and change come and go. "What is your life? It is even a vapour, that appeareth for a little time, and then vanisheth away" (James 4:14). To expect and to accept change is the better part of wisdom and faith. "For we walk by faith, not by sight" (II Cor. 5:7). In so doing, the Bible points the way to escape the tyranny of fear. Indeed, when we walk with God, we are always "of good courage" (II Cor. 5:6, RSV) even in the face of death, the greatest change of all. For, "as thy days, so shall thy strength be" (Deut. 33:25).

We must cultivate the habit of adaptation to the inevitable.

We must learn not only to accept the events and situations that come, but to adjust to them and use them. We fear and resist new conditions because we do not know how to deal with the unfamiliar. But God has given to every one of us more powers of adjustment than we realize or use. The human mind and the human spirit have the God-given capacity to take even the worst that comes and thrive on it. Many Bible characters proved this to be so. And countless men of faith have since validated its truth.

The very business of living is a risky affair. Accidents, illness, death, financial loss, and the criticism of our friends are all real enough. Our answer to them is not to pretend that they do not exist. Neither is it to run roughshod over them by assuming a blustering harshness. Nor can we escape from them by taking to drink or by retreating from reality into a protective shell of isolation, distrust, and cantankerousness.

In other words, it is the way we react to the changing fortunes of life and to the world about us that determines whether we are ruled by fear or by faith. Take the case of the European and American shoe salesmen who were on a cruise ship. It landed at an African port near the equator. The European salesman cabled his home office as follows: "No market here. Just a lot of barefoot natives." But the American sent back this message: "Market wide open. Only one person in a hundred wearing shoes." [5] So it is with many of us. Those who are held in the grip of the fear habit see nothing but the worst possibilities in any situation. But those who have faith enough to be adaptable see in the same situation opportunities for growth and development. God has given us all the power to rise above our inevitables! "God hath not given us the spirit of fear; but of power, and of love, and of a sound mind" (II Tim. 1:7).

This does not mean a weak submission to the winds of fate. But it does mean that God closes some doors only to open others if we have the faith to see them and walk through them. This happened many times, for example, in the life and travels of Paul. When Paul and Timothy set out from Lystra they went through Phrygia and Galatia. They wanted to go into Asia. But something kept them from it. Then they wanted to go into Bithynia. But something happened to keep them from going. The record says that they were prevented from going by the Spirit. Whatever the circumstances, they did not complain because they could not have their way. They were willing to follow the guidance of God. They were thus directed to Troas where Paul had the vision of a man of Macedonia who called to them to come over and help. And then began one of the most fruitful parts of Paul's work (Acts 16:1–13). If we only knew it, God speaks to us through closed doors as well as through open ones. The inevitable events that block our way are often our greatest opportunities.

Dr. O. T. Binkley, professor of Christian ethics at Southeastern Baptist Theological Seminary, gave these marks of an emotionally mature person: "1. He knows how to make decisions and accept the consequences of his decisions. 2. He faces an unalterable situation in which he has a deep personal interest with poise and a minimum of conflict. 3. He is willing and able to work with people with whom there is some disagreement. 4. He accepts constructive criticism without rationalization. 5. He undertakes to do what needs to be done today without excessive regret over the past and without excessive anxiety about the future. 6. He has a reasonably objective attitude toward reality." [6]

These are the marks of the person who has developed the habit of adjustment and adaptation to the inevitable. "I will not fear what flesh can do unto me" (Ps. 56:4). It reduces the fear habit to a harmless minimum. It gives us power over ourselves and over our work and world. For even in "tribulation, or distress, or persecution, or famine, or nakedness, or peril, or sword . . . we are more than conquerors through him that loved us" (Rom. 8:35, 37).

We can develop the habit of being governed by facts instead of fancies.

Most of those who are held in the spell of the fear habit are like the businessman who had this motto over his desk: "My mind is made up. Don't confuse me with the facts." The truth is that most of our fears are not about actual existing situations. They center around imaginary circumstances and events that we are afraid might happen. And they are often colored by prejudice. When the facts are known, we find either that our fears are groundless or that we can easily cope with the dreaded event whatever it may be.

When the Israelites were in search of the promised land, ten spies were sent out to look for it. They came back and reported to Moses that they had found it to be a land of milk and honey. There was, however, one thing wrong. The people in the land were "giants." "And there we saw the giants, the sons of Anak, which come of the giants: and we were in our own sight as grasshoppers, as so we were in their sight" (Num. 13:21–33). At this report the Israelites were fearful and wanted to turn back. But Joshua and Caleb thought otherwise. Far from being dismayed, they knew the "giants" to be mere men. "Rebel not ye against the Lord, neither fear ye the people of the land; for they are bread for us: their defence is departed from them, and the Lord is with us: fear them not" (Num. 14:9). Like the spies, we so often regard ourselves as we think others see us. And then we say that they think of us that way. We need to have the level heads and common sense of Joshua and Caleb. To say nothing of their faith in God. This always cuts our enemies down to size. It reduces as well our fear because we see our enemies in their true light and not in the exaggerated perspective of a fearful mind and imagination.

Jacqueline Cochrane, the first famous woman flier, in her autobiography *The Stars at Noon,* tells how she conquered fear early in life. It was during her early childhood in Florida. She had been down the road playing with some other children. She started home. Night came on. She had to pass a cemetery. A ghost was said to lurk there. As little Jacky started to go along a raised wooden walk, the "ghost" loomed up before her. She retreated and studied the situation. She had to choose between going on and going back to the jeers of her friends. She decided to go on. She said: "Yelling at the top of my lungs, I charged. As the ghost rose to grab me, I plunged in to grapple with it. It proved to be a calf with its hind legs stuck down through a broken board. I had won. Since then all ghosts in my life have turned out to be just scared calves caught by their hind legs." [7] Most of us would say the same if we were honest about it.

Dr. Guy Means gave tests and questionnaires to one thousand women students of the University of Alabama and the Woman's College of Montgomery. He found that the normal woman has an average of seventy-eight fears! These included fear of icepicks, rabbits, stairs, volcanoes, grasshoppers, and caves. The women also listed fear of marriage, failure, disappointment in love, being alone at night, changeable moods, losing self-confidence, and fear of the future and life in general.[8]

Other results of this study showed Dr. Means that the greatest factor that makes for self-control and stability is knowledge. We leave our fears behind when we are governed by facts and not by illusions, dreams, superstitions, and fantasies of our own creation. Most fears originate in, or are magnified by, our imagination. God gave us our intelligence to use. He surely wants us to deal with things as they are. Knowledge of ourselves. Knowledge of the nature and laws of the world we live in. Knowledge of history. Knowledge of other people. Knowledge of our own physical condition. Knowledge of God. These are the things that show up so many of our fears as merely scared calves caught by their hind legs. Most of our fears have little factual foundation. And for those that do, the truth is always easier to deal with than a fear-ridden imagination. "If ye continue in my word, then are ye my disciples indeed; and ye shall know the truth, and the truth shall make you free" (John 8:31, 32). Jesus was here calling for a growing faith that meant release from sin. But it also means that the mature child of God is free of the petty, irresponsible fears that annoy our days and nag our hearts.

Paul was a prisoner on board a cargo ship bound from Egypt to Rome where he was to stand trial. The ship went aground on a reef in a storm. The two hundred and seventy-six men on board were terrified. But Paul remained calm. He stood in the midst of the officers and said: "And now I exhort you to be of good cheer: for there shall be no loss of any man's life among you. . . . For there stood by me this night the angel of God, whose I am, and whom I serve, Saying, Fear not, Paul; thou must be brought before Caesar: and, lo, God hath given thee all them that sail with thee. Wherefore, sirs, be of good cheer: for I believe God, that it shall be even as it was told me" (Acts 27:22–25). Paul's calmness and subsequent good advice carried weight. And in the end all were saved. To be sure, God makes his angels watch over those who are faithful to him. This does not always mean that we will be spared. But it does mean that we can be calm and brave and can thus devise better ways and means to make our way out of an emergency than if we give in to panic and hysteria.

We can establish the habit of complete trust in the loving care of a great God.

Here is the basic antidote to counteract fear. It is one of the key messages of the Bible.

God spoke to Isaiah in words with real meaning for all of us when he said, in words quoted at the beginning of this chapter: "Fear thou not; for I am with thee: be not dismayed; for I am thy God: I will strengthen thee; yea, I will help thee; yea, I will uphold thee with the right hand of my righteousness." As if in reply, the prophet speaks in another place, "Behold, God is my salvation; I will trust, and not be afraid" (Isa. 12:2).

The Psalms are full of expressions of trust in God as a remedy for fear. "The Lord is my light and my salvation; whom shall I fear? the Lord is the strength of my life; of whom shall I be afraid?" (27:1). This trust is no vain or idle thing. "For he shall give his angels charge over thee, to keep thee in all thy ways" (91:11). It shows us the sure way out of even the worst of our fears. "Though an host should encamp against me, my heart shall not fear" (27:3).

The New Testament brings this idea of trust into full flower. Jesus frequently told his disciples that they need have no fear. He said that God cares for the lilies and the birds and the grass and he will care for us. "Therefore I tell you, do not be anxious about your life, what you shall eat or what you shall drink, nor about your body, what you shall put on. Is not life more than food, and the body more than clothing? . . . Which of you by being anxious can add one cubit to his span of life? . . . If God so clothes the grass of the field, which today is alive and tomorrow is thrown into the oven, will he not much more clothe you, O men of little faith?" (Matt. 6:25–30, RSV). This dramatic passage does not mean that we should be improvident and lazy. But it does focus sharp attention on a major emphasis of Jesus' teaching. And that is the need for man to conquer fear of life by a complete and abandoned sense of trust in the loving care of God.

Paul sounds the same note many times. "For ye have not received the spirit of bondage again to fear; but ye have received the Spirit of adoption, whereby we cry, Abba, Father" (Rom. 8:15). The author of Hebrews puts it plainly: "The Lord is my helper, and I will not fear what man shall do unto me" (13:6). And in I John 4:18 there is that memorable passage: "There is no fear in love; but perfect love casteth out fear."

This kind of complete confidence in a great and good God gives direction and stability to life. We need to try it out and develop it. We can build faith habits as well as fear habits. And the attitude of trust in God can become a habit of great power and permanence. We will find that it works much better than the habit of fear. It builds up a resistance to the fears that plague our days. The trust habit keeps us from being lonely by keeping us in touch with the Father above. Trust in God is sure protection for the hidden dangers that lie in wait for all of us.

In 1947 New York harbor was fogbound. All traffic was stopped. A mighty ocean liner was delayed thirteen hours reaching dock a mile away. A harbor ferry was lost for seven hours. Forty ships awaiting entrance to the harbor did not dare turn a propeller. In the thick and dangerous fog, only one ship moved. It was *Transfer 21*, a tugboat of the New York, New Haven and Hartford Railroad. It was guided by new radar equipment. And all through the thick fog it made its way as usual, moving three hundred and two railroad cars on schedule between Brooklyn and New Jersey.[9]

Something like this is possible for those who have learned the radarlike habit of contact with, and trust in, God. We go about our business as usual even though the fog lies heavy all about. We have no fear of lurking and unseen dangers. We have an unseen guide to show us the way. Piloted by the constant presence of God we travel without fear. "Mine eyes are unto thee, O God the Lord: in thee is my trust; leave not my soul destitute" (Ps. 141:8).

This basic habit of trust in God counteracts our fears by leading us from fear to faith. The Psalmist spoke of foes and enemies who would swallow him up. Yet, he said: "What time I am afraid, I will trust in thee" (56:3). And when we act as if we have faith, we find that we do! There are many times when many of us need to hear the word of God speaking to us as he spoke to Jacob of old: "And behold, I am with thee, and will keep thee in all places whither thou goest" (Gen. 28:15). In the over-all message of the Bible this applies to the individual as well as to the Hebrew people.

In chapters 6 and 7 of the Book of Judges there is the story of Gideon who put to flight the Midianite horde that threatened Israel. God called him to free his people and when he was sure of God's leadership he was fearless in his plans. At first there were some thirty thousand men in his army. But he told those who were afraid, to leave. And twenty-two thousand left. Then he weeded out the others until he had a band of only three hundred men. These surprised the enemy in the dead of night with the noise of their broken pitchers and the light of their lamps. The enemy fled. So it is that those who are sure of God need have no fear. And when men of faith use their heads they can put to rout any enemy, however superior in numbers. Those who retreat in fear never win the battle.

Additional biblical references: Pss. 27; 46:1, 2; 107; 121:104.

Isn't sin an old-fashioned idea?
Am I to blame for what happens?
How can I overcome a sense of guilt?

5 WHEN WE NEED TO GET RID OF THE DEVIL

A MISSIONARY, THE Reverend L. Fison, described how a witch doctor got rid of the devil in a Fiji Island native. The medicineman passed his hands over the patient's body until he detected the presence of the evil spirit by the fluttering of his fingertips. He then tried to get the devil down to a foot or hand. Much patience and care were required, because the spirits are very cunning. Then, said the witch doctor, "When you have got the demon into a leg or an arm which you can grasp with your fingers, you must take care or he will escape you. . . . But when you have drawn him down to a finger or a toe, you must pull him out with a sudden jerk, and throw him away, and blow after him lest he should return." [1]

The idea of the devil as the personification of evil in human life is an ancient one. It comes into the Bible from the demonology of primitive man. The devil was responsible for much disease, misery, and wrongdoing. History records many quaint and cruel methods, devices, and superstitions to get rid of the devil. One of these in the Old Testament was the scapegoat sent into the wilderness laden with the sins of the people (Lev. 16:8, 10, 26).

In our modern world we pride ourselves on being rid of the idea of the devil. But the trouble is we find that the thing the devil stood for, the fact of evil, is still with us! It thrives in the heart of the sophisticated American as well as in the body of the Fiji Islander. And it is quite as cunning! The job of getting rid of the devil is just as difficult and requires just as much patience and care for the modern man as for the witch doctor.

The Bible faces squarely and without compromise the fact of sin in human life. In it the devil is the personification of wickedness. But also in the pages of the Book, we find that by the power of God we can get rid of the devil, pull him out and throw him away and blow after him so he will not return!

The Bible warns us against the deadly nature of sin.

The fact of sin blights human personality and human society. It always leaves its mark. We can no more escape from the effect of our sins than the criminal can escape from his fingerprints. The science of fingerprinting is a modern device in crime detection. It was in 1901 that Sir Edward R. Henry, commissioner of police of Scotland Yard, devised a system for classifying and indexing the prints. It is in use today throughout the world. Its uncanny accuracy is based on the fact that no two human fingers have ever been found that will produce an identical print. Mathematicians have said that the chance for positive identification is sixty-four billion to one where one finger matches a print in twelve comparative points. With ten fingers to work with, the odds in favor of positive identification could not even be figured by a mechanical brain. In other words, every human being has a built-in detective agency! [2]

The Bible was centuries ahead of Sir Edward R. Henry. It tersely insists that the transgressions of the moral laws of God leave an impression from which none escapes: "Be sure your sin will find you out" (Num. 32:23). It declares that the results of sin are destructive: "The way of the transgressor is hard" (Prov. 13:15, ARV). "The wages of sin is death" (Rom. 6:23). It says that sin comes between men and God: "Your iniquities have separated between you and your God, and your sins have hid his face from you, that he will not hear" (Isa. 59:2). It points out that sin undermines society: "Righteousness exalteth a nation: but sin is a reproach to any people" (Prov. 14:34).

In the New Testament, Satan, the adversary, is identified with Beelzebub, the chief of the devils (Matt. 10:25; Mark 3:22; Luke 11:15), and with the devil of Christ's temptation, of which we will speak later. Demonic visitations were associated with such things as dumbness (Luke 11:14–16); deafness (Mark 9:25); blindness (Matt. 12:22); and epilepsy (Matt. 17:15). Mary Magdalene was said to be possessed of seven devils (Luke 8:2). Thus, while demon possession is not identical with sinfulness in the Bible, the use of the devil as a personification of evil is typical of the usage of the day in dramatizing abstract ideas and explaining evil conduct.

For instance, the betrayal of Jesus by Judas is charged to the devil. "Now the feast of unleavened bread drew nigh, which is called the passover. And the chief priests and scribes sought how they might kill him; for they feared the people. Then entered Satan into Judas surnamed Iscariot, being of the number of the twelve. And he went his way, and communed with the chief priests and captains, how he might betray him unto them" (Luke 22:1–4).

Paul takes into account Satan and his power to lead men astray (I Cor. 7:5). He speaks of the "fiery darts of the evil one" (Eph. 6:16, ARV). He calls Satan "the serpent" (II Cor. 11:3).

Thus the Bible tells of an ugly and evil power at work in the world that seeks to thwart the purposes of God among men.

To many modern-minded people this sort of thing is terribly old-fashioned. The idea of sin, to say nothing of the devil, is supposed to be out of date. We live in a day when moral license is sanctified by pseudo-psychology and encouraged by salacious popular novelists. We pride ourselves on our freedom from moral restraints. We like to think that science has delivered us from sin. All this is sheer folly! In every generation and under whatever guise and by any name, sin is still with us. The idea of the devil as such may be an ancient folk tale. But the reality of sin and its effects on human life is as modern as today. To close our eyes to it and deny its bitter, ugly, vicious presence is to display a stupidity unbecoming to the mind of man. We do not need to take the word of the Bible for it. We have but to read the record.

Take the case of Lillian Rutstein, known professionally as Lillian Roth, the dancer and actress. She was about as modern as they come. She was a child star at five and the toast of Broadway at twenty. She made as much as thirty-five hundred dollars a day and had made and lost a million before she was thirty. She was married five times. In her autobiography *I'll Cry Tomorrow,* Lillian Roth frankly tells the story of the path that took her downward to the brink of suicide. "Alcohol," she said, "creeps insidiously into your life, so insidiously you aren't aware of it until it's too late." At first it was four or five drinks a night. Then a pint. Then a drink or two every four or five hours. Then every two hours. Finally every hour.

"As the years went on, something terrifying happened. . . . Your body reached a point of revolt. Then, still worse, the shakes . . . and with the shakes, agony. . . . And, after the shakes, the horrors, delirium tremens, when you heard sounds that were not there and saw things that did not exist, your being one gigantic, inflamed, tortured mass of mental and physical anguish. . . . Your medicine is your poison, and there is no end but madness." [3]

This is the pursuit of pleasure in the modern manner? No! This is what sin does to human life! It is but a symbol of the way sin works in any of its many forms. As with alcohol, so also lust and greed and pride and hate and envy creep insidiously into the lives of men. We entertain them at first because they are friendly and attractive. But their sly and innocent appearance is frighteningly deceptive. For they lead us with a viselike grip down the way of physical and mental anguish whose end is dwarfed and twisted personalities.

In the parable of the three soils, Jesus speaks of the sower sowing seed. Some falls by the wayside. Other seed falls on rocky, thorny, and good ground. On the rocky soil it withers. On the thorny soil it is choked with brambles. On the wayside it is devoured by the birds. Only that on the good soil flourishes. The Master then declares that it is the devil that comes into human hearts and causes the seed of the word of God to fail to take root in the human heart. "*Then cometh the devil*" (Luke 8:12). This sly one tempts men and clutters them with cares and pleasures until God's word has no chance to grow. This is the nature of sin and is what makes it so vicious and evil. It ever so gradually leads us away from God!

The results are written large, not only in the Bible, but in the pages of the daily press. We may choose not to believe in sin. But, the stark truth is, according to J. Edgar Hoover, that our nation harbors three times as many criminals as college students. Three major crimes are committed every minute. A murder is committed every forty minutes. There are sixty suicides daily. And there are more barmaids in America than college girls. Whatever we choose to call it, it looks as if the devil is still very much around! We are foolish to think we can hide him or hide from him.

The Bible tells us that the source of sin is the human heart.

We need to know this if we are to get rid of the devil. For we are finding that we can not exorcise him with our glib excuses and our sophisticated explanations. We are like the farmer and the pig that

Lincoln told about. It seems that a farmer built a fence to keep in his pig. But the fence was so crooked that every time the pig bored a hole through it, he found himself on the same side from which he started! We love to set up many plain and fancy reasons to bottle up or explain away our sins. But they prove full of holes. And our sins are back again on our hands!

For instance, there is the fence of self-expression. We are taught to be deathly afraid of what are called frustrations and guilt complexes. To avoid these horrible things we are to do as we please without regard to the laws of God or the rights of man. Then there is the fence of sex freedom dating back to Freud. Said Dr. Edward Spencer Cowles, a psychiatrist: "Young people are encouraged to throw to the winds the 'inhibitions' taught them in their homes and to become sexually promiscuous. There is a widespread belief that continence is dangerous to health, that innocence is weak and ridiculous, and that decency in behavior and in speech is evidence of the repression of gross sexuality." [4]

There is the fence, also, of illness. We like to say that people are not bad; they are only sick and therefore not to blame for their sin. The argument is that they need treatment instead of punishment. Likewise, we find the fence of the lowest common denominator. That is, conduct becomes a matter, not of how we ought to behave, but of how most people do behave. Thus we are not concerned with righteousness or integrity or truth or honesty as such. But rather with the common practice and with how much we can get away with. Still another fence is that known as the big blame. We become experts in the evasion of personal responsibility. Parents are to blame! Heredity is to blame! Environment is to blame! An unhappy childhood is to blame! Emotional immaturity is to blame! Poverty is to blame! Maladjustments and frustrations are to blame!

The trouble is these elaborate fences never allow the devil pig to escape! He is always right back again in our back yard! Or, to recall a parable of Jesus, we clean the house of one devil only to have it occupied by seven more (Matt. 12:45)! As Elsie King Moreland put it: "The Big Blame makes man an automaton, his actions determined or predetermined by forces over which he has no control. It underwrites crime and subsidizes sin. It robs the individual of self-restraint, self-reliance, and self-respect. It destroys his conscience by removing his sense of guilt. And therein lies its greatest danger. For without a sense of guilt, man has no need of forgiveness. And without a need of forgiveness, man has no need of a God who forgives." [5]

In the face of all this, the Bible puts the responsibility for sin on the heart of man. And, with all due regard for special cases, this is where it belongs. We are personally responsible for the consequences of our own acts. Unless and until we are willing to recognize this, we can never get rid of the devil. "Keep thy heart with all diligence; for out of it are the issues of life" (Prov. 4:23). Jesus said that man is not defiled by failure to observe ritualistic custom for "out of the heart proceed evil thoughts, murders, adulteries, fornications, thefts, false witness, blasphemies: These are the things which defile a man" (Matt. 15:19, 20). "Cleanse first that which is within the cup and platter, that the outside of them may be clean also" (Mat. 23:26). And Paul declared that "every one of us shall give account of himself to God" (Rom. 14:12).

Indeed, the heart of the Bible teaching at this point is the teaching of Jesus that the root of sin is in the human heart. His metaphor of the "good tree" and the "corrupt tree" in Matthew 7:16–20 means this. That is, figs are not produced by thistles, nor good deeds by an evil heart. Moreover, God judges us not so much by the deed itself as by inner motives and attitudes. The story of Jesus dealing with the woman taken in adultery and with her accusers is an example of this (John 8:3–11). "He that is without sin among you, let him first cast a stone at her." The rebuke of Jesus was directed at the Pharisees who were so smug and sure in their self-righteousness. There are many devils, and spiritual pride is one of the greatest. We are all sinners, the Bible says, because in one way or another we have turned to our own way and away from God. But God does not leave us there. Jesus offered complete forgiveness to the woman. This forgiveness itself is a power that cleanses our hearts and helps us get rid of our devils.

We are only fooling ourselves when we always try to put the blame for our wrongdoing on factors and circumstances outside ourselves. Every one of us must deal with the devil in his own heart. "The sin of Judah is written with a pen of iron; with a point of diamond it is engraved on the tablet of their heart. . . . The heart is deceitful above all things, and desperately wicked: who can know it?" (Jer. 17:1, 9 RSV).

The Bible charges us to find in God the power to renounce sin.

The basic cause of sinfulness is godlessness. When men neglect, deny, or choose to disregard any final, divine standard of conduct, moral chaos sets in. The records of the courts prove this. Judge Julius H. Miner, of the Circuit Court of Cook County, Illinois, said: "Having sat in judgment on thousands of offenders, murderers, robbers, rapists, burglars, etc. . . . I have observed that over 85% of the criminals were non-churchgoers. . . . I have also presided over the divorce court for five consecutive years and have commiserated with more than 120,000 litigants over their domestic difficulties and those of their children. Here, too, I have found the same high percentage (85%) of non-churchgoers. . . . And out of 8,000 delinquent children called to the attention of the FBI, only 42 attended Sunday School regularly." [6]

We may place the blame for human wrongdoing on whatever convenient scapegoat that suits our imagination. But in the main we are only rationalizing. For the plain fact is that the devil comes in when God goes out. It is true, of course, that we cannot treat all disturbed people as criminals. But it is also true that we cannot excuse all immoral acts simply as the inevitable results of external conditions or mental lapses. When we permit economic maladjustment or family and personality disorders entirely to condone or justify our immoral behavior, we are blind to the truth and are headed for disaster.

Our freewheeling generation needs to know that there are eternal standards of right and wrong. These come from God. They have not been repealed even to excuse crazy, mixed-up kids. "Thou shalt have no other Gods before me. . . . Honor thy father and thy mother. . . . Thou shalt not kill. . . . Thou shalt not commit adultery. . . . Thou shalt not steal. . . . Thou shalt not bear false witness. . . . Thou shalt not covet" (Exod. 20:3 ff.). These laws of God are sharp and clear cut. They mean what they say. Jesus summed them up when he said that we should love God with all our heart and our neighbors as ourselves.

These laws of God are written into the very fabric of our lives and the life of society. They are basic to healthy personalities and a sound civilization. When we tamper with them, we pay for it in unhappy lives, broken homes, and a chaotic social order.

It is well for us to know that all men are tempted and that to be tempted is not to sin. It is possible for us to see through the disguises of sin and to find in God the power to challenge the wiles of the devil. This is the way Jesus dealt with his temptation by the devil, perhaps the supreme example in the Bible of how men get rid of the devil. The tempter was subtle in his appeals to Jesus. He sought to reach the Master at the points of his deepest needs and highest hopes. In all three instances Jesus used the same weapon of defense, so well expressed in his third reply: "Get thee hence, Satan: for it is written, Thou shalt worship the Lord thy God, and him only shalt thou serve" (Matt. 4:1–11). Jesus not only used God as his shield. He countered the appeal of the devil with the claims of God. Thus he carried the battle into the enemy's territory and put him on the defensive and the devil departed. The fact is, no devil on earth is cunning enough to win in any encounter with God speaking through a dedicated life. Jesus' encounter was in his mind and the evil force was invisible. But it was none the less real. And the victory none the less conclusive. Our own encounters with the devil and with God may never be seen of men. But God knows they are real enough. And with him we can win.

There was the man possessed of the devil of an unclean spirit whose name was Legion. He sought help in his torment of mind from the Master. And Jesus said to him, "Come out of the man, thou unclean spirit." And the man was freed from his uncleanness (Mark 5:2–16). So it is that the divine moral authority of the Saviour can cleanse our evil dispositions and we come into our right minds again. Indeed, the chief resource of God against the evil of the world is Jesus Christ, who "was manifested, that he might destroy the works of the devil" (I John 3:8).

The Bible thus not only shows us the divine laws of God. It also shows us how God gives us strength to live by them. The break with evil things must be complete. "No servant can serve two masters: for either he will hate the one, and love the other; or else he will hold to the one, and despise the other. Ye cannot serve God and mammon" (Luke 16:13). "Abstain from all appearance of evil" (I Thess. 5:22). "Denying ungodliness and worldly lusts, we should live soberly, righteously, and godly, in this present world" (Titus 2:12). The Bible tells us that God does not leave us alone in our sins. "The Son of man is come to save that which was lost" (Matt. 18:11). Jesus taught the disciples to pray for deliverance from "the evil one" (Matt. 6:13, RSV). Peter charged the people: "Repent ye therefore, and be converted, that your sins may be blotted out" (Acts 3:19). The Bible insists that we can get rid of the devil by a positive commitment to God. "Be strong in the Lord, and in the power of his might. Put on the whole armor of God, that ye may be able to stand against the wiles of the devil. . . . Stand therefore, having your loins girt about with truth, and having on the breastplate of righteousness. . . . Above all, taking the shield of faith, wherewith ye shall be able to quench all the fiery darts of the wicked. And take the helmet of salvation, and the sword of the Spirit, which is the word of God: Praying always . . ." (Eph. 6:10, 11, 14, 16, 17, 18).

Here is the way to get rid of the devil! Here is a ringing challenge to modern man from the pages of the book of life! We have temporized too much with his Satanic majesty. We have tolerated sin and coddled the sinner. We glamorize vulgarity and sadism and homosexuality when we should revolt against them. We have thought it smart and modern to be broad-minded about drug addiction and infidelity, and crookedness in high places. Too many modern Christians are in fact moral cowards in dallying with personal temptations and vices. We need a new toughness of moral fiber and a new alignment with the plain and godly virtues. Without God we are lost in a welter of obscenity, greed, violence, indecency, and moral cynicism. But when we have the courage to take a stand on God's side we will find that the powers of heaven are on our side. Active, positive devotion to God is the one, sure realistic way to leave sin behind. It is then that the devil is put to rout! "Be blameless and harmless, the sons of God, without rebuke, in the midst of a crooked and perverse nation, among whom ye shine as lights in the world" (Phil. 2:15).

King Nebuchadnezzar, of Babylonia, created a giant golden image and ordered that all the people should bow down and worship it. All did so except the three chosen young men from the captive people of Israel. These had been picked and trained for important responsibilities in the empire. They were getting ahead in the world. The temptation must have been great to go along with the order and bow down before the image. But they refused to do so, even when they were threatened with being burned in a fiery furnace if they refused. They said they would do homage to no god save one. They were cast into the furnace but were not harmed for God watched over them and brought them out alive. Their names, of course, were Shadrach, Meshach, and Abednego (Dan. 1, 3). Their temptation is that of many men today—namely, to compromise with their godly convictions to save their skins or to get the worldly power they think is theirs. Trial by fire may not be ours. But in a thousand ways God watches over those whose loyalty to him makes them turn their back on the glittering prizes of expediency or moral compromise.

Additional biblical references: Isa. 1:10–20; Rom. 5:6–8; Rom. 1:18–3:10; I John 1:5–10.

How may I meet the challenge of the years?
Can I grow older without growing old?
Why worry about the future?
What are the marks of maturity?

6 WHEN THE YEARS GO SWIFTLY BY

THE AMERICAN INSTITUTE OF PUBLIC OPINION interviewed men and women of all ages on an interesting question. They were asked: "Would you like to live to be one hundred years old?" Fifty-seven per cent answered in the affirmative. Thirty-two per cent said they definitely would not like to live to be one hundred. And 11 per cent could not make up their minds. Far more men than women wanted to live to this ripe old age. And this in face of the fact that men are shorter lived than women. The survey showed that, as a rule, the older a person gets the longer he wants to live. Many more people in their forties wanted to live to be one hundred than those in their twenties. And the highest percentage of would-be centenarians was found among those who were past fifty.

Most of us want to keep on living. The strange part of this survey, therefore, is the fact that almost one-third of the people have no desire to live to ripe old age. Here are some of the reasons given: "Just sitting around and becoming old and useless would be no fun." . . . "Nobody loves you when you're old and gray." . . . "I might be sick and helpless—just a burden on someone." [1]

If these were the inevitable consequences of age, many of us, too, might not vote to live long. But such a dismal fate need not be. Not many of us, whatever our age, are anxious to grow older. But the years go swiftly by in spite of all we can do. "My days are swifter than a weaver's shuttle" (Job 7:6). And when they do, we can learn to shape the future in the present so that the last will be "the best for which the first was made." The Bible has wise counsel for us here. It suggests that we prepare for the future before it comes. It advises us that the years can teach wisdom when we live with God. It gives us a key secret of mature living—namely, that life is spiritual rather than material. And though our bodies decay, our spirits may be renewed day by day and year by year, at the inexhaustible fount of the divine Spirit.

When the years go swiftly by the Bible advises us to keep our minds and hearts alive and growing.

By a strange coincidence two interesting books were placed on a display table side by side in Marshall Field's book department in Chicago. One was called *Add Years to Your Life*, by Dr. Peter J. Steincrohn. The other was *Add Life to Your Years*, by Dr. Ernest Boas.

These two titles standing together pose an important problem for us all. As we get more years to live we need to know more about how to live them. Medical science is adding years to our lives. But these extra years mean little unless they are enriched with spiritual insight, understanding, and faith. Indeed, if we do not thus add life to our years, we may well find that the years we add to our lives are empty and bitter.

This is so because life is of the spirit and not of the flesh. The more years we live the more we must know that this is true. "Is not the life more than meat, and the body than raiment?" (Matt. 6:25). "It is the spirit that quickeneth; the flesh profiteth nothing" (John 6:63). To come to maturity without recognizing this is to rob the years of beauty and power. Yet there are many who do. And one of the most pathetic sights in the world is to see men and women come into the fuller years clutching frantically at the baubles and husks of other days.

It is so pathetic because it is so unnecessary. "So teach us to number our days, that we may apply our hearts unto wisdom" (Ps. 90:12). The wisdom to know that the only lasting supports and the only enduring values are those of the spirit. But more than that. It is also wisdom to renew and revitalize them when they become dull and weak as they will surely be. The confidence of youth easily becomes the stubbornness of age. Ambitions unrealized can turn idealism into cynicism. The unreasonable accidents and tragedies of the years can harden into stone the gentlest of hearts. Love loses its luster when it is undernourished. The once generous and unselfish soul can become petty and cantankerous. And faith in God and in life, when it is not renewed from day to day, dissolves into doubt and skepticism.

These things need not be. For God has provided that the spirit of man may be renewed, restored, and re-created to meet the demands of the changing years. "Create in me a clean heart, O God; and renew a right spirit within me" (Ps. 51:10). "He shall be unto thee a restorer of thy life, and a nourisher of thine old age" (Ruth 4:15). The righteous "still bring forth fruit in old age, they are ever full of sap and green, to show that the Lord is upright; he is my rock, and there is no unrighteousness in him" (Ps. 92:14, 15, RSV). "Restore unto me the joy of thy salvation" (Ps. 51:12). This should be our constant prayer as the years go swiftly by.

It is no idle petition. For God can renew our spirits as surely as he renews our bodies. This is a scientific fact as reported by Dr. Paul C. Aebersold to the Smithsonian Institution. He is director of the Isotopes Division of the Atomic Energy Commission. Said Dr. Aebersold: "Medical men used to think of the human body as an engine that takes in food, air and water mainly as fuel. Only a small part of the intake was thought to go for replacement of engine wear. Now, investigations with isotopes have demonstrated . . . that individuals . . . are continually changing." He said the studies show that the human body is 98 per cent "born again" every year. The atomic turnover in our bodies is quite rapid and quite complete. In the course of a week or two, half the sodium atoms will be replaced with other atoms. In the course of a year nearly all of the atoms in the body will be replaced by other atoms taken in our air, food, and drink.[2]

If our bodies need making over, so do our souls, minds, and spirits. They need not only to be strengthened. They need to be renewed and re-created. Our faiths can grow and remain fresh and vital even as the years go swiftly by. "Though our outward man perish, yet the inward man is renewed day by day" (II Cor. 4:16). As we live with God and walk in his way, fragile beliefs become strong convictions and weak hopes become steady assurance. If isotopes show that body atoms can be replaced, so the Bible shows that faith can replace fear, hope can replace despair, and trust can take the place of doubt.

When the years go swiftly by the Bible suggests that we change our pace to suit our changing needs.

"When I was a child, I spake as a child, I understood as a child, I thought as a child: but when I became a man, I put away childish things" (I Cor. 13:11). Paul is here recommending a principle that holds in any span of life. He is telling us to accept the mandate of our years. In other words, to grow up in our thinking, our faiths, and our actions. The current worship of youth and things youthful tempts many people into making fools of themselves as the years come and go. To be childlike in spirit is one thing. To be childish in old age is something else. The man of faith need not weep over the youthful days that have gone. Nor should he vainly try to bring them back. For maturity brings its own opportunities and responsibilities and satisfactions. We need to welcome these and accept them and adjust to their needs and demands. "Days should speak, and multitude of years should teach wisdom" (Job 32:7).

Here is good counsel for all of us as the years come and go: "Bid the older men to be temperate, serious, sensible, sound in faith, in love, and in steadfastness. Bid the older women likewise to be reverent in behavior, not to be slanderers or slaves to drink; they are to teach what is good, and so train the young women to love their husbands and children, to be sensible, chaste, domestic, kind, and submissive to their husbands, that the word of God may not be discredited" (Titus 2:2–5, RSV). Men of faith have an obligation to see that the word of God is not brought into disrepute through them. This is an increasing responsibility as we grow older. For strangely enough, life often falls apart in later years. Older people have temptations, too. "There is no fool like an old fool." We all need to resist the temptation to the cynicism and bitterness that often come in later years.

Dr. Joseph W. Still, a physiologist of George Washington University school of medicine gave wise counsel in an address before the fifth annual conference of the American Association of Rehabilitation Therapists. He said that "doctors should advise their patients to sprint up to 25 years, to trot from 25 to 40, to walk from 40 to 60—and after 60 they can dawdle at golf." He declared that such a system of gradually slowed-down activity can do much to assure a long and satisfying life. At the same conference Dr. James F. Conner said that older people themselves must "reject the idea that growing old is bad." He stated that "pessimism probably kills more old people than disease." [3]

One of the wisest ways to meet the challenge of the passing years is to accept the days as they come without undue worry about the future. The most familiar modern expression of this technique is that of the noted physician, Sir William Osler. In his famous lecture, "A Way of Life," he said: "In the summer of 1871 I was attending the Montreal General Hospital. Much worried as to the future, partly about the final examination, partly as to what I should do afterward, I picked up a volume of Carlyle, and on the page I opened there was the familiar sentence–our main business is not to see what lies dimly at a distance, but to do what lies clearly at hand. A commonplace sentiment enough, but it hit and struck and helped, and was the starting point of a habit that has enabled me to utilize to the full the single talent entrusted to me." [4]

Jesus had the same idea long before either Osler or Carlyle: "Therefore do not be anxious about tomorrow, for tomorrow will be anxious for itself. Let the day's own trouble be sufficient for the day" (Matt. 6:34, RSV).

It is not the work but the worry that kills. It is not the future but the fear of the future that takes the joy out of life. It is not the troubles that come, but the stress and strain they cause that makes us old before our time. It is not the fact that we do not have enough that makes us unhappy. It is the driving ambition to get more and more that keeps us from enjoying what we have. In all of this we are our own worst enemies as the years go swiftly by. We need to slow down, to do our very best day by day, and trust God for the rest. If we do not find happiness and fulfillment in the tasks at hand it is likely we will never find them in some vague and uncertain future.

It is good to expect much from life and to work for it. But it is still better not to expect too much and to find serenity in what we have. We do well to learn this early enough to discover that it is not in gold but in God that our peace and security are to be found. Dr. Raymond Pearl found of some two thousand persons over ninety that they had only one outstanding trait in common: they were not given to worry.[5] This should also be a trait common to all who love God and trust him. When we walk the years with him we will find the simple tasks, the simple virtues, the simple pleasures, the simple faiths are those worth living by and bring the richest rewards.

When the years go swiftly by the Bible urges us to keep our faith to the end.

"He that endureth to the end, the same shall be saved" (Matt. 24:13 ARV). West Florida's oldest resident, Leonard Finch, of Chipley, celebrated his one hundred and twelfth birthday in the presence of one hundred descendants. He gave this recipe for longevity: "Look after your own business. Work hard. Put your trust in the Lord. He will never let you down. Let liquor alone and don't forget to pray." [6] It is a good recipe for anyone in any span of life. To be sure, God does not guarantee old age to those who obey his laws and live as in his presence. But he does assure us he will not desert us along the way if we are faithful to him. "I have been young, and now am old; yet have I not seen the righteous forsaken" (Ps. 37:25). Work may become a bore. Friends may go back on us. Money comes and goes. Pleasures can pall. Loved ones sometimes disappoint. Dreams often come to naught. But those whose faith is in the righteousness and love of the eternal God, will find strong sure support to life down to the very end. This is the one thing we can count on. And it is the one thing most worth having as the years go swiftly by. "Be thou faithful unto death, and I will give thee a crown of life" (Rev. 2:10).

The trouble is we give up too soon. Too many times our faith in God gets worn and thin by exposure to life. Then something happens and we throw it all overboard. We think God has deserted us. But the fact is, we have deserted him.

Dr. Cyrus Sturgis, a noted physician of the University of Michigan, tells of a patient of his, a wealthy Boston lawyer. It was in 1925. The patient had pernicious anemia. At that time there was no cure for this malady. All the doctor could do was to keep the patient alive with blood transfusions. The lawyer patient told Dr. Sturgis he wanted to be kept alive that way just long enough to finish a book he was writing. So, for almost a year the patient was kept alive by receiving over forty blood transfusions. When the book was finished, Dr. Sturgis urged the lawyer to continue the transfusions in the hope that some new cure might be discovered. The patient scoffed at this. The transfusions were stopped at his request. In a few weeks he died. And just six weeks after his death, Dr. George Minot announced his lifesaving liver treatment for pernicious anemia! Had this patient persisted for a few more weeks he might well have had many more years to live.[7]

It is so with the ways of the spirit of man. There is much to baffle us and wall us in. We are crushed by disappointment or despair. There seems to be no way out and no road ahead. And then we give up the one thing we need most in a crisis. We surrender our hope and faith. We quit going to church. We become cynical. We turn away from God. And something dies inside us. For we have thrown away the one thing that can save us in the end. Many a soul in distress has found that it has been darkest just before the dawn. God has many good things in store for us that we can not see. "He giveth power to the faint; and to them that have no might he increaseth strength" (Isa. 40:29). Our God is a dependable God! Thank God this is so! "Thy word is true from the beginning: and every one of thy righteous judgments endureth forever" (Ps. 119:160).

Perhaps the most important thing for us as the years come and go is to have something big enough and holy enough to give ourselves to without reserve and forever. This is the meaning of the Christian commitment. It is no tentative or temporary expediency, to be discarded if things do not come our way. It is for keeps. It needs to be so. For as the Bible often points out, life is a fleeting thing. "All flesh is grass . . . The grass withereth, the flower fadeth" (Isa. 40:6, 7). We need some splendid dedication to make it all worth while. "No man, having put his hand to the plow, and looking back, is fit for the kingdom of God" (Luke 9:62). Paul put the matter clearly when he said that God "will render to every man according to his works: to those who by patience in well-doing seek for glory and honor and immortality, he will give eternal life; but for those who are factious and do not obey the truth, but obey wickedness, there will be wrath and fury" (Rom. 2:6–8 RSV).

Amid the shifting scenes and terrifying uncertainties of life and living there is only one sure, enduring thing to which we may anchor and which will bring stability and confidence to our years. And that is our faith in God and his eternal laws. "Know therefore that the Lord thy God, he is God, the faithful God, which keepeth covenant and mercy with them that love him and keep his commandments to a thousand generations" (Deut. 7:9).

In his autobiography, *Books and Bidders,* Abraham S. Wolf Rosenbach, the famous collector, said: "On February 14, 1493, Columbus carefully prepared as complete an account of his marvelous voyage as was possible under the circumstances. He wrote the details of his journey on a stout piece of parchment, wrapped it carefully in a piece of waterproof cloth, then placed it in an iron bound barrel and threw it into the raging ocean. . . . If I thought there were one chance in a million of finding it, I would take my power boat, the First Folio, and cruise in the neighborhood of the Azores forever." [8]

If a lost parchment of Columbus can claim such devotion, how much more shall the word of life claim ours. "Seek ye first the kingdom of God and his righteousness; and all these things shall be added unto you" (Matt. 6:33). This is our priceless treasure. We are wise if we cruise for it forever. When the years go swiftly by we do well to transfer our ambitions from attainable goals to an eternal vision—though its attainment we never realize. "Mark the perfect man, and behold the upright: for the end of that man is peace" (Ps. 37:37).

According to I Kings 3:5–15, the Lord appeared to Solomon in a dream and told him to ask for whatever he wanted. It was at Gibeon where Solomon had gone to make sacrifices after becoming king. In his dream he replied to God that he was as a child and needed most of all an understanding heart to judge between good and bad among God's people. This prayer pleased the Lord. "And God said unto him, Because thou hast asked this thing, and hast not asked for thyself long life; neither hast asked riches for thyself, nor hast asked the life of thine enemies; but hast asked for thyself understanding to discern judgment; Behold I have done according to thy word: lo, I have given thee a wise and understanding heart. . . . And I have also given thee that which thou hast not asked, both riches and honor. . . . And if thou wilt walk in my ways, to keep my statutes and my commandments, as thy father David did walk, then I will lengthen thy days." All of us may well make Solomon's humble prayer our own. And when we ask of life and of God only the most important things, we are likely to get more than we ask as the years go swiftly by.

Additional biblical references: Rom. 8:35–39; John 15; Gal. 5, 6; Ps. 39:4.

Why doesn't God make me well?
Can my mind make me sick?
How can our faith keep us healthy?
Is it right to expect healing miracles?

7 WHEN WE ARE SICK IN MIND AND BODY

IT HAS BEEN reliably estimated that twenty-five million people in this country suffer at any one time from some kind of chronic physical ailment. These ailments cause a loss of almost a billion man-days of work a year. They result in nearly a million deaths in a year.[1] This terrific drain on the economy and on human well-being is a concern common both to medicine and to religion.

Dr. Edward A. Strecker, a physician, has said that "fully fifty percent of the problems of the acute stages of an illness, and seventy-five percent of the difficulties of convalescence, have their primary origin, not in the body, but in the mind of the patient." And Dr. Stanley Cobb, of Massachusetts General Hospital in Boston, found that ninety-six per cent of his patients showed serious resentments, seventy-five per cent were profoundly depressed, and sixty-eight per cent were burdened with a deep sense of guilt.[2] Thus mental health is a factor of real importance to physical health.

The Great Physician had much the same idea some nineteen hundred years ago. He, too, was interested in the whole person. He, too, knew the powerful effect of the mental outlook on the physical body. Jesus, however, did not start with medicine. He started with faith: the faith of the patient. There was the case of the woman who had been sick for twelve years. She had tried all medical remedies of the time. Then she heard of Jesus. She came upon him as he was walking along, followed by a crowd. Reaching forward she touched the hem of his garment. She immediately felt that her body had been healed. Jesus asked who it was that had touched his clothes. Then the woman came and confessed what she had done and why. "And he said unto her, Daughter, thy faith hath made thee whole; go in peace, and be whole of thy plague" (Mark 5:25–34).

It was not the touching of the garment that made her well. It was her faith. Jesus gave this one reason in many of the cases of the cures reported in the Gospels. To the centurion Jesus said, "Verily I say unto you, I have not found so great faith, no, not in Israel . . . as thou hast believed, so be it done unto thee. And his servant was healed in the selfsame hour" (Matt. 8:10, 13). At another time some blind men came to him. He first asked them: "Believe ye that I am able to do this?" When they replied in the affirmative he touched their eyes, saying, "According to your faith be it unto you. And their eyes were opened" (Matt. 9:28, 29). When the Canaanite woman kept insisting that he heal her daughter possessed of a demon, he finally said: "O woman, great is thy faith: be it done unto thee even as thou wilt" (Matt. 15:22–28).

It must be understood that Jesus was no divine healer in the ordinary sense. He urged people not to tell of the benefits they received from him. This in itself is in sharp contrast to the healing charlatans who prey on the public today in the name of religion. The healing ministry of Jesus was a definite part of his teaching ministry. He did not deal in magic. He dealt in faith. He knew well the dynamic, cleansing, re-creating power of faith as a healing agent of amazing influence. Whatever our interpretations of his healing miracles and whatever our lack of ability to reproduce them, all of us need to discover the curative powers of this healing faith. In the Bible the value of faith for mental and physical health comes to focus in the New Testament. It is there the word of the psalmist comes to life. "Bless the Lord, O my soul, and forget not all his benefits: Who forgiveth all thine iniquities; who healeth all thy diseases" (103:2, 3).

The Christian faith recognizes the real existence and interrelation of both body and spirit.

Our mental attitudes are often the expression of a sick body. On the other hand, those who insist that the mind is everything and who deny the existence of the body, are guilty of evading the facts of life. Such a position is neither Christian nor scientific. Many unbelievable tragedies, not to say murders, have been committed in the name of religion by misguided people who have refused to use medical aid to save human lives. The human spirit is real. But so is the human body! Said St. Paul, "Know ye not that your body is the temple of the Holy Spirit? . . . Glorify God therefore in your body" (I Cor. 6:19). The Christian religion has never denied the real existence of the physical world nor the reality of disease, pain, and suffering. Someone has said that we should not be more "spiritual" than God himself, who gave us our bodies and who fashioned the raw material of many medicines.

The word "health" in the Bible usually includes both spiritual and physical soundness. "Beloved, I pray that in all things thou mayest prosper and be in health, even as thy soul prospereth" (III John 2 ARV). When Paul was on the ill-fated voyage to Rome, he counseled those on shipboard to break their fast as food was as necessary to their well-being as spiritual discipline. "Paul besought them all to take meat, saying, This day is the fourteenth day that ye have tarried and continued fasting, having taken nothing. Wherefore I pray you to take some meat; for this is for your health" (Acts 27:33,34). Health of body and soul are related in the thinking of Jesus. When he ate in the house of Levi the scribes and Pharisees questioned his action. "Why do ye eat and drink with publicans and sinners? And Jesus answering said unto them, They that are whole need not a physician; but they that are sick. I came not to call the righteous, but sinners to repentance" (Luke 5:27–32).

The Bible makes no effort to deny the reality of disease. Indeed, the list of diseases recorded in its pages is a long one. Some of these are: alcoholism (Prov. 23:30–35); consumption (Lev. 26:16); skin diseases (Exod. 9:9; Deut. 28:27, 35; Isa. 1:6); dropsy (Luke 14:2); epilepsy (Matt. 17:15, RSV); fevers (John 4:46–54); foot disease (II Chron. 16:12); leprosy (Lev. 13:1–17; Kings 7:3; Mark 1:41); mental disorders (I Sam. 21:13; Acts 26:24); paralysis (Mark 2:1–12); pestilence (Ezek. 6:11).

So also the Bible, along with the emphasis of Jesus on spiritual healing, takes into account the work of physicians. The Old Testament refers to them in Gen. 50:2; Jer. 8:22; II Chron. 16:12. Only Luke, the beloved physician, is mentioned by name in the New Testament. However, there are other references to physicians, even by Jesus himself (Mark 2:17). And Jesus on at least one occasion used an application of clay as a healing factor, either symbolical or real (John 9:6).

The fact is, of course, that neither the materialists nor the mentalists have a corner on the truth. For some disease is physical in origin; some is mental in origin; some is traceable to both. In the treatment of any sickness the reasonable man seeks to use the full truth of God wherever he finds it: both in the ministrations of the physician and in the ministry of religious faith. God made man a unit. The real meaning of salvation is wholeness. God certainly wants us to use all available methods of therapy in our search for health. There is nothing in the Bible that keeps us from using our intelligence in this as in any area of life.

Regardless of the extremists, ample records are available to show the powerful effect of harmful emotions and mental states on health. The most damaging of these states of mind are anger, resentment, hate, guilt, fear, anxiety, and worry. We can not live with them long, consciously or unconsciously, without suffering from the poison that they feed into our nerves and glands.

High-pressure living also has its inevitable effect on the health. New York's Life Extension Examiners examined 25,000 executives of American corporations averaging 45.6 years of age. Only 20 percent were in normal good health. The American Fidelity and Casualty Company found that the average businessman dies six years before his time. Standard Oil Company (N.J.) had 340 of its executives report for medical checkup. Of these, 235 had something wrong, with 192 having ills that affected their work and efficiency.[3] It is not hard work that does all this. It is the nervous tension, anxiety, and fear that often come with responsibility and ambition.

Heart disease has increased until it is the number one killer. From a heart disease death rate of one out of thirteen in 1900, it has risen to about one in four. Much of this comes from poor human relations. Said an authority in *Life* magazine: "The chief personality characteristic of persons with hypertension (high blood pressure) is resentment. When resentment is chronic, chronic hypertension and heart trouble follow." [4]

In view of all this, no wonder Dr. Frank Hutchins, a nerve specialist, said, "Seventy per cent of the medical cases need new mental and spiritual attitudes for health." [5] No wonder Jesus could say,

"Thy faith hath made thee whole" (Matt. 9:22)! No wonder Paul urged us to glorify God in our bodies! No wonder mental health is important to physical health! No wonder Jesus healed the bodies of men by bringing to them a new and vital mental attitude of love, forgiveness, and faith! Here, then, in the Bible itself, are vital basic, spiritual resources for those who are sick in mind and body.

The case of the healing of a man possessed by a demonic spirit is an important one for the healing record. The Oriental belief in the demonic possession as a cause of disease was widespread at the time of Jesus. There are many accounts of spirit healing and healers in other literature of the day. This no doubt strongly influenced the people and the writers of the Gospels. In fact, many of the healing miracles of Jesus dealt with ailments which today would be known as mental and nervous diseases. In this case it says that the people were amazed at the "authority and power" by which "he commandeth the unclean spirits, and they come out" (Luke 4:33–37). It is so even today. And when we are free of the evil thoughts and tempers and attitudes that poison our spirits, we are often well on the way to being made whole.

The Christian faith recognizes that healing mercies
are possible but are not necessarily
a sign of superior faith.

The urgent desire of the sick to be healed has opened the way to much quackery in the field of faith healing. Many modern miracle workers hold out the hope of divine healing in the name of Christ to those who will claim to have the faith. When no healing occurs it is said that the patient does not have enough faith. This traffic in human misery by religious quacks is often pathetic and misleading. Sometimes it is based on a wholly misleading view of Scripture. It capitalizes on the power of suggestion and sometimes, of course, does have results for the suggestible. But for many choice Christians of great faith, backed by years of devoted service to God, all this is a mockery of religion. Any number of genuinely Christian people have been ill for years without relief in spite of their beliefs.

The point is well illustrated by the case of a young girl, a friend of Leslie Weatherhead of London, who tells the story. She was taken to Lourdes, the shrine of healing of the Catholic Church, and given a silver cross which the priest had "blessed." She was too ill to join in the processions. The priest told her therefore to hold the cross tightly when the "Host" was elevated and have faith that she would recover. She tried as best she could but came home to die. As she lay dying she gave the silver cross to Dr. Weatherhead. He was deeply moved when she said to him: "I want you to keep it, for it taught me a great lesson. I have learned not to hold the cross and try to believe that I shall be healed, but to yield myself utterly to the Crucified and not mind whether I am healed or not." Commenting on the experience, Dr. Weatherhead said: "That attitude of believing in Christ whether healing comes or not is far more worthy of the name 'faith' than the attitude which assesses our own faith, or Christ's power, or both, by the phenomenon of a healed body." [6]

This does not mean that apparently miraculous healing does not take place. In the loving and wise providence of God there have been many well-authenticated cases where the power of a great faith has brought healing that has been beyond the reach of medicine. We are glad and grateful that this is so. There are spiritual laws operating in these realms which we must neither presume upon nor belittle.

Take the case of Albert Cliffe, a Canadian chemist. Some years ago he had a severe attack of ulcers. The doctor told him he would die in about a month, and advised him to take care of himself the best he could during that time. He was a member of the church and a Christian. He began to read his Bible and books on prayer and faith. Then he said that he offered this prayer at first: "Lord, I pray for healing, if it be thy will." But later on he said to himself: "Why should I put it that way? God knows what his will is. I do not need to qualify it. Anyway, I have everything to gain and nothing to lose. I am going to die in a month." So he changed his prayer. And now he said, "Lord, heal me, period!" He also began affirming to himself: "I believe I am going to be healed."

That was over twenty years ago. Albert Cliffe became a well man. He started teaching a Sunday School class. It grew from twenty-four to over a thousand. In the years that followed, he wrote several books and gave new hope and faith and healing to many people.[7]

There are many such instances of healing faith which bring inspiration and hope. They are usually in the area of functional diseases whose origin is traceable to disturbed emotions. Organic diseases and germ diseases can defy the most ardent faith. But even here attitudes of faith and courage will speed recovery.

We are all learners in the school of divine healing. We need more faith to seek God's healing power. We need, also, more complete understanding and trust in his spiritual and physical laws that govern us all. The true key to the Scriptures in healing is to exercise our faith in both Christianity and science without that gullibility which is neither Christian nor scientific.

The Christian faith recognizes the need of developing a positive, realistic faith as a continuing asset for good health.

Consider the story of Jesus' healing the blind beggar near Jericho. The beggar heard a crowd passing by and asked what it was all about. Upon being told that Jesus was passing by, he cried out to him for mercy. The people rebuked him and told him to be quiet. But he cried out again. Jesus heard him and asked what he wanted. The beggar asked that he receive his sight. "And Jesus said unto him, Receive thy sight: thy faith hath saved thee. And immediately he received his sight, and followed him, glorifying God: and all the people, when they saw it, gave praise unto God" (Luke 18:35–43). This is another instance wherein Jesus declared that the suppliant's faith was responsible for the healing. Many scholars gloss over these healing miracles of Jesus by using them as symbolic of Jesus as healing the spiritual needs of men. Thus it is easy to say in this case that we are all spiritually blind and that our inner eyes are opened by the truth the Master taught. It is also easy to sidestep the issue by saying that our modern miracles of medicine under Christian auspices represent the healing work of Jesus today. These things are true but they do not account for the accounts of healing in the Gospels. We cannot discard them any more than we can say that all healing must come by faith alone.

"Thy faith hath made thee whole," said Jesus. "Glorify God in your bodies," said Paul. They are both saying, in effect, that God has made us for healthy living. It follows that we can have healthier minds and bodies as we have faith enough to observe God's laws of body and spirit. Regardless of our belief or disbelief in healing miracles, we may all share in the miracle of preventive faith. The

New Testament is the greatest textbook on mental health ever written. In fact, Dr. William S. Sadler has said that over half of all human illness could be prevented by Christian living as outlined in the Bible.[8]

Mental health means more than thinking good thoughts. It means that we use our God-given common sense as well. Good health involves such things as good food, plenty of rest, some exercise, and proper weight. It is just as religious for us to give attention to such things through the years as it is to pray to God to heal us of some disease caused by neglect or overexhaustion or overindulgence.

The Bible brought to light long before modern psychosomatic medicine that our wholeness of body and mind depends on our right relationship with God, with our fellow men, and with ourselves. For instance, the psalmist sensed that sin was the cause of his sickness: "There is no soundness in my flesh because of thy indignation; there is no health in my bones because of my sin" (Ps. 38:3, RSV). It is sin, or rebellion against God, that causes many kinds of sickness, physical, social, and mental. Thus the total personality and conduct are matters of concern for those who are sick of mind and body. Jesus one time specifically effected a cure by releasing a palsied man from his sin by declaring his sin had been forgiven (Matt. 9:1–8; see also Mark 2:1–12). Thus our wholeness comes not merely as the result of some clever psychological exercise or formula, but as the result of the power of God to restore us to a right relationship with him and with our fellow men. And this restoration takes place as our sin and guilt are purged by the forgiveness of God and of those whom we may have wronged. This is not an easy or simple matter. But we will never be whole of mind and body unless we first are cleansed of the sin which poisons our systems. Many a mind has been cleared and many a body restored when a sick soul has penitently confessed his sin and found divine and human forgiveness. For it is when a feeling of guilt is suppressed and buried within us that it causes untold ills, often subconsciously and unconsciously.

A vital faith in God, in ourselves, and in life itself has definite curative powers. God surely wants us to be healthy and is always with us in our fight for health. Psychology and psychotherapy may remove many morbid fears and emotions. But that alone is not enough to heal. We need something to believe in and live for. This is what the religion of the Bible can give us. As A. J. Hadfield, the English psychiatrist, put it: "In some cases I have attempted to cure nervous patients with suggestions of quietness and confidence, but without success until I have linked these suggestions on to that faith in the power of God which is the substance of the Christian's confidence and hope." [9] This quiet, strong confidence in the eternal, saving, life-giving, loving God is both the beginning and the basis of a healing faith. Modern psychiatry and medicine are at long last confirming that simple statement in Acts: "Jesus Christ maketh thee whole" (9:34).

Additional biblical references: Ps. 91; Matt. 5:1–16; II Cor. 12:7–10.

How can I find peace of mind?
What are the sources of real serenity and poise?
How important is a calm spirit?

8 WHEN WE NEED INNER QUIETNESS

DR. DAVID I. MACHT and his associates at Sinai Hospital, Baltimore, report an interesting experiment in the *Journal* of the American Medical Association. They found that nervousness and apprehension speed up the clotting time of the blood. In a person who is normally calm and cool the blood clots in from eight to twelve minutes. In those who are somewhat anxious, this is shortened to four to five minutes. In those who are very nervous and upset, the time is actually cut to one to three minutes.[1] Thus inward upheavals are actually a threat to life. This is especially true for persons suffering from high blood pressure or hardening of the arteries.

If states of anxiety have this effect on the blood, they also are certainly harmful to the general well-being of the normal person. When our inner lives are distraught, tense, and worried, things happen to us. We are not at full strength. Our efficiency is lowered. Our tempers are strained. Our attitudes are warped. And our dispositions are below par. The need for inner quietness thus is one of the basic needs of life.

It is a need that increases daily. We live in a noisy world and in hectic times. The pace is uneven. The tempo is stepped up. The claims on our time and attention are beyond number. The ills and accidents that come our way upset our plans and composure. Our minds are pulled this way and that by conflicting ideas and causes that seek our loyalty. Forces and movements beyond our control make the future uncertain. To be sure, we need to come to grips with life and not retreat from it. We must strive and achieve. But we need help if we are going to retain a balance and quietness that make for secure, happy, healthful, creative living.

Our best and most dependable help comes from the Bible. For in its pages are divine sources of strength and quietness. In it we discover the way to blessed inner peace that comes to those who are spiritually minded.

The Bible reminds us that inner quietness is an inside job.

Much of our inward unrest comes because we have keyed our peace of mind to the attainment of outward desires. We become strongly attached to certain plans or people or programs. We allow our own inner well-being to depend upon riches and other outer circumstances. When these fail us our inner world is turned topsy-turvy. "Where your treasure is, there will your heart be also" (Luke 12:34). We had better not let our peace of mind hinge on what happens to us on the outside. If our calmness and poise hinge on the weather, or the size of our bank account, or what the neighbors think, or the health of Uncle Harry, or the existence of the H bomb, or the political party in power, we are doomed to disillusionment. "A man's life consisteth not in the abundance of the things which he possesseth" (Luke 12:15). The trouble is we can have everything come our way and still be dissatisfied inside. Paul put the idea in a brief, simple sentence: "To be spiritually minded is life and peace" (Rom. 8:6).

But many people never find this solution. They look all about for some magic cure-all for their distress of spirit. And never find it. Herbert Agar in his book, *A Time for Greatness*, protested against the idea of the advertiser who implies that "there must always be an answer to every problem and that answer is something money can buy." For instance, in the midst of a world war, morale was made to be something to be bought over the counter. One advertisement asked this question: "In bewildered times, where shall a man turn to replenish the wells of his courage, to repair the walls of his faith?" The answer was: beer! [2]

The notion that we can find quick peace of mind in a potion is an ancient one. There is nothing new in the modern vogue of "happiness pills." The *Spectator* in England carried an ad a long time ago which read: "Famous drops for Hypocondriack Melancholy: Which affecting cure on the Spot . . . comforting the Brain and Nerves, composing the hurried Thoughts, and introducing bright lively ideas and pleasant Briskness instead of dismal Apprehension and dark Incumbrance of the Soul. . . . Price 3s 6d a Bottle with Instructions. Sold only at Mr. Bell's, book-seller at the Cross Keys and Bible in Cornhill, near the Royal Exchange." [3]

How stupid can we get? To look for serenity of spirit on the medicine shelf is to look in the wrong place. Peace of mind does not come in a bottle.

Nor does inner quietness come from a perfect environment. Take the case of Mr. Danielson, one of the six men who sailed a balsa raft across the Pacific. He wrote about it in the book *Kontiki*. While on the trip he had a wonderful time on a balmy, peaceful Pacific island. After he had returned to the United States, he could not stand the turmoil and the inner tension it created. Taking his wife with him he went back to this lovely Pacific isle to live. He had plenty of money from his book. The coconuts were sweet and the natives kind. The weather was perfect. There was nothing to worry about: no taxes, no politics, no job, no competitors. Not even any Communists or newspapers. Mr. and Mrs. Danielson stuck it out for a year. Then they headed for home.[4] They found no peace in paradise! Escape from struggle is not the same as peace of mind in the midst of struggle.

Likewise, there is no peace in much hurrying about, even in the doing of good things. Many who are constantly on the go are in reality trying to take their minds off themselves simply because they do not want to face themselves. This may well be one interpretation of the little story of Jesus with Martha and Mary. Martha was busy with preparations for the meal when Jesus visited their home and resented her sister Mary's sitting and talking with Jesus. She complained about it to the Master. Whereupon Jesus said to her: "Martha, Martha, you are anxious and troubled about many things; one thing is needful. Mary has chosen the good portion, which shall not be taken away from her" (Luke 10:38–42, RSV). It is not by bustling about that we best serve God or find him. Those who open their minds and hearts to the wisdom and love of God have found the "good portion," the inner sense of poise and contentment that is an anchor to life. And we will continue to be "anxious and troubled about many things" until we find it by sitting at the feet of Jesus Christ, the Lord of life.

This means that we will find peace no place unless we find it in our own hearts. And this we may find no matter how hard pressed we may be or how unlikely our situation. It is when we become too strongly attached to *things* that we invite trouble. Inner quietness comes rather from a sense of detachment. We need to stand back from the things of life and look at them objectively. Few things matter as much as we think they do. We can get along without many if not most of the things we think our happiness depends upon. It will do us good, in our perennial pursuit of plunder, to ponder the words of Jesus: "Therefore I tell you, do not be anxious about your life, what you shall eat or what you shall drink, nor about your body, what you shall put on. Is not life more than food, and the body more than clothing?" (Matt. 6:25, RSV).

Inner quietness is an inside job! That is, it is a spiritual quality. Its first requirement is that we make peace with ourselves. For as Paul said: "The fruit of the spirit is love, joy, peace, patience, kindness, goodness, faithfulness, gentleness, self-control; against such there is no law" (Gal. 5:22 RSV). We look in vain for inward poise so long as our minds are bitter, our consciences tarnished, our loyalties divided between good and evil, and our hopes attached to the things of the world. As the writer of Ecclesiastes put it: "Better is a handful with quietness, than both the hands full with travail and vexation of spirit" (4:6).

The inner life is all-important in the teaching of Jesus. The heart is thought of as the directive center of the will, feeling, conscience, and thought. The "pure in heart" are to see God (Matt. 5:8). Those of "honest and good heart" are the good soil which produces best (Luke 8:15). The heart is where man's treasure lies (Matt. 6:21). Thus it is our inner lives that need purifying and regulating if we are to be balanced and creative personalities.

Paul felt the need of the unification of the inner life disturbed by inward conflicts with evil. "For the good that I would, I do not: but the evil which I would not, that I do. . . . I delight in the law of God after the inward man: But I see another law in my members, warring against the law of my mind. . . . O wretched man that I am! who shall deliver me from the body of this death? I thank God through Jesus Christ our Lord. So then with the mind I myself serve the law of God; but with the flesh the law of sin" (Rom. 7:19, 22–25). He found release from this inner conflict through the saving power of Jesus Christ. "For the law of the Spirit of life in Christ Jesus hath made me free from the law of sin and death" (Rom. 8:2). There is no surer route to inner quietness than this.

Paul knew well that the pressures of outward life force us to inner perplexity and confusion. But he knew also that the way to cope with the situation lies within ourselves rather than on outside circumstances. "And be not conformed to this world: but be ye transformed by the renewing of your mind, that ye may prove what is that good, and acceptable, and perfect, will of God" (Rom. 12:2). This capacity for inner renewal is one of the greatest weapons of the spirit. It is what goes on within us that determines the quality and stability of our lives.

The Bible suggests that inner quietness may be developed through trustful prayer.

Many of us are upset more by the minor irritations of living than by the major tragedies that come. We are like the Denver housewife who asked to be excused from jury duty. This was her reason: "Three children, 12, 6 and 1. Dirty diapers, dirty dishes, dirty clothing, dirty faces. School, ironing, cleaning, cooking, washing, and also consulting the best book on psychology to know more about why they behave like demons." She was excused!

But it is not as easy to be excused from the anxieties that beset the soul in anxious and harried days. We need some inner protection from the poisons of sin and pride and selfishness and jealousy and greed and hatred and resentment. And this sort of inward immunity comes from the habit of continuing and trustful prayer. "Thou wilt keep him in perfect peace, whose mind is stayed on thee: because he trusteth in thee" (Isa. 26:3). When our minds are stayed on him, nothing can hurt us. Millions of weary and perplexed souls have found a deep and abiding peace of mind when they turned their burden over to God. "But as for me, my feet were almost gone; my steps had well-nigh slipped. . . . Whom have I in heaven but thee? and there is none upon earth that I desire besides thee. My flesh and my heart faileth: but God is the strength of my heart, and my portion for ever. . . . It is good for me to draw near to God: I have put my trust in the Lord God, that I may declare all thy works" (Ps. 73:2, 25, 26, 28).

Bennett Cerf tells an interesting story about Dean Godolpin of Princeton University. The Dean's home was on the location on which was to be built the imposing new Firestone Memorial Library. Therefore the house was moved from one side of the campus to the other. The house was moved while the Dean was inside reading. He was completely unaware of the commotion. That evening, when he came out of the house, his only comment to his wife was: "Isn't the house facing in the wrong direction?" [5]

Here is a parable of life and of trustful prayer. When we live close to God day after day we become unaware of the commotion about us. When we are surrendered to God's will we do not even notice the shifting movements that go this way and that. It is our own stubborn wills and the determination to have our own way that cause so much inner upheaval. And it is only when we are willing to commit our ways into the care and keeping of God that the jolts and disturbances and tensions die away. It is then that the inner quietness comes that passes all understanding. We can have it when we get ourselves out of the way and let God take over. We need to know that it is not in huffing and puffing that we grow strong inside. But that "in quietness and in confidence shall be your strength" (Isa. 30:15).

"Rejoice in the Lord always; again I will say, Rejoice. Let all men know your forbearance. The Lord is at hand. Have no anxiety about anything, but in everything by prayer and supplication with thanksgiving let your requests be made known to God. And the peace of God which passes all understanding, will keep your hearts and your minds in Christ Jesus. Finally, brethren, whatever is true, whatever is honorable, whatever is just, whatever is pure, whatever is lovely, whatever is gracious, if there be any excellence, if there is anything worthy of praise, think about these things. What you have learned and received and heard and seen in me, do; and the God of peace will be with you" (Phil. 4:4–9, RSV). No finer or more complete prescription for inner quietness will be found anywhere!

The Bible assures us that inner quietness is a strong and sturdy thing when it has divine support.

Temporary peace of mind may be found by taking certain drugs. Or by practicing some form of mysticism or self-hypnotism. Such things are the stock in trade of many cults. But the quietness that comes from artificial means or from self-suggestion is likely to be a negative, empty, and undependable quietness. We cannot fool ourselves for long. The inner quietness that the Bible talks about comes from God. It is solidly based on an understanding and acceptance by the mind of the reality, the presence, and the laws of God. These laws govern life, morally, mentally, spiritually, and physically. When we try to live against them we are inwardly confused and at odds with ourselves. When we find them for ourselves and live by them we will find peace. For it means that we are at one with the universe. "They that trust in the Lord shall be as Mount Zion, which cannot be removed, but abideth for ever" (Ps. 125:1).

A well-known example of this idea in the Bible is to be found in the speech of Eliphaz in the Book of Job. In the midst of much weighty argument Eliphaz gives toward the end this simple and warm counsel: "Acquaint now thyself with him, and be at peace: thereby good shall come unto thee" (22:21). In this plain statement Eliphaz, perhaps unwittingly, goes to the heart of the matter for many of us. For there can be no real peace for any man until we bring to an end the estrangement that so often exists between us and God. It reminds us of Augustine's famous statement that God has made us for himself and that we are restless until we rest in him.

We miss the point, therefore, when we think of peace as something to be manufactured ourselves. The inner quietness that we really want and need is the peace of God. To understand this and to find it we must come to know something of the providential nature and loving care of the eternal God. Then we will realize that "your Father knoweth what things ye have need of, before ye ask him" (Matt. 6:8). And that all we need to do is to accept what is already ours. "Great peace have they which love thy law: and nothing shall offend them" (Ps. 119:165).

We catch a glimpse of the wonder of God's care in the lowliest of creatures. Take the case of the European eel. Each fall adult eels leave the fresh waters in Europe and come down to the sea. Then, guided no one knows how, they cross almost three thousand miles of the open Atlantic to their spawning grounds in the depths of the weed-strewn Sargasso Sea. There they lay their eggs. And from there the newly hatched eels take the long journey home to European waters. It takes them three years to make it. But unerringly they make their way back to the fresh waters. There they live for ten years until the cycle begins again.[6]

What is behind all this? Nature? Instinct? Yes, but who set it all up and planned it and controls it? How does the chick know when to break the shell? Who tells the rosebud when to blossom? These things do not come by accident. The eternal creative God is in charge of things. He cares for his creation. Is it too much to expect, then, that he cares for us, too? He who watches over the birds of the air and the lilies of the field and the eels under the sea is surely great enough and loving enough to watch over us. We can rest secure in his guidance and love. "Be still, and know that I am God" (Ps. 46:10). This is the beginning and end of our inner quietness. For only when we know him can we be really still. For when our trust is in him our nagging worries slip away and our fretfulness subsides.

Engineers of the Westinghouse Electric Corporation have predicted the use of phosphorescent substances on wallpaper and in paint. These substances have the power of absorbing the sun's rays and then giving them off again after a period of time. Thus the light absorbed by the walls in a house during the day would be radiated by the walls at night. We would need no artificial lighting. There would be no problem of efficiency. We would use at night only a small fraction of the light stored up during the day. Even in wintertime the daylight intensity is about 2,400 foot-candles. Whereas only 100 foot-candles give plenty of light for a room at night.[7]

Here is a parable of inner quietness. If we can store up and use the light of the sun, why can we not absorb within our souls something of the infinite power and divine peace of the great Father God to give us quietness and confidence? Even on dark days! But it cannot be done without the phosphorescent substances of faith and trust and goodness. We must clear our minds of debris through forgiveness. We must do all we can ourselves. And we must leave the ultimate with him. Then we will find the rooms of the spirit strangely illuminated with the wondrous peace and beauty of the divine presence. "The work of righteousness shall be peace; and the effect of righteousness, quietness and assurance for ever" (Isa. 32:17). "They that know thy name will put their trust in thee: for thou, Lord, hast not forsaken them that seek thee" (Ps. 9:10). "I will both lay me down in peace, and sleep: for thou, Lord, only makest me dwell in safety"

(Ps. 4:8). It was this divine peace that Jesus left as his ultimate gift to his disciples. "My peace I leave with you, my peace I give unto you: not as the world giveth, give I unto you" (John 14:27). And Paul declares that peace with God is the sum of the blessings found in Christ. "Therefore being justified by faith, we have peace with God through our Lord Jesus Christ: By whom also we have access by faith into this grace wherein we stand, and rejoice in hope of the glory of God" (Rom. 5:1, 2).

Then there is the story of Jesus' stilling the storm on the Sea of Galilee. He was with the disciples in a ship. A sudden storm arose. The disciples were afraid and called to him for help. "And he saith unto them, Why are ye fearful, O ye of little faith? Then he arose, and rebuked the winds and the sea; and there was a great calm" (Matt. 8:23–27). Such quick storms were not unusual on the Sea of Galilee. The story is taken literally to suggest the power of the Master over natural forces. But from that day to this it also has been interpreted as a symbol of the authority of Christ to quiet the turbulent storms that often arise in the hearts of men. Many of us are panicky and helpless before them, even as the disciples in the boat. In such times there is no place to turn save to the Lord of life himself. Uncounted disciples through the years have in times of great stress sought him in faith and never in vain. For in him is the divine power to rebuke the tempest and bring a calmness within such as comes from no other place on land or sea.

Additional biblical references: Ps. 51; Isa. 31:1–5; John 14; Eph. 2:12–18; I John 1:5–10.

Why not give it up as a bad job?
How can I get hold of myself again?
Can we successfully go it alone?

9 WHEN WE LOSE FAITH IN OURSELVES

IN CHARLES LINDBERGH'S book about his famous flight to Paris he makes an interesting observation. He points out the dangers to a trans-Atlantic flier in flying too high or too low. If the plane is too high, the wings may become iced and the control of the plane is lost. If it is too low, a sudden heavy fog might easily cause a quick dip that would send the plane into the ocean. The distinguished flier said that the success of his solo flight depended upon avoiding the two extremes.[1]

Life is like that. Especially so with reference to our faith in ourselves. Sometimes we think too much of ourselves or only of ourselves. When this happens the wings of our spirits become iced over with the heavy weight of egotism, self-pride, and self-righteousness. From these things come the superiority complexes that make prigs and snobs and tyrants. But more often than not we are tempted to fly too low. We tend to devalue ourselves. We run ourselves down. We underrate our own capacities. These things obscure our vision and a crash landing is often the result.

It is at this point that the Bible comes to our aid in a real way. It tells us to think well of ourselves. But it cautions us not to think of ourselves more highly than we ought to think. In the Old Testament Isaiah says that when God is our strength we can all keep going. Some may fly higher than others. But even though we have to walk we will have strength for the journey (Isa. 40:31). In other words, no man need have cause to lose faith in himself. And Paul declares triumphantly that he has learned that in Christ he is able to do, or withstand, anything (Phil. 4:13).

There is an old English word called *inwit*. It means self-understanding. The Bible helps us toward inwit. It faces us with ourselves as well as with God. It shows us who we are and how we operate. From this self-understanding at its highest level comes the renewal of our faith in ourselves.

The Bible helps us recover our self-respect.

Far too many of us lose faith in ourselves because we live like Packey Lydon. Packey is an engineer for the Chicago Tunnel Company railroad which carries freight and ashes underneath the city. For forty-eight years Packey has been wandering around in a tunnel beneath Chicago's Loop. He has traveled 1,383,200 miles without setting foot in bus, streetcar, cab, train, ship, or plane. All this travel has been along 40 miles of track 125 feet underground.[2]

Most of us would not like Packey Lydon's job. Yet many of us persist in living in some dark tunnel of self-abasement. There have been many influences that have driven the spirit of man underground. The terror of war and the brashness of science. The worship of the gods Freud and Marx. The naked materialism that reduces life to the operation of the animal functions. And then there is what someone has called *pan-phobia;* fear of everything! These things and their evil offspring have taken us around and around and around forty short miles of track. It is an endless ride in the darkness. To it there is neither beginning nor ending. On it there can be no lifted vision or alluring hope.

Likewise there are more immediate matters that take away our self-confidence. These include the discouragements and defeats that come from failure, illness, and frustration. It does not take much, sometimes, to shut out the light and send us into the dark tunnels.

As a result we become discouraged. We run more to surface sophistication than to inner security. We go in for toughness rather than goodness. We become hard and cynical instead of being patient and understanding. And so, gradually, we lose two attitudes of supreme worth—namely, reverence for life and respect for self. When we do not think much of ourselves, we do not act like much.

Here is where the Bible helps us. It restores our self-respect by assuring us that we can be the children of God, no matter what may be our lot. And that we may live always within the providence and care of God. We are not merely creatures of the hour or of the earth. We may likewise become citizens of eternity. In our bodies and spirits we carry the mark of the beast but also of the eternal. We are not doomed to be denizens of darkness. We can belong to the light. We have the capacity for victory! We can be on the side of the angels! This is so, the Bible says, because man is made in the image of God, only a little lower than the angels, and has qualities that can resemble the qualities of God himself (Gen. 1:26–28, 9:1–7; Ps. 8:5; John 1:1–13).

There is much in the Bible that tells of sin and disillusionment which separate man from God. Man is designed to walk with God. But he has the power of choice. He is disobedient and departs from the path. His nature is corrupted by a deep-seated evil. "Being filled with all unrighteousness, fornication, wickedness, covetousness, maliciousness; full of envy, murder, debate, deceit, malignity; whisperers, Backbiters, haters of God, despiteful, proud, boasters, inventors of evil things, disobedient to parents, Without understanding, covenant-breakers, without natural affection, implacable, unmerciful: Who, knowing the judgment of God, that they which commit such things are worthy of death, not only do the same, but have pleasure in them that do them" (Rom. 1:29–32). See also John 3:3–6; I Cor. 2:14; James 3:1–10. But God does not leave man alone in his wickedness. Man is capable of being saved. In fact, the Bible records the persistent purpose of God to save men from evil. In other words, God is on our side!

Thus, against this backdrop of the sordid aspects of human nature, there is the triumphant story of the spirit of God in man. It begins in the first chapter of Genesis: "God created man in his own image, in the image of God created he him" (1:27). It continues with the shout of the psalmist: "Thou hast made him [man] a little lower than the angels, and hast crowned him with glory and honor" (8:5). And it reaches its climax in the words of the Master: "Ye are the light of the world" (Matt. 5:14).

It is this divine origin and undergirding of human life that gives dignity to our days. It gives us the divine right to believe in ourselves, because it gives us the divine power to overcome our sins, weaknesses, temptations, and disillusionments. This makes possible an inner spirit that cannot be routed. For when we find God we can respect ourselves as the children of God. Then we are unconquerable.

This capacity of man to respect himself is part of the permanent possession of the race. No cruel turn of history and no godless human philosophy has been able to crush it out. Nor has man's own sinful rebellion against God. After speaking of the human degradation of the concentration camps in Germany during World War II, Mme. Olga Lengyel wrote: "Yet I saw many internees cling to their human dignity to the very end. The Nazis could debase them physically but they could not degrade them morally. Because of them I have not entirely lost my faith in mankind." [3]

We are, therefore, partakers of a great heritage. We are not meaningless specks of atomic dust. We are potentially the children of the most high God! We will never achieve this full, vast potential until we look up and let God claim us. We can be worth more, and can amount to more, and can count for more, than we allow ourselves to think. "Therefore, brethren, we are debtors, not to the flesh, to live after the flesh. For if ye live after the flesh, ye shall die: but if ye through the Spirit do mortify the deeds of the body, ye shall live. For as many as are led by the Spirit of God, they are the Sons of God. . . . The Spirit itself beareth witness with our spirit, that we are the children of God: And if children, then heirs; heirs of God, and joint-heirs with Christ; if so be that we suffer with him, that we may be also glorified together" (Rom. 8:12–17).

William Faulkner is neither purist nor religionist. But when he accepted the Nobel Prize in Stockholm, he stated his faith: "I believe that man will not merely endure: he will prevail. He is immortal, not because he alone among creatures has an inexhaustible voice, but because he has a soul, a spirit capable of compassion, and sacrifice and endurance." [4] Certainly he has! *It is there because God gave it to him!* Because of it we can dare to have faith in ourselves. On no other basis can we explain life or find confidence and courage to stand up to it and conquer.

"Ye are the salt of the earth: but if the salt have lost his savor, wherewith shall it be salted? it is thenceforth good for nothing, but to be cast out, and to be trodden under foot of men. Ye are the light of the world. A city that is set on a hill cannot be hid. Neither do men light a candle, and put it under a bushel, but on a candlestick; and it giveth light unto all that are in the house. Let your light so shine before men, that they may see your good works, and glorify your Father which is in heaven" (Matt. 5:13–16).

The Bible shows us the importance of self-control as a way to self-confidence.

When self-respect goes, so does self-control. When we do not think much of ourselves we do not much care what we do or what happens to us. We are likely to think of ourselves as the tool of circumstances. Or that we are at the mercy of impersonal forces and events. We will never regain faith in ourselves until we let God take us in hand. No healthy person need always be the cringing victim of his sins, fears, and phobias. God can give us the power to control our minds and wills. We need not remain the hapless victims of evil forces. We will be the masters of ourselves, regardless of the reverse turns of the wheel of fortune, when God becomes our master. This is the message of the Bible. It brings new life to defeated men.

At the same time, as we have said, the Bible does not indulge in cheap optimism about man's nature. It warns of the dire results of the evil that is in our hearts. Man is akin to God but he also is subject to sinful tendencies (Isa. 1:4–15; Jer. 17:1–10; Rom. 7:7–25).

But with it all, man can be redeemed and is worth redeeming. God stands ready but man must do something about it too. Dale Carnegie tells the story of a friend of his. This young man suffered a nervous breakdown brought on by constant worry. He had worried about his health, his finances and his ambitions until he became a nervous wreck. He was forced to quit his job. He was in continuous mental agony. He felt he was deserted by everyone. He retreated from life and could not even talk with his own family. In this depressed state of mind this man decided to go to Florida, hoping that a change of scene would help him. As he got on the train, his father handed him a note in a sealed envelope telling him not to open it until after he had arrived. In Florida he found he was more wretched than ever. Finally he opened the note from his father. It read: "Son, you are 1500 miles from home, and you don't feel any different, do you? I knew you wouldn't, because you took with you the one thing that is the cause of all your trouble, that is, yourself. It is not the situations you have met that have thrown you; it is what you think of those situations. 'As a man thinketh in his heart, so is he.' When you realize that, son, come home, for you will be cured."

This young man told Dale Carnegie that his father's letter made him angry. He was looking for sympathy, not counsel. That very night as he walked down a side street in Miami he came to a church where services were going on. He drifted in, not having any other place to go. But he heard a sermon that changed his life. It was on the text, "He that is slow to anger is better than the mighty; and he that ruleth his spirit than he that taketh a city" (Prov. 16:32). This word from the Book verified the word from his father. It swept away the accumulated litter from his brain. He said: "I realized what a fool I had been. I was shocked to see myself in my true light: here I was, wanting to change the whole world and everyone in it—when the only thing that needed changing was the focus of the lens of the camera which was my own mind. The next morning I packed and started home. A week later I was back on the job . . . God has been good to me both materially and mentally." [5]

It is a parable as from the Bible itself. *He that ruleth his spirit is greater than he that taketh a city.* Here is a powerful dynamic for faith in ourselves! For, as another verse of Proverbs puts it, "He that hath no rule over his own spirit is like a city that is broken down, and without walls" (25:28). And when we take ourselves in hand, we find divine support.

This matter of the self-discipline of the mind and will and emotions takes courage and effort of a high order. There is nothing magical about it. But it does not come from our own puny human efforts alone. It comes from God. "They that wait upon the Lord shall renew their strength; they shall mount up with wings as eagles; they shall run, and not be weary; and they shall walk, and not faint" (Isa. 40:31). "Be strong in the Lord, and in the power of his might. Put on the whole armor of God, that ye may be able to stand against the wiles of the devil" (Eph. 6:10, 11). These are wise counsels that have stood the test of long experience. For a host of men have found personal victory when God has mastered their passions, their thoughts, and their actions.

Paul himself was one of these. Scholars who take a dim view of self-discipline as being something less than Christian should take a lesson from the Apostle. Paul was a man of fire, passion, and strong will and he had to keep himself well in hand to maintain his confidence as a messenger of God. Let him speak for himself: "Every man that striveth for the mastery is temperate in all things. Now they do it to obtain a corruptible crown; but we an incorruptible. I therefore so run, not as uncertainly; so fight I, not as one that beateth the air: But I keep under my body, and bring it into subjection: lest that by any means, when I have preached to others, I myself should be a castaway" (I Cor. 9:25–27). See also RSV.

There is more self-discipline in Christianity than some people seem to think! "If any man will come after me, let him deny himself, and take up his cross daily, and follow me" (Luke 9:23). "Strait is the gate, and narrow is the way, which leadeth unto life" (Matt. 7:14). "Herein do I exercise myself, to have always a conscience void of offence toward God, and toward men" (Acts 24:16). "The fruit of the Spirit is love, joy, peace, patience, kindness, goodness, faithfulness, gentleness, self-control; against such there is no law. And those who belong to Christ Jesus have crucified the flesh with its passions and desires" (Gal. 5:22–24, RSV).

God has made man his own free moral agent. The power to choose the quality of our own souls and the direction of our own lives is in our hands. Therefore, we do well to heed the word of the psalmist when he said: "Be ye not as the horse, or as the mule, which have no understanding: whose mouth must be held in with bit and bridle" (32:9). Thank God we are more than horses and mules, dumbly subject to the bit and bridle of accident. We are free men but, as Paul said, "All things are lawful unto me, but all things are not expedient" (I Cor. 6:12). Our freedom is protected by our self-restraint.

The parable of the prodigal son is generally thought of as an illustration of the conversion of a wayward man. But it likewise points up the way men lose confidence in themselves and then regain it. The prodigal started out with a brave heart and great hopes. But the temptations were many and his will was weak. He wanted to enjoy life! It was not long before his self-control was gone and then his self-respect. He was ashamed and miserable. But he did not stay that way! He made up his mind he would swallow his pride and go back to his father. And his father received him with open arms and gave him back his status as a man. But he had to have the self-control to make the first move! (Luke 15:20) It is the story of Everyman. We find our self-confidence only as in humility and penitence we are willing to find our way to the Father's love, accept his forgiveness, and take our place as a child in his household.

The Bible tells us that the key to self-confidence is self-surrender.

This is a paradox of life that many, if not most, of us miss completely. We have had the idea that faith in ourselves meant merely faith in ourselves. And so we have read books on psychology. We have repeated clever slogans. We have built atom bombs. We have filled our banks with gold. We have passed no end of laws. And yet we are unsure of ourselves. Our human satisfactions do not seem to mean much because we have missed the deeper meaning of life which also brings the only real satisfaction. And that is that man's true purpose in life is to honor God and serve him. It is not in ourselves but "*in him* we live, and move, and have our being; as certain also of your own poets have said, For we are also his offspring" (Acts 17:28). And it is only as we learn to lose our lives that we truly find them. We are God's children. We belong to him. And until we identify ourselves with his divine purposes our faith in ourselves is a weak and misplaced thing. We become sure of ourselves only as we become possessed of an inspired purpose. We get the things we want most only as we give ourselves away. This is a law of God and of life.

Our faith in ourselves breaks down when we do not have anything bigger than our own petty selves to have faith in. We have to get ourselves off our own hands. "Trust in the Lord with all thine heart; and lean not unto thine own understanding" (Prov. 3:5). It is this that makes men strong. The men who have the most confidence in themselves are those who are most willing to admit their own self-dependence. Said J. Edgar Hoover, in commenting on this word from the Word: "When man 'leans on his own understanding' . . . when he lives by his own strength—he forgets God and claims he is his own master. The result is untold suffering. . . . To 'trust in the Lord with all thine heart' is a mark of strength. And it is the only path to happiness, success and true fulfillment." [6]

And yet there are those who strut about and make loud noises only to cover up an inner lack of confidence. They are like the men T. S. Eliot wrote about:

> We are the hollow men
> We are the stuffed men

Leaning together
Headpiece filled with straw. Alas!

Shape without form, shade without colour,
Paralyzed force, gesture without motion; . . .[7]

These are they who are wise in their own conceits. But who are terribly ignorant of the deeper springs of being. They sneer at those who would make life better. They catch no lofty vision of service to humanity. They are coldly aloof to the appeal of dedicated living. They are like the character in the play by Robert Ardrey, *Sing Me No Lullaby*, who says: "If Abraham Lincoln were alive today he'd take two Nembutals and go straight to bed."

In this view of life there can be no faith in ourselves! For faith in self goes when we lose faith in God. When we have no controlling purpose save to satisfy our own personal needs we find ourselves as hollow men, stuffed with straw, the force within us paralyzed and motionless. Abraham Lincoln would *not* take Nembutals were he alive today! Nor will any normal person who has caught a glimpse of the possibilities of the Kingdom of God. The Creator made us for superior living. In his service no life need be ordinary or useless. It is not common, but uncommon people that God needs to redeem a commonplace world.

Every man owes a debt to humanity he can never repay. And personal tragedy comes when a person denies the claims of the spirit or ignores the pain and suffering of mankind. Such isolation of soul makes for inner emptiness. We can have no real faith in ourselves until we see ourselves as sharing and bearing the common lot of mankind. It is nobility of purpose and height of ideal that gives self-confidence. "Seek ye first the kingdom of God . . ." (Matt. 6:33). We never come into our own until we give ourselves away. "He that loveth father or mother more than me is not worthy of me: and he that loveth son or daughter more than me is not worthy of me. And he that taketh not his cross, and followeth after me, is not worthy of me. He that findeth his life shall lose it: and he that loseth his life for my sake shall find it" (Matt. 10:37–39). Our greatest key to personal power is to give our lives to God. The "new man" is to come into his own as an ambassador on behalf of Christ (II Cor. 5:17–20).

Those who live with God and for God are among the unconquerable. It is not in our strength we can do all things. But in his! When we surrender our wills to his will we find a capacity for great living beyond human dreaming.

The Bible tells of the time Joshua called together the people and challenged them to choose their God. He told them that they would have to give up their other gods if they served the one true God. "And if it seem evil unto you to serve the LORD, choose you this day whom ye will serve; whether the gods which your fathers served . . . or the gods of the Amorites, in whose land ye dwell: but as for me and my house, we will serve the LORD" (Josh. 24:14–25). Life is full of choices for us all. But often we are not brave enough to make the good and wise choice. We let ourselves be pushed around by events. We worship whatever gods happen to be handy. No wonder we lose faith in ourselves. There is no high and pure standard to guide us and hold us to our best. But when a man decides for God against the world he lays the foundation for faith in himself.

Additional biblical references: Ps. 27; Ps. 139; Prov. 3:5–18; Matt. 13:44–46.

How can a God of might also be a God of love?
Why does a good God allow evil to flourish?
Is God indifferent? Cold? Friendly? Approachable?

10 WHEN WE WONDER WHAT GOD IS LIKE

A ROVING REPORTER stopped six people on the sidewalks of New York and asked them what they thought was the most important happening in history. Five of the replies came from adults. They were quite varied. "The settlement of Jamestown by the English." "The defeat of the Saracens at Tours." "The splitting of the atom." "The defeat of the Japanese." "The invention of the wheel." The sixth answer came from a fourteen-year-old schoolboy. He said, "The birth of Jesus Christ." [1]

The lad answered more wisely than he knew. For history is no bare record of events. It is the story of people. And the most influential person who ever lived was Jesus of Nazareth, born in Bethlehem. Many reasons might be given why this is so. And all of them would be important. But the one reason that rises above all others is that Jesus showed men what God is like. "He that hath seen me hath seen the Father" (John 14:9).

This, of course, is the most ancient question to puzzle the mind of man. What is God like? Thomas Heywood put it and give his answer in haunting lines:

> I asked myself what this great God might be
> That fashioned me.
> I answered: The all-potent, sole, immense,
> Surpassing sense;
> Unspeakable, inscrutable, eternal,
> Lord over all;

The only terrible, strong, just and true,
Who hath no end, and no beginning knew.[2]

But the answer of Thomas Heywood is only a partial and incomplete answer to his own question. There are many answers like it in the Old Testament.

One of the key principles to keep in mind in understanding the Bible is that it is a record of the changing and developing ideas of man about the nature of God, as well as about many other aspects of religious faith. There is a great difference between the idea of God in Judges and in John. In the first chapter of Genesis God is described as the Creator of the universe and of man (1:2–31). This was a tremendous advance over the shadowy concept of the Great Spirit of primitive man. God as Creator also finds expression in the Psalms. "The heavens declare the glory of God; and the firmament showeth his handiwork" (19:1). This Creator was not thought of only as brute force. He is the supreme ruler of the Jewish people. "The Lord your God is God of gods and Lord of lords, the great, the mighty, and the terrible God, who is not partial and takes no bribe" (Deut. 10:17, RSV).

The idea of God as a judge and lawgiver gradually took shape and form over the centuries. The record is found in Exodus and Deuteronomy. There is the dramatic story of God's giving the Ten Commandments to Moses on tablets of stone (Exod. 20:1–21). They show God to be a supreme being of righteousness and of law. The great moral principles expressed in the Commandments still hold as divinely ordained rules of life. When men violate them they reap the reward of their disobedience. For God is a God of justice and judgment as well as of love and peace. Many of the woes of life and society are brought about, not because God wills it or wants it, but because of man's deliberate turning away from the plain laws of life written into the texture of the universe by the great God of all men.

But God's justice is tempered with mercy as seen in Hosea. And in Isaiah and Psalms the idea of an ethical God as a spirit and a shepherd come to the fore. The famous 23rd Psalm is a compact statement of the kindlier aspects of the nature of God as a considerate guide, a provider for our needs, a protector against our enemies, a restorer of weary souls, a comforter in time of sorrow, and a rewarder after death. It is no wonder that such a beautiful and tender expression of faith has made God real for millions of questing hearts.

Then still later the book of Jonah suggests that God's concern and forgiveness extend to Israel's enemies. And the Book of Ruth is a beautiful story of racial tolerance. Prophets such as Amos, Micah, and Jeremiah stress the moral nature of God and plead for social justice among all peoples as the essential purpose of God. The "Eternal" in much of the Old Testament thought is characterized by such words as righteous, just, holy, long-suffering.

These Old Testament answers as to what God is like all have their truth and their appeal. But they still did not completely satisfy the mind and heart of man. There is only one answer that does. It came from God himself, when he sent his son into the world. "And the Word was made flesh, and dwelt among us, (and we beheld his glory, the glory as of the only begotten of the Father,) full of grace and truth" (John 1:14). This is the climax and fulfillment of all that had gone before. In it we find that God is like Jesus Christ. This has deep meaning for us all in our understanding of the nature of God.

In Jesus' revelation of the seeking God we find the climax of man's ancient search for him.

From time immemorial men had sought God in many weird ways and faraway places. They had built him temples and altars and had sacrificed all manner of costly things to gain his favor. Then, one night in Bethlehem, a child was born. And forever after, men have known that God is seeking them. "Canst thou by searching find out God?" (Job 11:7). It is a fruitless search until it takes us to Bethlehem. And then we know it is God who seeks us out and finds us in Jesus Christ. The great creator of the universe came to earth in human form to make his home among men. This is the epic story of the ages!

It is a timeless story that is familiar to the whole world. It is the story of the birth of a baby in a manger beside a wayside inn, attended by two plain people, by sheep and shepherds, and by a few men of uncommon wisdom who brought gifts from afar. The universal and perennial appeal of this event so long ago is evidence enough that God was in it. Generation after generation of men of all kinds and descriptions have found here, often without realizing it, the answer to their questioning search for God. Here the vague hopes of the Old Testament become a glorious reality (Luke 2:1–20).

The Cloisters is a beautiful showroom of medieval art in New York, a part of the Metropolitan Museum of Art. Its director, James J. Rorimer, is an expert on medieval art. For some thirty years, Mr. Rorimer had been looking for something—something he was not sure even existed. It seems that there were in the United States two superb fifteenth-century tapestries thought to be the work of Jan van Roome of Brussels. Each piece was held by different owners. But Mr. Rorimer began to study them. He saw that they both featured the same principal characters. The borders were identical in design and each had been restored along one side. The expert decided there must be a missing middle section that would tie together the two separate pieces. It was for this middle section that he looked so long.

Finally, in 1953, Mr. Rorimer found the missing piece in the Walters Art Gallery in Baltimore. He arranged for the Cloisters to acquire the three separate pieces. They matched perfectly in design, color, and thread count. It was found that the complete original tapestry, thirty feet long and eleven feet high, had been commissioned by Emperor Maxmillian of Austria. It had been cut into three sections sometime about 1850 and the various parts found their separate ways to the United States. Carefully put together and cleaned, the tapestry is one of the most beautiful works of its kind in the world.

There is a stranger part, still, to this strange story. In the key center section, missing so long, the artist-weaver illustrated a popular medieval legend. He shows the Emperor Octavian asking the Tiburtine sibyl whether any king as great as he would ever live. The sibyl replies by showing the Emperor a vision of the Christ Child! [3]

The story of this tapestry is the story of the race in more ways than one. In their search for the one true God, men have found many expressions of his presence woven into the tapestry of the world. It is not unusual for men to bow before shrines of science or nature or humanity. These are all beautiful. They all contain some segment of divinity. Yet they are marginal. They all have something in common. But there is a section missing. It is the key center section and on it is the picture of the Christ Child. When this is in place, the search is ended and the entire panorama becomes of one piece. For when

God sent his only son into the world he gave the key to his own nature and being.

In the coming of Jesus men saw that God did not dwell on Mount Sinai nor in the temples nor even with the mightiest of the emperors. No longer is God a lofty and unapproachable being, outside of the universe and removed from the struggle of men. The New Testament God is a God who is humble enough to take the form of a child. He enters into the human arena. He takes part in the struggles and suffering of his children. He cares enough for us that he sent his own son to tell us what he is like and to show us the way to him. God does not wait for us to find him. He is with us. "One God and Father of all, who is above all, and through all, and in you all" (Eph. 4:6). He knows our indifference and willfulness, as well as our needs. "Your Father knoweth what things ye have need of, before ye ask him" (Matt. 6:8). He wants to claim us for his own. "Fear not, little flock; for it is your Father's good pleasure to give you the kingdom" (Luke 12:32). He stands ready to share with us his abundance. "Eye hath not seen, nor ear heard, neither have entered into the heart of man, the things which God hath prepared for them that love him" (I Cor. 2:9). God is equal to any possibility. He cuts through our stuffiness, our snobbishness, and our selfishness with the appealing presence of the Christ Child. Is there any more sublime and effective route to the hearts of men?

The parables of the lost coin and the lost sheep are two familiar illustrations of the seeking God in the Gospels. If even one sheep out of a flock of one hundred is lost, the shepherd searches for the one lost sheep until it is found. The same with the woman who has lost one of ten pieces of silver. She sweeps the house carefully until she finds it (Luke 15:3–10). Of such is the nature of God. Even though we may become lost in our own conceits and sin, God's love seeks us out and finds us and God rejoices when we return to him. This is routine to most of us. But in the time of Jesus it was a fresh and startling idea about the nature of God. He is a God of love!

In Jesus' portrait of the loving God we find the secret of the true greatness of the Creator.

The glimpses of the truth about God's greatness that men find in Judaism, in Hinduism, in Buddhism, and in Islam are all fragmentary and marginal. There is something missing at the center. And that something is Jesus Christ, symbolic of the love of God. The description of the divine being by Isaiah is a high and noble thing. "The Lord is our judge, the Lord is our lawgiver, the Lord is our King; he will save us" (33:22). If that were all the Bible has to say about the nature of God, it would be good. But not good enough! The supreme answer comes from the writer of John: "For God so loved the world, that he gave his only begotten Son, that whosoever believeth in him should not perish, but have everlasting life" (3:16). And in I John it is reduced to three short words: "God is love" (4:8).

This may seem to most of us a commonplace idea. We become so familiar with it that we lose its full meaning. But it is one of the most sublime ideas of all time. The mighty Creator, the One who is from everlasting to everlasting, the Great Eternal Spirit, the Infinite Power of the universe, the One in whose hands reside the destinies of the whirling worlds, the majestic and almighty force that hangs the stars in their places and that establishes the order by which all things are governed, what is he like? Is he detached and impassive mind? Is he brute and inscrutable strength? Is he indifferent, cold, remorseless law, or harsh, stern judge? The Old Testament sees him as the embodiment of righteousness and truth and law. This was a great advance over much that had gone before. But it is only when we come to Jesus that we know the true answer. For in Jesus we make the supreme discovery that God is love and we know that he loves us. God loves us! That is what the Bible means!

The idea of God as a loving Father has its beginnings in the Old Testament, of course. "Like as a father pitieth his children, so the Lord pitieth them that fear him" (Ps. 103:13). "Have we not all one father?" (Mal. 2:10). But it comes to life and to flower in the New Testament. Jesus early thought of God in this way. "Did you not know that I must be in my Father's house?" was the question the boy of twelve put to Mary and Joseph when they sought him out in the temple (Luke 2:49, RSV). His teachings were full of references to God the Father. They might be summed up in his introduction to the Lord's Prayer: "When ye pray, say, Our Father" (Luke 11:2). Paul likewise used this idea of a loving Father in all his dynamic ministry. "To us there is but one God, the Father, of whom are all things, and we in him" (I Cor. 8:6).

God the Father cares for us, even the least of us. This is one of the reassuring messages of the New Testament. "Are not five sparrows sold for two farthings, and not one of them is forgotten before God? But even the very hairs of your head are all numbered. Fear not, therefore: ye are of more value than many sparrows. . . . Consider the ravens: for they neither sow nor reap; which neither have storehouse nor barn; and God feedeth them: how much more are ye better than the fowls?" (Luke 12:6, 7, 24).

Why should God care? Why should he be concerned? Said Martin Luther: "If I were as our Lord God . . . and these vile people were as disobedient as they now be, I would knock the world to pieces." [4] We are so human we fail to see that this is the very nature of love: that it loves even if there is no love in return. Not only did God send his son into the world to show his love, but in Jesus himself we see the nature of the love of God: genuine, understanding, sacrificial, patient, suffering, forgiving. God loves the leper, the outcast, the hurt, the sinner, the oppressed. And even on the Cross Jesus prayed for God's forgiveness for those who put him to death (Luke 23:24). Do we want to know what God is like? The Bible tells us he is like Jesus Christ! No scientist, no philosopher, no educator, no historian, no sociologist, no statesman, no religionist has a better or more profound answer than that.

The tragedy is that we so often fail to understand this. We like to follow our minds instead of our hearts. We like to worship power. The power of guns, of gold, and of bigness. We forget that love is the greatest power of all. We philosophize and speculate. We make a production of everything. Even the story of the love of God in Christ. The Christmas television program by the Fred Waring group required sixty-five entertainers before the cameras. And behind the cameras there were ninety-four persons at work. There were fourteen stagehands, four cameramen, two camera prop men, four men at the camera controls, four sound men, two sound boom men, a four-man lighting crew, four stage managers, four directors, three commercial writers, five commercial prop workers, sixteen ushers, three house managers, two advertising agency contact men, seven publicity men, two business representatives, two writers, two script girls, one ticket girl, one producer, five musical arrangers, two music librarians, one attorney, and one chef.[5]

All of this to say: "Unto you is born this day in the city of David a Saviour, which is Christ the Lord" (Luke 2:11)! The original production was much simpler. But it was a scene etched indelibly upon the heart of the world. Simply because in exquisite simplicity without fuss and fanfare it told of the love of the Father God for all men. Why must we always call in prop men and writers and camera crews to dress up the gospel and doctor up our religion and rationalize our faith? The love of God shames us for our own callousness and our crass sophistication. We need but to lay aside our stiff pride and unlock our hard hearts. The loving God is waiting to possess us and bring us peace. "Cast all your anxieties on him, for he cares about you" (I Peter 5:7, RSV).

In Jesus' demonstration of a saving God we find God meeting man's deepest needs.

"For God sent not his Son into the world to condemn the world; but that the world through him might be saved" (John 3:17). Saved from its sin, its ignorance, its cruelty, its despair. "For the Son of man is come to seek and to save that which was lost" (Luke 19:10). Lost in the blind alleys of superstition, ritualism and dogma, self-love and self-worship.

The objective of many religions, both ancient and modern, has been the appeasement of an angry or tyrannical god. The real objective of Christianity, however, is the fulfillment of human life. "I am come that they might have life, and that they might have it more abundantly" (John 10:10). In sending Jesus into the world, God the Father is saying that he is not satisfied with our legalisms, our burnt offerings, our self-righteous conformity to a religion of rote and custom. He is saying rather that we are saved as our minds, hearts and wills are claimed by Jesus Christ. For in Jesus we find God to be a saving God, lifting the fallen, sustaining the weak, redeeming the sinful, reclaiming the wanderer. In Christ we see God giving new stature and dignity to human life. In Jesus Christ we find that human life has boundless possibilities for growth and achievement. In a word, the Christian God is not against us; he is for us! He is on our side! In his power we are saved from our worst and we can find our best. He judges us not by outward conformity but by inward motive.

"God is a Spirit: and they that worship him must worship him in spirit and in truth" (John 4:24).

No generation has needed this message more than ours. The message of the saving power of the saving God of Jesus Christ. For many of the gods we thought could save us have proved to be false messiahs. Materialism and Humanism and Militarism and Science, all have claimed their worshipers and have done their best. But they are toppling from their thrones.

The deep spiritual need of modern man is reflected in many ways. But it is seen no more clearly than in what is known as "modern" art. In trying to interpret it, Robert Beverly Hale, of the Metropolitan Museum of Art, gave this explanation: "If our art seems violent, it is because we have perpetrated more violence than any other generation. If it deals with weird dreams, it is because we have opened up the caverns of the mind and let such phantoms loose. If it is filled with broken shapes, it is because we have watched the order of our fathers break and fall to pieces at our feet." [6]

It is true that such times as these baffle those who see them only from a human perspective. But the insight of the man of God sees beyond the broken shapes and the shattered order. The Christian has faith to believe that out of this chaos will yet come a better day and a nobler humanity. He believes this because he believes in the Christian God that can save men from themselves and who can make even the wrath of men to praise him. This is no vague and wistful wish. It is based on the solid fact of the nature of God as found in the Bible and in the testimony of history. It is a sturdy faith that disillusioned modern man can and must recover.

The fabulous electronic brains of today are perhaps the last word in man's ingenuity. Take the one called Mark IV, for instance, at Harvard University. It is used ordinarily to figure out fantastic problems in physics and aerodynamics. But recently it was put to a new test. The Reverend John W. Ellison, of Winchester, Massachusetts, asked Mark IV to help him find and classify the variations in texts of the various ancient manuscripts of the New Testament. The corresponding verses of different manuscripts were given code numbers. The first code he fed to the machine went, in part, like this: 01—20; 03—12; 07—16; 09—16. But in spite of variations, the basic answer to this problem came out the same. It was as follows: "And this shall be a sign unto you; Ye shall find the babe wrapped in swaddling clothes, lying in a manger" (Luke 2:12).

Strange work for an electronic brain! If we are wise we will know that the problems that haunt the brains of men today will find their solution only when we rediscover the wonder, beauty, and saving power of a God of love who came down to earth in Bethlehem. When the skills and ingenuity and machines of men are brought into the service of Christ we will find the cleansing, the order, the direction, the salvation, and the peace that are our deepest needs. This the Bible can do for us. For in it we find that the Creator God is not only the guiding power in history but that he is also the "God and Father of our Lord Jesus Christ" (I Pet. 1:3) and the God of redeeming power and love who seeks to make all people his children (John 1:12, 13).

Additional biblical references: Exod. 20; Pss. 19:1–4, 90:1, 2; Matt. 7:9–12; I Cor. 8:5, 6; Eph. 1:3–14.

Should I hold out against the impossible?
Can mere man win against the forces of the universe?
What must I do in an emergency?

11 WHEN THE ODDS SEEM STACKED AGAINST US

WALLACE KIRKLAND, author of *Recollections of a Life Photographer*, was recuperating from a long hospitalization. During this time he said he designed a new man to cope with modern miracle medicines and injections. "Instead of skin on his forearms, he would have a composition covering, a sort of rubberdermis. On this would be charted the veins that lie beneath. There would be no nerves on this covering. Above the center of each vein would be a small blue dot, like a tiny bull's eye. . . . This would show internes just where to insert the needle. And a small spigot would be permanently set in the vein for drawing blood. . . . To take care of pills, I would have a kangaroo sort of pouch, into which would go all pills. Here, too, would go the anti-biotics, the pro-biotics, the coagulants, the anti-coagulants. . . ." [1]

Most of us, too, have wished that we might be able to make ourselves over. And, for that matter, make our world over. We are sure we could do a much better job and make things easier on ourselves. When things go wrong, we could use some indestructible parts. A cast-iron stomach often could come in handy. A plastic heart would escape the anguish of being broken. Nerves of copper wire would never jangle. And, if we had our way, we would bypass, by some mechanical pouch, the bitter pills of disappointment, failure, discouragement, and futility that poison the system. Moreover, if the events of life would only act as we order them, things would go much smoother; or at least we like to think so. It is so simple to blueprint the Kingdom so as to avoid all suffering and poverty and conflict.

But all this is not to be. We live in a real, unpredictable, sometimes cruel world filled with suffering and defeat. We are not made of rubber composition, and our Utopias and Shangri-las are illusions. We are subject to all the pains of the flesh. We are creatures of the spirit that can be crushed and beaten and twisted and frustrated. Indeed, to all of us come times when the odds seem stacked against us. It is then we need to realize that "man is born unto trouble, as the sparks fly upward" (Job 5:7). Sometimes, as Eliphaz here suggests, we bring trouble on ourselves by our own sins. But at other times there seems no reason for it.

At all such times the Bible has real help for us. To be sure, it shows us no easy or magical way out, for there is none. But it does show us tested techniques to triumph over trouble.

When the odds are against us we can cover their threat by accepting their challenge.

In 1954 Oberlin College gave the honorary degree of LL.D. to Theodore E. Steinway, president of Steinway and Sons, makers of fine pianos. The citation for the degree read: "At the time of the centenary last year, the Steinways had produced 342,000 pianos, used and abused by pianists from Liszt to Rubinstein the Second. In one of their concert grands, 243 taut strings exert a pull of 40,000 pounds on an iron frame. Theodore E. Steinway gives constant proof that out of great tension may come rich harmony." [2]

This has been a guiding principle of men of faith through the centuries. The Bible shows that God has built into the human spirit the capacity to face heavy odds and to use them to accomplish great things. God does not make the way smooth and easy for us. "Man that is born of a woman is of few days, and full of trouble" (Job 14:1). But neither does he intend that men be overcome by adversity. The man of God has enough of the stuff of courage and stamina and intelligence to accept the challenge of his limitations and handicaps and turn them to good account. That is what Abraham did when he faced the wilderness not knowing whither he went. This is what David did as he faced Goliath. This was the secret of Paul's power as he influenced a world even from behind prison bars. Indeed, out of tension *can* come richer harmony. It comes when men, in spite of their handicaps, venture to "face the music" and achieve in spite of everything.

As a rule we pity those who suffer under some severe affliction of health or circumstances. But those who have the courage to face it head-on deserve our admiration instead. There is a little story of Naaman. The record says that he was an important and brave man, *but he was a leper*. Someone has suggested that we should turn the story around and start with that fact. Then we would say that *in spite* of being a leper, Naaman was "captain of the host of the king of Syria, was a great man with his master, and honorable, because by him the Lord had given deliverance unto Syria: he was also a mighty man of valor" (II Kings 5:1). Naaman's leprosy then becomes not a blight on an otherwise able man. But it makes his achievements all the more commendable and inspiring.

There are many things about this business of living upon the earth that we cannot understand. But the record of the Bible and the record of the race hold out the truth that life is a challenge. And when the challenge is greatest the victories are the finest. God has built into human life the deathless power to face the worst and make the best of it. "This is the victory that overcometh the world, even our faith" (I John 5:4). This has been true from Naaman the leper to Jacqueline the waif.

Jacqueline Cochrane was born and raised under the handicap of bitter poverty in the cypress swamps of Florida. She had no home life. She received no education. She was a waif of Sawdust Road. She did not even have a pair of shoes until she was eight years old. Yet she fought her way up as a pioneer airplane pilot and later became the wife of the financier Floyd Odlum. In her autobiography, *The Stars at Noon*, this courageous woman revealed her secret: "Flying got into my soul instantly but the answers as to why must be found somewhere back in the mystic maze of my birth and childhood and the circumstances of my earlier life. Whatever I am is elemental and the beginnings of it all have their roots in Sawdust Road. I might have been born in a hovel, but I determined to travel with the wind and stars." [3]

So it is and always will be. Handicaps of birth, poverty, disease, or disaster need not be the end. They can be the springboard to a better life. This is basic to the Judeo-Christian faith. "None of them that trust in him shall be desolate" (Ps. 34:22). "I take pleasure in infirmities, in reproaches, in necessities, in persecutions, in distresses for Christ's sake" (II Cor. 12:10). It is also basic to our American heritage. Failure on an early bleak New England farm did not mean government subsidies. It meant that the family walked beside a wagon for two thousand miles to set up again somewhere to make a meager living by endless toil, thrift, and self-reliance while enjoying the self-respect that freedom brings. We need more of that elemental quality today.

A sudden attack by the Syrians threatened Samaria. Elisha's servant was panic-stricken. But Elisha saw all about them the protecting care of God. He reassured his servant with unforgettable words: "Fear not, for they that be with us are more than they that be with them" (II Kings 6:16). Isaiah's declaration of God's sustaining power fortifies the human spirit across the centuries: "He giveth power to the faint; and to them that have no might he increaseth strength. Even the youths shall faint and be weary, and the young men shall utterly fall: But they that wait upon the Lord shall renew their strength" (Isa. 40:29, 30, 31a).

Paul conquered the odds that were against him by accepting them and using the suffering they brought to the glory of God. Paul not only endured his troubles, he actually rejoiced in them! He recognized their discipline as a means of increasing his insights and strength. "We glory in tribulations also; knowing that tribulation worketh patience; And patience, experience; and experience, hope: And hope maketh not ashamed; because the love of God is shed abroad in our hearts by the Holy Ghost which is given unto us" (Rom. 5:3–5). The Apostle knew that even in apparent defeat there can be victory. "Who shall separate us from the love of Christ? shall tribulation, or distress, or persecution, or famine, or nakedness, or peril, or sword? . . . Nay, in all these things we are more than conquerors through him that loved us" (Rom. 8:35, 37). Suffering of itself does not necessarily bring strength. But when it is undergirded by a faith like that it cannot hurt us. Indeed, from such a faith as this comes the stuff that makes men victorious over great odds. God always gives men of faith the power, though they be born in hovels, yet "to travel with the wind and stars."

Jeremiah exemplifies the courage of those who stand up for their convictions and what they believe to be the will of God regardless of the odds against them. After Josiah died Jeremiah came out of retirement to predict the destruction of the Temple because of the sins of the people. The priests and prophets were horrified. They wanted to put Jeremiah to death. But he persisted in speaking his piece. His life was spared but he suffered much hatred and persecution because he stood by what he believed. He was beaten and put in the stocks where the people could laugh at him. But still he spoke, sure that God was on his side. He was wise enough to counsel submission to the rule of Babylon, but the leaders of the people accused him of treason. After the fall of Jerusalem and the burning of the Temple, Jeremiah's stubborn faith seemed to have been to no avail. But during those years, when the odds were all against him, he found that God was with him whenever he was and he learned that men did not need to go to the Temple to find God (Jer. 15, 20, 26, 29). This was one of the greatest advances in religious faith in the Old Testament. Indeed, the stirring example of this man in the face of overwhelming opposition is one of the most inspiring stories of the Old Testament. The victories of faith are not always visible.

When the odds are against us we can discover alternatives while waiting out the crisis.

Dr. Richard A. Kern, head of the department of medicine of Temple University School of Medicine, reports that more than twenty-five thousand people in the United States commit suicide each year. Suicide is highest among divorced persons, lowest among married, and the more children the less self-destruction by parents. The rich take their lives oftener than the poor, and leaders more than the led. And there is more self-killing in good times than in bad. These facts are contrary to popular belief. Dr. Kern declares it is not sickness, but fear of sickness that leads to suicide. It is not a depression, but a depressive mood that does the damage. It is not love, but loneliness that brings life to an end. In fact, Dr. Kern's study of the subject convinces him that troubles, even sickness, can actually prevent suicide. He quotes an old saw: "There's nothing like a few fleas to keep a yellow dog from brooding over the fact that he is a yellow dog." [4]

The results of this study point up the tremendously valuable idea that our *attitude* toward our frustration is vastly more important than the thing itself. Crises call for calmness, not hysteria; patience instead of petulance; activity instead of dumb despair. It is our faith in God, in ourselves, and in life itself that can keep us steady and stable in any crisis. And it is then that we can find unexpected and unsuspected alternatives which lead out and around and over and ahead. "No chastening for the present seemeth to be joyous, but grievous: nevertheless, afterward it yieldeth the peaceable fruit of righteousness unto them which are exercised thereby" (Heb. 12:11). That is, the discipline of pain is for the moment, but if endured in faith, good will come of it. "We know that in everything God works for good with those who love him, who are called according to his purpose" (Rom. 8:28, RSV).

God has things in store for us that we do not sometimes see. He has a way of closing one door in order to open others. The psalmist said confidently, "Thou wilt show me the path of life" (Ps. 16:11). And when we are willing to follow God's guidance we will find an amazing thing. Whereas life has many turns and ups and downs, it need never lead down blind alleys nor up against stone walls. For the Bible assures us that life is good and that God is good and that he never forsakes his children. So long as life lasts there are always, in the loving providence of God, new ways and different choices. We cannot blame God because we are too blind or stubborn to see them. But we will find that he undergirds us even though we may not know him (Isa. 45:5). The wise man is willing to change his plan of attack. Just because we are Christians does not mean that we should not use our common sense!

Some time after Paul's great conversion experience on the Damascus Road he stayed for a time in Damascus preaching Christ. He apparently had no intention of going anywhere else at the time. Then the Jews in the city plotted against him to kill him. But Paul heard of their plot. The odds were certainly against him then. He was not willing to be so easily trapped. So, while his enemies watched the gates of the city day and night, Paul devised an alternate plan. He had himself let down over the wall in a basket (Acts 9:23–25). He was simply using his head to further his cause.

Jesus himself used and gave this same counsel. There were times when the people did not receive him and he could do no work among them. Instead of fighting it out, he moved on to some other place where they were more receptive. And in his instructions to his disciples he told them to shake the dust off their feet whenever they were not favorably received (Mark 6:11). His was a great message and task but he did not want to throw pearls before swine (Matt.

7:6). In other words, he advised his followers that when circumstances thwarted the work of the kingdom in certain cases, they were to devise other ways of doing the job.

This is true in our common life as well as in the work of the Kingdom. The famous picture of "Praying Hands" by Dürer has brought inspiration to millions. The story of the hands themselves will inspire us more. They are those of a friend of the artist. He was an artist, too, but was not successful. So this friend decided to work at other things in order to help support Dürer while he got his start as a painter. The picture shows the hands to be those of a toiler, unfit for any more painting. But even so they became immortalized on canvas.[5] It is often so. When our dreams fail we can help the dreams of others to come true. And in so doing we will find our own fulfillment.

The man of faith knows that there is no situation so barren and hopeless but that something remains to build upon. Modern industry gives us an example at this point. It makes much use of residue materials formerly thought to be of no value. For instance, the Eastman Kodak Company now recovers 2,500,000 ounces of silver annually from spoiled films and from the tiny punchings from the perforations in movie films.[6] This exceeds the production of any silver mine in the world! It is a modern parable of an ancient truth of God. "Behold, I have refined thee, but not with silver; I have chosen thee in the furnace of affliction" (Isa. 48:10). In such a furnace much is burned away. Plans are thwarted. Hopes are dissolved. The things we lean on crumble away. But in the furnace of affliction much also remains. In the strange alchemy of God even the tragedies of life can be redeemed and made to yield their fruits of insight, understanding, and faith. In the midst of crisis we may even find in the punchings and the spoiled footage a source of new plans and hopes which will be of surprising value in renewing our interest in the possibilities of life. Therefore, we can say with Paul: "We are troubled on every side, yet not distressed" (II Cor. 4:8).

When the odds are against us we can rediscover the divine supports of life by falling back on the love and power of God.

When our own supports give way there is nothing more thrilling than to test the divine supports to life and find that they are solid and secure. And there is no stronger assurance the Bible gives us than the fact that this is so. "God is our refuge and strength, a very present help in trouble" (Ps. 46:1). Countless weary and troubled souls have walked with confidence a rugged road because of this simple and sure faith.

The great eleventh chapter of Hebrews spells out the story of many in the Bible who overcame every conceivable obstacle by the faith that was in them. It tells of Abel and Enoch and Noah and Abraham. It recounts that "by faith Moses, when he was come to years, refused to be called the son of Pharaoh's daughter; Choosing rather to suffer affliction with the people of God, than to enjoy the pleasures of sin for a season; . . . By faith he forsook Egypt, not fearing the wrath of the king: for he endured, as seeing him who is invisible" (24–27). The record goes on to mention others, all of whom by faith did great deeds for God in the face of heavy odds: "They were stoned, they were sawn asunder, were tempted, were slain with the sword . . . [wanderers] being destitute, afflicted, tormented." These did not receive the promises. Nevertheless, because of them we are "compassed about with so great a cloud of witnesses. . . ." Therefore, "let us lay aside every weight, and the sin which doth so easily beset us, and let us run with patience the race that is set before us, Looking unto Jesus the author and finisher of our faith; who for the joy that was set before him endured the cross, despising the shame, and is set down at the right hand of the throne of God" (11:37–12:2).

In spite of all this, many who believe in God when all is well, never seek or find his help when the odds are stacked against them. Perhaps a homely analogy will help.

W. P. Knowles is an expert on deep breathing. He tells us that a heavy object such as a suitcase can be lifted much easier if we take a deep breath first. No one knows where the weight goes. It is like picking up a box, expecting it to be full and finding it empty. Normally, says Mr. Knowles, we breathe sixteen times a minute or 23,040 times a day. This is enough for our normal needs. But in in emergency we create a surplus of carbon dioxide and make no conscious provision for the intake of extra oxygen to burn it up. This causes panting and weariness. Mr. Knowles declares that rhythmic breathing, with the shoulder blades pulled together to free the lungs of the extra work of pushing up the chest walls, will work wonders in lessening fatigue, offsetting thirst and cold, and in lifting depression of spirits. Why depression of spirits? "Because," says Mr. Knowles, "you have stimulated and inspired your brain and eased the nerve tension with a fuller supply of oxygen."

The United States Army used W. P. Knowles to teach the tricks of deep breathing to the officers and men in World War II. This letter from General Lumsden proves that it works. It was written after his tank corps played an active part in the desert battle of El Alamein under General Montgomery. "Without constant resort to the rhythmical breathing you taught me, I could not have withstood the stresses and strains during the fighting half so successfully. It revives one physically in an amazing way." [7]

So it is that God has given us all a simple, built-in method of relieving physical tension and fatigue and restoring courage in emergencies. It is surely not so strange, then, that we have also a built-in spiritual capacity to help us cope with the baffling issues that block and burden life. It is to open our cramped and drooping spirits to God and let the life-giving, purifying, supporting presence of the divine, flood the dark crevices of the soul. Our bodies are revived as fresh oxygen burns up the accumulated carbon dioxide. Likewise our spirits are revived and made strong as we put ourselves in the hands of God. "Be strong in the Lord, and in the power of his might" (Eph. 6:10). His presence will burn out the dross of anger, discouragement, and resentment that poison and fatigue us. "He healeth the broken in heart, and bindeth up their wounds" (Ps. 147:3). When we give up and let God take over, the odds are never against us. They are always on our side. "My God shall supply all your need according to his riches in glory by Christ Jesus" (Phil. 4:19). In other words, when the odds seem stacked against us, we need to turn the burden over to God. Let him carry the load. "The eternal God is thy refuge, and underneath are the everlasting arms" (Deut. 33:27). This brings release of strain and tension. It also brings solutions. Why do we fuss and fight, strain and worry so much in our own strength? God is ready and able to help if we let him have a chance. "He shall give his angels charge over thee, to keep thee in all thy ways" (Ps. 91:11). This does not lessen our burden nor relieve us of struggle. But it does make us equal to any worthy responsibility.

Glenn Clark suggests a spiritual breathing exercise which in a sense combines these physical and spiritual techniques for restoration. He tells us to think these words as we breathe rhythmically: "I am breathing out old memories; I am breathing in new ideas. I am breathing out old prejudices; I am breathing in new truths. I am breathing out old fears; I am breathing in new courage. I am breathing out old resentments; I am breathing in new forgiveness. I am breathing out old sorrows; I am breathing in new absolution. I am breathing out old obsessions; I am breathing in new freedom. I am breathing out old love of self; I am breathing in the life and love of God." [8]

In some such way as this we fortify ourselves for the demands of any conflict. The war is not called off. But we find that we do not fight our desert battles of El Alamein alone. God is with us. And with him any man is conqueror. "My flesh and my heart faileth: but God is the strength of my heart, and my portion for ever" (Ps. 73:26). The things we possess do not help us much. They are at best fleeting. But our real help is in the greatness and permanence of God who never fails us. "He that dwelleth in the secret place of the Most High shall abide under the shadow of the Almighty" (Ps. 91:1).

Paul was an aggressive and vigorous champion of Christ on many fronts over many years. During these adventurous years he met and overcame many odds. In this passage he sums them up in one outburst. "Of the Jews five times received I forty stripes save one. Thrice was I beaten with rods, once was I stoned, thrice suffered I shipwreck . . . in journeyings often, in perils of waters, in perils of robbers, in perils by my own countrymen, in perils by the heathen, in perils in the city, in perils in the wilderness, in perils in the sea, in perils among false brethren; in weariness and painfulness, in watchings often, in hunger and thirst, in fastings often, in cold and nakedness" (II Cor. 11:16–31).

Let no one say that to follow Christ is not a demanding enterprise! But thank God the Christian faith is an asset of great power in the face of great odds!

Additional biblical references: Ps. 46; Eph. 6:10–24; Phil. 1:3–26, 3:12–16.

Is the world coming to an end?
Do I dare plan for tomorrow?
What is God doing about the future?

12 WHEN THE FUTURE LOOKS FORBIDDING

A MODERN ARTIST, Ivan Le Lorraine Albright, painted an unusual picture which received considerable attention. It shows what appears to be the wreck of a room, in complete disorder, strewn with a jumble of indistinguishable objects. He calls it: "Poor Room—There is No Time, No End, No Today, No Yesterday, No Tomorrow, Only The Forever, and Forever, and Forever, and Forever, Without End." [1]

Is this a picture of the future of the poor earth—desolate, exhausted, and forbidding? There are those who seem honestly to think so. Joseph Alsop, for instance, voiced the fear that is real in many minds when he said, "We have perhaps three or four years to enjoy ourselves, if we go on with business-as-usual, politics-as-usual, and self-delusion-as-usual. The joyride, one hopes, will be very agreeable. But at the end will come a big bang, or more likely a small, self-pitying whimper. And our world, the free world of the West, will then come to an end." [2] A more scholarly pessimist was Dr. E. A. Hooton, for twenty years chairman of the department of anthropology at Harvard. His lifelong thesis was that man and civilization are headed back to the jungle. One of his books was called *Twilight of Man*. And then there are those glib predictions that it will be only a matter of time until the new nuclear weapons will destroy all living things on this planet. These modern pessimists are part of a long succession going back to Ecclesiastes and beyond.

With all due respect to the sincerity of these predictions, there is one antidote to them all. It lies in the divine perspective to be found in the Bible. "Judge me, O God, and plead my cause against an ungodly nation: O deliver me from the deceitful and unjust man. For thou art the God of my strength. . . . O send out thy light and thy truth: let them lead me. . . . Why art thou cast down, O my soul? and why art thou disquieted within me? hope in God" (Ps. 43: 1, 2, 3, 5). God is our deliverer from the injustices and enemies of life and when we dare try to see our world from God's perspective, our dismay is turned into hope. It is then that the man of faith can answer the prophets of doom with the words inscribed on the National Archives Building in Washington: "What Is Past Is Prologue." It is so with modern man! He faces beginnings; not endings. The Bible gives this assurance because it declares that this is God's world, that God is in history and that the destiny of mankind is in the hands of God.

When the future looks forbidding, God's perspective gives us the long view.

The Bible opens with the magnificent statement of the first verse of the first chapter of Genesis: "In the beginning God. . . ." And the next to the last chapter of Revelation opens with a tremendous vision: "And I saw a new heaven and a new earth . . ." (Rev. 21:1). It is as if the whole Bible were trying to lift up our sights. In the history of the Hebrew people, we glimpse something of the faithfulness of the eternal God toward his children. In the songs of the psalmist we hear the praises of a God who is the creator of all things and who is from everlasting to everlasting. In the admonitions of the prophets we find faith in the goodness of the universe and in the permanence of truth and justice. In the New Testament we see in the dramatic scenes of the death and resurrection of Jesus the abiding conviction that God's universe is one in which love and righteousness triumph forever over hate and evil.

In the turmoil and confusion of today, men desperately need this longer view. From a purely human and material viewpoint we seem to be hemmed in on every side. But from the perspective of the all-wise providence of the living God, it is a different story. For from that lofty vantage point we see our times as but a moment in the never-ending reaches of time itself. And we see in the upheavals of our day, not the end of all things, but the forecast of a new earth to come. Such a perspective gives us a quietness and confidence beyond the reach of the bitter tragedies of the day. "Hast thou not known? hast thou not heard, that the everlasting God, the Lord, the Creator of the ends of the earth, fainteth not, neither is weary?" (Isa. 40:28). This God is our God still. He bids us see in the long reaches of time the fulfillment of his purposes. We are in despair until we lift our eyes to the eternal hills that are the signposts of the timeless laws and order of God. Against this vast backdrop the upsets of the hour lose much of their terror.

In the great 90th Psalm the writer gives expression to the fleeting nature of human life against the vastness of the eternal God and the endless sweep of his universe. "Lord, thou hast been our dwelling place in all generations. Before the mountains were brought forth, or even thou hadst formed the earth and the world, even from everlasting to everlasting, thou art God. . . . For a thousand years in thy sight are but as yesterday when it is past, and as a watch in the night" (1, 2, 4). The same idea, of course, appears many times in the Book. In Isaiah the voice of God speaks in rebuke to the people for their sins and their worship of false gods: "For thus saith the high and lofty One that inhabiteth eternity, whose name is Holy" (57:15). In the New Testament there is a school of thought which felt that the end of the world was near and at that time God would set up a new heaven and a new earth. But even here the emphasis is on the infinity of God's power and dominion. Paul, in writing to Timothy, offers this praise to God for his mercies to him: "To the King of ages, immortal, invisible, the only God, be honor and glory for ever and ever" (I Tim. 1:17 RSV).

This biblical perspective is not just a vision of the ancients. It is supported by our most thoughtful modern scientists. British biologist Julian Huxley, no theist certainly, in his book *Evolution in Action* declares that man is not "just an animal." He says that man has a boundless future. Said he: "To the historical specialist, the five or six thousand years of civilization seem intolerably long. But this is a minute interval to the biologist. Man is very young; the human deployment is in an explosive and very early phase. Man is the result of two thousand million years of biological evolutions; he has every prospect of an equal or even greater span of psychosocial evolution before him." Against such a long future, Huxley sees man's current problems as only temporary. "Man can now see himself as . . . one of the few possible instruments of progress in the universe at large. . . . He need no longer regard himself as insignificant in relation to the cosmos. He is intensely significant." [3] This has been the conviction of men of God for centuries and is at the heart of the Bible message.

When the future looks forbidding, therefore, the man of faith needs to peer a long way into the past and toward the long future. We need something like the great Palomar telescope to get the perspective of history as well as of the physical universe. It is said that if the Palomar instrument could be focused from California to New York City it could make the people on the streets there look as if they were but seven feet away!

Such a long look shows us not how far we have to go, but it shows us how far we have come. The age of scientific chemistry began with Antoine Laurent Lavoisier with the correct interpretation of the process of oxidation. He was executed by the guillotine in 1794. But in the intervening one hundred and fifty years, man has accomplished more than during all the previous millenniums of recorded and unrecorded history.

Indeed, it was only a few short years ago that Oliver Wendell Holmes said: "If the whole materia medica . . . could be sunk to the bottom of the sea, it would be better for mankind—and all the worse for the fishes." [4] Yet, within a generation, distrust of medicine has given way to trust of a high order. In fact, one authority stated in 1953 that 80 per cent of the items of medical therapy available to the physician at that time were unknown ten years before! So it is that Jesus spoke a word of infinite wisdom when he predicted that men would work greater wonders than those he himself performed (John 14:12). And so it is, also, that the long view toward what has gone before gives us more faith in the things to come.

All this means that the man of faith has both the right and the obligation to take the forward look. It has always been so. When the Israelites were wondering what to do about their troubles in Egypt, "The Lord said unto Moses, Wherefore criest thou unto me? speak unto the children of Israel that they go forward" (Exod. 14:15). We do not need some miracle like the crossing of the Red Sea as on dry land to convince us of God's leadership. This story carries a great message. It is that God does stand by us when we stand by him. He opens the way for us in ways unforeseen and often mysterious when we have the faith to move ahead at his behest, even though the difficulties seem insurmountable. It was such a faith that led Abraham to heed the call of God to go out into an unknown place (Gen. 12:1–5). It is such a faith that has sustained many faithful souls as they have sought to know and follow the will of God in the days ahead of them. They have the assurance that Moses gave to Joshua in a difficult assignment: "Be strong and of a good courage. . . . And the Lord, he it is that doth go before thee; he will be with thee, he will not fail thee, neither forsake thee: fear not, neither be dismayed" (Deut. 31:7–8).

When the future looks forbidding the perspective of God shows us that man's mastery over nature is a means of building the Kingdom.

The idea is widespread, even in religious circles, that modern science has gone too far too fast. There are even those who want to turn back the clock or at least declare a holiday for further research and development. But the man of faith cannot share that viewpoint. He remembers that the Bible says that God created man to subdue and have charge over all created things (Gen. 1:26). He recalls the words of the psalmist: "Thou madest him to have dominion over the works of thy hands; thou hast put all things under his feet" (8:6). He remembers that the later Isaiah, twenty-five hundred years ago, foresaw a minimum span of life of one hundred years and the creation of a prosperous world without war or bloodshed (65:16–25). He calls to mind the prayer of Jesus: "Thy kingdom come. Thy will be done in earth . . ." (Matt. 6:10).

It is folly to say that science is Antichrist and that the discoveries of science, even atomic energy, are opposed to the will of God for men. For the fact is, at long last modern man is in a position to subdue the earth and to bring into being that "new earth" which has been the dream of men of God through the centuries. Far from being an enemy of faith, science is an ally of faith. It gives to men the tools by which may be realized the prayers of their hearts. There is nothing in the Bible that is opposed to scientific progress.

Jacob Rosin and Max Eastman, in *The Road to Abundance*, state the key to the matter in these words: "We must get accustomed to knowing that the resources of our planet are practically limitless. . . . Most wars have been motivated by a desire to redistribute the earth's natural resources. The distribution mentality will soon be obsolete. For no problems of distribution can exist in a world of absolute abundance. . . . Want, fear and greed now rule the world and threaten the destruction of our civilization. Chemistry, with the help of physics, can save it by creating a new world of abundance." [5]

This is no matter of wishful thinking. As Stuart Chase has said, for the first time in history man has the resources and know-how to banish poverty and want from the face of the earth.

Up to now, for instance, we have been using only a fraction of the energy at our disposal. And we have worried lest we exhaust our coal and petroleum supplies. But now man is harnessing the sun. Every three days the sun gives us more energy than all the coal, gas, oil, and timber in the world combined. And Lawrence R. Hafstad of the Atomic Energy Commission said that all the deposits of uranium on earth will yield only as much atomic energy as we receive from the sun in less than one hour. Nobel prize winner Sir John Cockcroft announced at the 1954 meeting of the British Association for the Advancement of Science that there is enough available energy to keep man supplied for more than nine hundred thousand billion years!

John Jay Hopkins, chairman of the General Dynamics Corporation, has given a breath-taking vision of what can be done in reclaiming backward areas with atomic power. As commercial reactors are built, all Asia "could leapfrog the conventional fuel systems" and hurry on to higher living standards that would also "propel Africa, free Europe and Latin America into the 21st century. . . ." [6]

New foods and methods of production find us on the threshold of the age of plenty. Stanford Research Institute, as an example, has developed the single-celled algae plant called Chlorella. It produces 44,000 pounds of proteins per acre, as against 336 pounds for soybeans. It is believed this yield can be doubled. A one-acre algae farm can rival 100 acres of wheat or corn. And a new method of rice cultivation in India has increased production to the unheard of figure of 14,000 pounds of rice per acre. For the first time India has stopped importing rice and her impoverished farmers no longer will have to look upon poverty as a divine phenomenon.[7]

The basic raw materials of the future will be sea water, air, ordinary rock, and sunlight. The iron age is giving way to the age of light metal alloys, having the structural strength of steel. These are made from magnesium and aluminum, which in turn come from sea water and ordinary rock.

The advance of living standards has just begun in this country. The National Bureau of Economic Research, the top economic research organization of the nation, recently said that by maintaining the same rate of progress in the next eighty years as in the past eighty years, the average family income of about five thousand dollars will rise to twenty-five thousand dollars of present purchasing power. At present that is a level attained by only 1 per cent of the families.

Miracles are being performed, also, in the field of public health. In 1945 Italy had 411,600 cases of malaria. The wide use of DDT was so effective that during the first half of 1951 only 392 cases were reported. And there was not a single death from malaria reported in Italy in the following three years, whereas at the beginning of the century malaria killed nearly ten thousand Italians each year.

To be sure, science is no second Messiah. But with it men of faith have a golden chance to remove some centuries-old barriers to the Kingdom of God on earth. Dedicated to the meeting of human need, Christianity and science can and will usher in a new age of peace and plenty.

Such a faith puts us in the succession of many of the seers of the Bible. In one of the dark hours of Hebrew history the prophet Micah looked down the years and predicted the end of war and the rule of justice and peace among men under the providence of God. "And many nations shall come and say, Come ye, and let us go up to the mountain of Jehovah, and to the house of the God of Jacob; and he will teach us of his ways, and we will walk in his paths . . . and he will judge between many peoples, and will decide concerning strong nations afar off: and they shall beat their swords into plowshares, and their spears into pruning-hooks; nation shall not lift up sword against nation, neither shall they learn war any more. . . . For all the peoples walk every one in the name of his god; and we will walk in the name of Jehovah our God for ever and ever" (4:2–5 ARV).

Again, about a hundred years later, in the midst of his people's desperate straits, Jeremiah wrote even from prison of his faith in the future under God: "Thus saith the Lord; Again there shall be heard in this place, which ye say shall be desolate without man and without beast. . . . The voice of joy, and the voice of gladness, the voice of the bridegroom and the voice of the bride, the voice of them that shall say, Praise the LORD of hosts: for the LORD is good: for his mercy endureth forever" (33:10, 11).

In the midst of the desolation of the modern world we may well learn from such as these. We need to see beyond the turmoil of the moment the victories of the future. To be sure, the theory of unending progress has been rudely exploded in these years of global conflict and deep-seated, aggressive evil. But the fact remains that what we call progress is still possible! Under the guidance of God the upheavals of the present can be the heralds of a new and better day. Even the wrath of men can be made to praise God (Ps. 76:10)! And the outreach of God's truth and power is without end. "Thy kingdom is an everlasting kingdom, and thy dominion endureth throughout all generations" (Ps. 145:13).

When the future looks forbidding we can find confidence in the providence and power of the righteous and everlasting God.

In a world "full of calamity and conflict, famine and disease, war and rumors of war" it is easy for men to lose faith in the future. It has been so since the beginning of time. Two hundred years before Christ, the author of Ecclesiastes gives voice to the feeling of the pessimist: "For what good does a man get himself from all the toil and strain of his labour in this world? All through life his task is a sheer pain and vexation, day after day; the very night brings no rest to his mind" (Eccles. 22, 23, Moffatt).

Thus, even in the Bible we find a sense of futility that matches the mood of many people in our day. If evil checkmates goodness and if all our human gains are to be wiped out in the end, what is the use of trying? Why build for the future when there may be no future?

But men lose faith in the future only when they lose sight of God. And the Bible expresses the fundamental conviction that the great God is from everlasting to everlasting and that he guarantees the triumph of justice and truth over every obstacle and enemy. "Fret not over evildoers, envy not the lawless; soon like grass they fade, and wither like a green blade. Trust in the eternal and do right, be loyal to him within his land; make the Eternal your delight, and he will give you all your heart's desire" (Ps. 37:1–4, Moffatt). So spoke the psalmist. And the prophets of the eighth and seventh centuries B.C., living in the midst of war and poverty, disease and destruction, proclaimed without question that God would save his people from every evil thing and in the end fulfill their hopes.

This sturdy faith in a great and good God gives men courage. We need it today if we are not to be blinded by the tragedy and confusion of the hour. Our ultimate faith is not in the ingenuity of men but in the providence and power of God. Too many Christians and Christian thinkers have lost this divine perspective. They have been captured by the notion that the world is headed for destruction and that the end of the world is near in Christ's second coming. True, there are biblical references to the destruction of the world (II Pet. 3:7–10; Rev. 20:11; 21:1). Surely, however, God did not create the world to destroy it. Atomic war or universal tyranny may come. But they, too, should pass. And in the long reaches of time the power and providence and truth of God will surely prevail.

But neither global tyranny nor atomic destruction need come, for God has given man in Jesus Christ and in the Christian faith the one instrument by which the future may be stripped of its blight. Kenneth Scott Latourette in *A History of Christianity*, the most exhaustive modern study of the Christian faith in its universal setting, declares that Christianity, far from declining, is just beginning its influence. "The weight of evidence appears to be on the side of those who maintain that Christianity is only in the first flush of its history and that it is to have a growing place in the life of mankind." In spite of its striking losses in our generation, historian Latourette holds that "Christianity has moved forward. . . . It is entering into the lives of more peoples than it or any other religion has ever done. In the new and often terrifying stage into which the human race, bewildered, is being ushered, Christianity is more potent than in any earlier era." [8]

It is one of the strange paradoxes of history that there are times when it seems that the work of evil men and forces supports the sovereignty of God in the end. Such a time was that when Cyrus was displaying his wicked power. In it all God speaks to Isaiah: "Remember this, and show yourselves men: bring it again to mind, O ye transgressors. Remember the former things of old: for I am God, and there is none else; I am God, and there is none like me. . . . My counsel shall stand, and I will do all my pleasure . . . yea, I have spoken it, I will also bring it to pass; I have purposed it, I will also do it" (Isa. 46:8–11). In other words, there is one God and he is the Lord of history. His purposes are justice and righteousness and they will stand. All men and nations stand under his judgment. But in the end his truth will prevail.

Here, then, is the solid and unbreakable basis of our confidence in the future. We who are the children of God need to learn to live by the permanent instead of the passing. We must not worry so much about evildoers but rather concentrate our powers on the things that make for righteousness and peace. Those who dare so to believe will find their faith verified in the years ahead. Therefore, we venture to invest our lives and labors in the things that cannot be destroyed. "I will hope continually, and will yet praise thee more and more" (Ps. 71:14). This faith sustains us even down to the end of our days.

The Hebrews rebelled under the oppression of the Canaanites. In a battle of ten thousand men led by Deborah and Barak, they put to rout a much larger army under Sisera (Judg. 4:2–24; 5:19–21). The record indicates that a violent storm helped to sweep the Hebrews on to victory while at the same time blinding the army of Sisera. Thus the famous line in the song of victory: "The stars in their courses fought against Sisera" (5:20). The account is a gory one, but the meaning clear and timeless. In it they were declaring their faith that in the long run the universe itself backs up the fighters for righteousness and is against slavery and oppression. The record of the race proves the truth of this idea, even in spite of recurring wars and the temporary success of evil men. This is a moral universe because God made it so, and cruelty and evil are always doomed to defeat. When men or nations persist in defying the laws of God they are fighting the stars in their courses, pitting their puny powers against the eternal order of God.

The beautiful story of Jesus' appearing to the two men on the Emmaus Road after the death and resurrection illustrates the renewed hope that the living Jesus gave and still gives to all those who believe in him. The two travelers were puzzled and disappointed over the recent events. But when Jesus fell in with them, unrecognized at first, they took a new lease on life. They were excited that Jesus was still alive and they immediately retraced their steps to tell the disciples about it (Luke 24:13–35). Their experience symbolizes the tremendous fact that a great, new, divine, unquenchable hope came to the troubled world with the resurrection of Jesus. It turned the faces of the disciples forward. It was the powerful drive that established the early Christian church. And still today it gives body and thrust to man's faith in the future.

Additional biblical references: Matt. 7:21–27; Luke 12:22–31; II Tim. 3.

Is love still a valid rule in our modern world?
How can everybody be out of step but me?
Is it necessary to forgive and forget?
What can the Bible say about modern human relations problems?

13 WHEN WE FIND IT HARD TO GET ALONG WITH PEOPLE

A CARTOON IN *The New Yorker* shows two monks talking in a monastery cloister. A third monk, Brother Valentine, is passing by at some distance. As the first two monks look toward their brother going by, one says to the other: "I think my love for Brother Valentine is less than my love for anyone else in this world." [1]

This remark both sums up a common problem and is a key to its solution. For even the best of us find it difficult to get along with some people. And this in spite of the fact that we are supposed to love everybody. Yet we are all human. And there is no reason to expect us to love everyone with the same degree of love. We may love people in the religious sense without necessarily liking them. So also we may disagree with people and still love them.

The problem of human relations is a major one in today's world. It is no new problem. For people have always been "getting in each other's hair" since the days of the cave man. But it is much more acute these days because there are more of us and we are so dependent on one another. Harrison Brown states that during the last seven thousand years the number of human beings inhabiting the earth has increased from about ten million to twenty-four hundred million.[2] In its larger proportions, therefore, the problem becomes one of survival. Either we learn to live together or we all perish.

The problem comes to focus, however, as far as we are concerned, in our everyday treatment of our fellow men. There are so many troublesome Brother Valentines in the world. How are we going to get along with those whom, if we love at all, we love less than anyone else? The answer lies in the disciplines of the divine fellowship, which includes all who walk in love.

The Bible, especially the New Testament, has much to say to us here. Jesus declared that love of God and love of our fellows are the two greatest commandments. To fulfill the second takes some doing. It means that all of us need to be reminded of this discipline of love. Most of us are like the preachers described by Edgar DeWitt Jones: "The preacher for this day must have the heart of a lion, the skin of a hippopotamus, the agility of a greyhound, the patience of a donkey, the wisdom of an elephant, the industry of an ant, and as many lives as a cat." The whole trouble is that many, many people are entirely too sensitive, get hurt too easily, and are too harsh with their brothers who do not happen to believe as they do.

The Bible tells us that the brotherly, forgiving spirit is basic to our faith in God and man.

Respect for other people is not just a nice social custom in polite society. It has its roots deep in the Judeo-Christian ideas of God as heavenly Father and of all men as brothers. "Have we not all one father? hath not one God created us?" (Mal. 2:10). Answers to this leading question of Malachi are heard throughout the New Testament. "One is your Master, even Christ; and all ye are brethren" (Matt. 23:8). "A new commandment I give unto you, That ye love one another; as I have loved you, that ye also love one another" (John 13:34). "Be kindly affectioned one to another with brotherly love; in honor preferring one another" (Rom. 12:10). "Speak not evil one of another" (James 4:11). "Add . . . to godliness brotherly kindness and to brotherly kindness charity" (II Pet. 1:7).

It is important that we recognize that there is a direct relationship between good will, or brotherhood, and God. The brotherhood of man must be a human-divine fellowship undergirded by God. Otherwise our human relations are on a purely humanistic basis. And this can become sordid and dangerous. For instance, take Joseph Goebbels, in Hitler's Germany. He was a smart man and earned a Ph.D. from Heidelberg. But his hate complex began with his rejection of his religious faith. It is not surprising, therefore, that shortly before his twenty-eighth birthday he wrote in his diary: "I have learned to despise the human being from the bottom of my soul. He makes me sick at my stomach." [3]

When there is no recognition of God as Father and of men as his children, there is no basis of trust and confidence in our fellow men. This is the inherent danger with any humanistic philosophy, whether idealistic or materialistic. So it is that nine of eleven Russian cabinet ministers who held office in 1936 have been shot, as have five out of seven presidents of the last Soviet Central Executive Committee and forty-three of the fifty-three secretaries of the Communist Party Central Organization. Also, fifteen of twenty-seven top Communists who drafted the 1936 Constitution, seventy out of eighty members of the Soviet War Council, and all members of Lenin's first Politburo, excepting Joseph Stalin, met death by execution.[4]

All this means that hate rules and life becomes cheap when we lose sight of God as our Maker and the Father of all men. This holds true in our personal relations with others as well as in society. And the rantings of a Goebbels or the acts of a Soviet firing squad only prove its truth.

The Bible drives home this divine source of human kindness in a still more forceful way. For it declares without compromise that our faith in God is sterile and meaningless unless it exhibits a brotherly spirit, and issues in mercy and forgiveness.

The idea of forgiveness in social relationships appears early in the Bible. For instance, there is the forgiveness accorded by Joseph to his once jealous brothers at the request of the aged Jacob (Gen. 50:17). Another example is the forgiveness sought by Pharaoh from Moses and Aaron (Exod. 10:17).

Forgiveness of others is a cardinal point in the ethics of Jesus. One of its finest expressions is the parable of the unmerciful debtor (Matt. 18:21–35). The emphasis of the Master was on the inner motive of the heart. "Ye have heard that it was said by them of old time, Thou shalt not kill. . . . But I say unto you, That whosoever is angry with his brother without a cause shall be in danger of the judgment. . . . Therefore if thou bring thy gift to the altar, and there rememberest that thy brother hath aught against thee; Leave there thy gift before the altar, and go thy way; first be reconciled to thy brother, and then come and offer thy gift" (Matt. 5:21–24). He goes on to say that we are even to love our enemies and to forgive those who do us harm. "Ye have heard that it hath been said, Thou shalt love thy neighbor, and hate thine enemy. But I say unto you, Love your enemies, bless them that curse you, . . . That ye may be the children of your Father which is in heaven: for he maketh his sun to rise on the evil and on the good, and sendeth rain on the just and the unjust. For if ye love them which love you, what reward have ye? do not even the publicans the same? And if ye salute your brethren only, what do ye more than others? do not even the publicans so?" (Matt. 5:43–47). In fact, our own forgiveness by God is dependent on our forgiveness of others. Jesus follows his familiar word in the Lord's Prayer, "Forgive us our debts, as we forgive our debtors" (Matt. 6:12), with this stronger word: "For if ye forgive men their trespasses, your heavenly Father will also forgive you: But if ye forgive not men their trespasses, neither will your Father forgive your trespasses" (Matt. 6:14, 15).

This forgiving spirit is not an occasional, calculating thing. It is to be a genuine and continuing attitude of mind and heart. This is hard for many of us to understand, and harder still to activate. "Then came Peter to him, and said, Lord, how oft shall my brother sin against me, and I forgive him? till seven times? Jesus saith unto him, I say not unto thee, Until seven times: but, Until seventy times seven" (Matt. 18:21, 22).

Paul helps further to deflate the self-righteous people who are short on human kindness when he said: "Though I speak with the tongues of men and of angels, and have not charity [love] I am become as sounding brass or a tinkling cymbal" (I Cor. 13:1). "Ye yourselves are taught of God to love one another" (I Thess. 4:9). And in I John the whole matter is put clearly and bluntly: "He that saith he is in the light, and hateth his brother, is in darkness even until now" (2:9). "We know that we have passed from death unto life, because we love the brethren" (3:14). "If a man say, I love God, and hateth his brother, he is a liar: for he that loveth not his brother whom he hath seen, how can he love God whom he hath not seen?" (4:20).

All of this is strong medicine for all of us. The plain fact is that far too many of us are far too spiteful, fussy, and critical in our attitudes toward other people. This not only keeps us from getting along with them, but it also nullifies our faith in God.

The Christian religion is far more than a mere matter of treating our fellow men with kindness and respect. But it does include just that. And too many ardent religionists are apt to forget it. Yet the way we deal with our brothers is an acid test of our faith in God. The second commandment is as important as the first. They go together. We can not be saints at church and devils at home or in the office.

The familiar story of the good Samaritan is known to every child (Luke 10:30–37). But its message is overlooked by many of them and many of us. Jesus told it to a certain lawyer in further explanation of his famous saying that eternal life hinges on our love of God and of our neighbor. It points up the idea that anyone in need is our neighbor. We are to serve such a need, not out of a sense of duty, but simply because a fellow human being is in need and we want to help out. This quality of good will completely cuts across all lines of race and creed and makes brothers of all men. It has a strong application to our own day and time. And we cannot escape the injunction of the Master at the close of the story: "Go, and do thou likewise" (37). It calls to mind that other word of Jesus: "Inasmuch as ye have done it unto one of the least of these my brethren, ye have done it unto me" (Matt. 25:40). This is the magic key to better human understanding.

The Bible makes it plain that we must make allowances for human weakness and recognize our own.

The New Testament takes us sharply to task for the harsh judgments and criticisms we so easily make of others—often without knowing the circumstances. It reminds us that we are all human and are all subject to mistakes and that all stand in the need of mercy. "Why beholdest thou the mote that is in thy brother's eye, but considerest not the beam that is in thine own eye?" (Matt. 7:3). Paul tells us that when we idly criticize others, we only reveal our own weak points. "Thou art inexcusable, O man, whosoever thou art that judgest: . . . for thou condemnest thyself; for thou that judgest doest the same things" (Rom. 2:1). When certain self-righteous religious people brought a poor woman of the street to Jesus for his condemnation, he turned to them and said, "He that is without sin among you, let him first cast a stone" (John 8:7). It is no wonder her accusers slipped away in embarrassment and shame. So would we. Those who are so ready to accuse and to judge deserve the same stinging rebuke from the Master. For the Bible wants us to leave the judgment of others to God. "Why do you pass judgment on your brother? . . . For we shall all stand before the judgment seat of God" (Rom. 14:10, RSV). Few of us ever know the full circumstances behind the actions of others. And we who are so quick to bring the judgment of God to bear on men and society need to be careful that it is not our own opinions, born of frustration, prejudice, or hatred, that we pass off as the judgment of God. "Judge not, that ye be not judged. For with what judgment ye judge, ye shall be judged" (Matt. 7:1, 2). "Finally, all of you have unity of spirit, sympathy, love of the brethren, a tender heart and a humble mind (I Pet. 3:8 RSV). Why this kind of merciful, generous, forbearing attitude? Because God is a merciful God and we are his children. Shakespeare states this truth in the words of Portia in her plea with Shylock to be merciful with the moneylender. She declares that mercy

> . . . is an attribute to God himself;
> And earthly power doth then show likest God's
> When mercy seasons justice. Therefore, Jew,
> Though justice be thy plea, consider this,
> That in the course of justice, none of us
> Should see salvation: we do pray for mercy;
> And that same prayer doth teach us all to render
> The deeds of mercy.[5]

Ryllis Goslin Lynip reminds us that "this appeal to the noblest in man has its roots back in the prophet Hosea, who first conceived of God as a merciful judge. He was aware that God pities man's weakness . . . and forgives with the hope of winning them to higher levels of thought and action."[6] Jesus brought Hosea's ideas into dramatic reality when he prayed forgiveness for those who had nailed him to the cross. And his word in Luke is plain: "Be ye therefore merciful, as your Father also is merciful" (6:36).

This idea of consideration for others comes home to us, also, in countless everyday ways. Indeed, one of the major reasons for human friction is the simple failure to realize that all people are different, including ourselves. No one is perfect. Not even ourselves! No one is wholly consistent. Sometimes we are different persons than we are at other times. And for others to differ from us in minor matters does not necessarily mean that they are wrong and we are right. It is sheer folly for us to expect everyone to think and act alike, or as we do, or as we think they should. And to be in the wrong and refuse to acknowledge it is to invite heartache and disaster in human relations. Something is wrong with the person who is always right!

Stuart Chase, in his book *Roads to Agreement*, tells of the work of Captain James Saunders, U.S.N., retired. The Captain teaches the principles of agreement in a graduate class in Washington, D.C. As a demonstration he gives each member of the class a small piece of white paper and asks that he chew it and report the taste. The paper has been treated with phenylthiocarbimide. Some report the taste as bitter. Some say sweet. Some say their paper has no taste at all. A violent argument usually follows as to who is right. Then Captain Saunders tells them that phenylthiocarbimide is a chemical which tastes different to different people. And that stops the argument! They *all* are right! [7]

It is so with many of our most disagreeable arguments. Many of them are over personal interpretations. As a rule they are only opinions and are about things that do not matter much anyway. And they are easily ended when we grant the right of others to their own opinions growing out of their own peculiar personal make-up and background.

This means that we must not be so sensitive or so easily offended or so dogmatic or so belligerent. It means that we must not think that we are so important that everything centers in us. It means that we must give other people credit for at least as good intentions as our own. It means that we are to put the best possible construction on things we do not understand. It means that we can compromise gracefully. It means that we must have respect for others if we expect them to have respect for us. "Not rendering evil for evil, or railing for railing: but contrariwise blessing" (I Pet. 3:9).

The Bible emphasizes that the spirit of love, service, and understanding makes for successful human relations.

We are not expected, of course, to be good to others for the sake of any reward. Nor are we expected to compromise any moral ideals to win the favor of others. At the same time God has so ordered human nature and human society that hatred and bitterness toward others bring misery in return. "He that loveth not his brother abideth in death" (I John 3:14). Likewise, our kindness to others does not go unrewarded. "Blessed are the merciful: for they shall obtain mercy" (Matt. 5:7). "Love ye your enemies, and do good, and lend, hoping for nothing again; and your reward shall be great, and ye shall be the children of the Highest" (Luke 6:35). If we are generous and gentle, considerate and helpful, forgiving and cheerful, we will get the same treatment in return. For "whatsoever a man soweth, that shall he also reap" (Gal. 6:7).

The fundamental, practical, workable nature of this rule of human relations is at long last coming to be realized. Said Ordway Tead in *Good Business:* "More and more clearly every day, out of biology, anthropology, sociology, history, economic analysis, psychological insight, plain human decency and common sense, the necessary mandate of survival that we love all our neighbors as we love ourselves, is being confirmed and reaffirmed." [8] Perhaps the golden rule is right after all! "Therefore all things whatsoever ye would that men should do to you, do ye even so to them: for this is the law and the prophets" (Matt. 7:12).

Thus in the confusions and discoveries of modern life the tremendous fact is emerging that the laws of God are written into the very structure of life itself. The thing we are talking about is no vague and otherworldly ideal. It is an everyday necessity for human well-being and for successful living. Only our littleness of soul keeps us from seeing it.

And yet it is surprising how hard it is to learn this simple idea which can do so much for us. Owen Bristow tells of an investigation made by a group of vocational teachers. They wanted to learn what errors young people starting out on their first jobs should be warned about. These vocational teachers wrote to several thousand employers asking them to look up the last three persons dismissed and tell why they had been let out. The teachers expected a long catalogue of reasons. They were very much surprised when the returns showed that more than two-thirds of the persons losing jobs had been fired for one and the same reason. It was the same in every sort of business, for workers of all ages and both sexes. It amounted to this: "They couldn't get along with other people!" [9] Who ever said the Bible has no relation to life?

Two young children built a clubhouse in their yard. On the wall, scribbled in a childish hand, were the club rules. Rule No. 1 read: "Nobody act big, nobody act small, everybody act medium." [10] It is a good rule when we find it hard to get along with other people.

Cain asked a very modern question a long time ago: "Am I my brother's keeper?" (Gen. 4:9). The answer of the Bible and of history is the same: "*You had better be!*"

The poignant story of the little Book of Ruth is well known. Written in a time of hatred and distrust among peoples, it carries a message of good will toward peoples of differing faiths and nationalities. It is a glimpse into the possibilities of world friendship. And its method is that of subtlety and indirection. Ruth commanded respect as an individual even though she was an alien and came of a people hated by the Hebrews. She won this respect because of her unselfish devotion to others. It is a method that might well be adopted by aliens or minorities in any country. The book further suggests the need of co-operating with the inevitable, as far as human relations are concerned. There are many situations in which we have to live with others whether we like them or not. We might just as well accept one another and learn to get along with one another by the easier ways of consideration and co-operation.

Whatever else we may think of it, the biblical principle of brotherly love pays rich dividends when translated into the common ways of the day's work and the ordinary affairs of family and friends. Does this make it any less significant? "Bear ye one another's burdens, and so fulfil the law of Christ" (Gal. 6:2). When we lift our human relations to that high level of outgoing, positive concern we find life sweeter, finer, cleaner, and happier than we dreamed possible. But on the lower levels of self-centeredness, pride, envy, jealousy, and spitefulness we find that our tempers are short, our anger is poison, and that all life becomes unruly. No wonder the Bible urges us, all the way from the concern of the Hebrews for their own people—as in Deuteronomy: "Thou shalt open thine hand wide unto thy brother, to thy poor, and to thy needy, in thy land" (15:11)—down to Galatians which makes the principle universal: "As we have therefore opportunity, let us do good unto all men" (6:10).

Additional biblical references: Matt. 7:3–5; Rom. 12; I Cor. 13; I John 3:1–3, 4:7–21.

What is left for me when death takes one I love?
Why do we try to ignore the fact of death?
How may I find anything good in my grief?

14 WHEN SORROW SHADOWS THE SOUL

A YOUNG WOMAN in California wrote a letter to her former pastor, Dr. James Gordon Gilkey. It read in part: "My fiancé, a naval officer in the Pacific, has been killed in action. I know he died as he would have chosen to—in the service of his country. For that I am grateful. But of course I myself have now lost everything. Does the solution of my problem lie in mere resignation to my loss, or in something else? Is there anything I can 'go on' when the best things in life have now been taken away?" [1]

This young woman was voicing the vacancy that comes to all of us when death takes someone we love. And not one of us escapes if we live very long. Sometimes it is a cry that is born in bitterness and rebellion. Sometimes in honest wonderment. Sometimes in crushed anguish of soul.

We give little thought as a rule to the possibility of death stealing away our loved ones. It is a good thing we do not dwell on it. For continued morbid thoughts of the dark visitor can cast a pall over life. But sorrow is a universal experience. And we need to be prepared for it. Sometimes it comes without warning. Sometimes it sets up advance signals. Yet when sorrow does envelop us we need help. The kindness of friends is appreciated. The comfort of loved ones is a benediction. But in the end the issue has to be met in the silent sanctuary of the soul. And it is here that we need the ministry of the divine and the eternal support of the word of God.

Does the solution to our problem lie in "mere resignation"? Or is there something we can "go on"? The best answers to these and questions like them may be found in the Bible. We are foolish if our sorrow drives us away from God. In such hours we need him most of all. "O my God, my soul is cast down within me: therefore will I remember thee" (Ps. 42:6).

The Bible wants us to accept the reality of death.

"In the midst of life we are in death." Yet there are those who can never reconcile themselves to it. For instance, there is the case of a prosperous miller in a small Illinois town. He was a man of large business ability and had built a fortune of several million dollars. He was used to having his own way. Then his lovely and talented daughter died. She had been an only child and had had the very finest educational opportunities. Suddenly death came to her door. The father never accepted the fact. And twenty years after, the daughter's room in the old home was still kept just as she had left it. The same dresses hung rotting in the closets. Her grand piano in the living room had not been touched for twenty years. She was buried in a private family graveyard nearby the house, and for twenty years the father made a daily pilgrimage to the grave. Then his wife died and the same routine was repeated for many more empty years. In his later life this man was a broken, pitiable creature. He walled himself in. He was unloved by his associates. He was sour and cynical. His millions mocked him. His heart was desolate. He was a prisoner of his sorrow. And he was finally its victim.

Surely God does not intend sorrow to do this to us. When sorrow shadows the soul we must learn to accept it as a part of the business of living and loving. It is real enough. No philosophy of sweetness and light can avoid the devastating, gnawing loneliness that death leaves behind. And however long and desperately we may want to hold on to those who pass, there comes a time when we must accept the fact that they have gone. To rebel or to deny or to live in the past only invites more misery and more heartbreak. We need not be ashamed of our grief. It is a normal and natural thing. We would be less than human not to show it. But to be mastered by our grief is unhealthy, unnecessary, and unbecoming to a child of God.

The Bible offers little support to those people and to those cults that deny the reality of death. In Genesis we read: "Dust thou art, and unto dust shalt thou return" (3:19). In II Samuel: "Now he is dead, wherefore should I fast? can I bring him back again? I shall go to him, but he shall not return to me" (12:23). In Job: "Man that is born of woman is of few days, and full of trouble. He cometh forth like a flower and is cut down: he fleeth also as a shadow, and continueth not" (14:1, 2). In Jeremiah: "For death is come up into our windows, and is entered into our palaces, to cut off the children from without, and the young men from the streets" (9:21). And the psalmist declared that man's days are as grass and the winds pass over it and it is gone (103:15). But it is in the New Testament that the fact of death is most clearly put. Indeed, it has been said that no book in the whole world has faced the fact of sorrow so honestly and with such steady eyes as the New Testament. This is because at its heart is the Cross of Christ. In the Cross we find that death, even when it is cruel, untimely, and unreasonable, can be faced and overcome. And that even then we are not separated from the love of God. Paul speaks of death as an enemy of life which is conquered by the Risen Christ. "Then cometh the end, when he shall have delivered up the kingdom to God, even the Father; when he shall have put down all rule, and all authority and power. For he must reign, till he hath put all enemies under his feet. The last enemy that shall be destroyed is death. . . . So when this corruptible shall have put on incorruption, and this mortal shall have put on immortality, then shall be brought to pass the saying that is written, Death is swallowed up in victory" (I Cor. 15:24–26, 54).

All of this is to say that God has made death a part of the order of life and the universe. The man of faith must make it a part of his universe, too. We do well to get used to the idea and fact of death. We need to learn to live with it. We need to make it a part of our thinking and plans and philosophy. A philosophy of life that does not include a philosophy of death is inadequate and incomplete. Yet so many of us refuse to do this. We can be objective when sorrow comes to others. But when bereavement comes to us, we protest and complain and "take up arms against God and life." Yet it does us no good frantically to question why God has thus treated us so badly. Resentment against death, whatever may be the circumstances surrounding it, is never the key to overcoming sorrow. But acceptance always is. Grief must be recognized as a real force. As someone has said,

"Mourning, painful though it is, has to be faced if comfort is to follow." [2]

The simplest way to do this is to keep on going and living and working and loving. In one of his last letters home, Pieter Cammaerts who lost his life with the R.A.F. wrote this to his father: "You have your work to carry on, and if anything happens, you must go on without losing one day. You understand? Not one day. That'll keep you straight on the track." [3] After all, we do more honor to those who have gone by faithfully doing our duty than by giving in to our grief. We do well to call to mind the actions of Job after he had been told of the accidental death of his sons. "Then Job arose, . . . and fell down upon the ground, and worshipped, And said, . . . the Lord gave, and the Lord hath taken away; blessed be the name of the Lord. In all this Job sinned not, nor charged God foolishly" (Job 1:20–22).

The Bible assures us that we can find in God the peace and strength to carry us through our sorrow.

"He healeth the broken heart, and bindeth up their wounds" (Ps. 147:3). This is one of the great and enduring messages of the Bible. In the pages of the Book there are comfort and consolation to the endless procession of those who taste the depths of pain and sorrow. Their way is hard and they are bereft of loved ones. Yet God in his infinite power and love sustains them and sees them through. Even the Saviour is known as a man of sorrows and acquainted with grief. And the great Father God himself knew, in the experience of the Cross, the deep pain that comes to those who see their innocent sons die as the victims of the cruelty and stupidity of men. The Bible knows sorrow. But it also knows that God is equal to its mystery and anguish. It knows that God knows the answers, even if we do not, and that we can trust him. "Now we see through a glass darkly; but then face to face" (I Cor. 13:12).

"If ye endure chastening, God dealeth with you as with sons; for what son is he whom the father chasteneth not? . . . For they verily for a few days chastened us after their own pleasure; but he for our profit, that we might be partakers of his holiness. Now no chastening for the present seemeth to be joyous, but grievous: nevertheless, afterward it yieldeth the peaceable fruit of righteousness unto them which are exercised thereby. Wherefore lift up the hands which hang down, and the feeble knees" (Heb. 12:7–12).

"I will lift up mine eyes unto the hills, from whence cometh my help. My help cometh from the Lord, which made heaven and earth. He will not suffer thy foot to be moved: he that keepeth thee will not slumber. Behold, he that keepeth Israel shall neither slumber nor sleep. The Lord is thy keeper: the Lord is thy shade upon thy right hand. The sun shall not smite thee by day, nor the moon by night. The Lord shall preserve thee from all evil: he shall preserve thy soul. The Lord shall preserve thy going out and thy coming in from this time forth, and even for evermore" (Ps. 121).

Sorrow comes because of the vacuum created by loneliness. We sometimes find no help from any human being. But there is one to whom we may go. "Out of the depths have I cried unto thee, O Lord. Lord, hear my voice" (Ps. 130:1, 2). No one who voices such a cry is left without a hearing. And there is peace for broken hearts in the tender and merciful heart of God. When our own personal world is shaken to pieces and falls apart we need something more than human security and advice. We need the strong, solid support of the eternal love that cannot be moved. "O Lord, my strength and my fortress, and my refuge in the day of affliction" (Jer. 16:19). "Cast thy burden upon the Lord and he shall sustain thee: he shall never suffer the righteous to be moved." The words of the Shepherd Psalm have brought peace to millions: "Yea, though I walk through the valley of the shadow of death, I will fear no evil: for thou art with me; thy rod and thy staff they comfort me" (Ps. 23:4). Paul sums it up well: "Now may the Lord Jesus Christ himself, and God our Father, who loved us and gave us eternal comfort and good hope through grace, comfort your hearts and establish them in every good work and word" (II Thess. 2:16, 17 RSV).

Divine hope and comfort are real no matter the refinements of our theology, nor the status of our economic situation, nor the persecution that may be ours. On one of the highways of Vietnam a refugee peasant and his wife were trudging along to escape the invaders. Several of their loved ones had already been massacred. The man was named Ta Hop Toan. He was a Christian. A reporter along the way asked him what Christmas meant to him, for it was the Christmas season. He said: "It means that Christ came upon earth to help the poor." "And has he helped?" was the next question. The weary peasant paused a moment before answering. Then Ta Hop Toan said: "He gave me strength to carry my children." He had just carried two of them thirty miles, hiding by night in insect-infested jungles and hounded by communist soldiers. And Ta Hop Toan's wife, who, wounded and lame, had brought two more children and a few belongings, said: "He gave me strength to walk with pain." [4]

It was the response of the human heart across nineteen hundred years to the promise of the Master: "Come unto me, all ye that labor and are heavy laden, and I will give you rest" (Matt. 11:28). We know little about the meaning of death and suffering and why it comes sometimes as it does. But we do not need the answers to these questions to know that God can give us strength from above "to walk with pain." Even the desolate pain of a sorrowing heart. Millions of Ta Hop Toans have found it so.

"Peace I leave with you, my peace I give unto you: not as the world giveth, give I unto you. Let not your heart be troubled, neither let it be afraid" (John 14:27). This word from the Master brings us comfort in our times of sadness. It lets us know that God is in charge of things. It infers that our dear ones are safe within his care and keeping. Above all, it would have us know that those who love and who are within the love of God need have no fear of the here or the hereafter.

"Verily, verily, I say unto you, That ye shall weep and lament, but the world shall rejoice: and ye shall be sorrowful, but your sorrow shall be turned into joy. . . . And ye now therefore have sorrow: but I will see you again, and your heart shall rejoice, and your joy no man taketh from you. . . . These things I have spoken unto you that in me ye might have peace. In the world ye shall have tribulation: but be of good cheer; I have overcome the world" (John 16:20, 22, 33).

I would to God I knew some place
Where I could lock my love away
Secure from death, whose quiet face
Looked in upon us yesterday.
But lovers have nowhere to hide:
We cannot creep beneath a leaf
Or find a crack and slip inside
Beyond the fingers of this thief.

No bolted door, no cunning mesh
Of woven steel, no wall of stone
Can shield the petal of the flesh
Or save the living stem of bone.
But only this—if we possess
A love as strong and sure as death.
What matters one heartbeat the less?
One pitiable pinch of breath?
Death cannot grasp the sun nor cup
His bony hand around the sea,
Nor take love but to lift it up
From earth into eternity.[5]

The Bible counsels us to find in sorrow a means of new insight and power.

The comfort of the divine presence is important for the healing of broken hearts. But it cannot operate in a vacuum. Too many of us take advantage of sorrow by indulging in an orgy of self-pity. We do not accept the healing of the spirit and go on to other things. We want to be humored and coddled and petted and pitied. But surely God does not expect us to be defeated by our grief. Rather to find in it the materials of a finer, more useful, and more understanding life. This depends on our courage and faith. The world does not stop just because a loved one dies. Our responsibility is more to the living than to the dead. The victorious ones, therefore, are those who, in the face of all that life can do, put their faith in God and are not dismayed.

Josephine Butler and her husband were returning home from a vacation trip. They were looking forward to seeing their little daughter again. As they drove up the driveway the girl was standing on a balcony, waving a childish welcome. In her excitement she leaned over too far and fell to her death. It was a tragic homecoming. And for a time the light went out of that home. Then the mother said that she decided "to find a keener sorrow than my own" and to minister to it. So she glorified her grief by becoming the friend and helper of all little girls. Her tragedy thus became the source and secret of one of the most inspiring lives of her time. It was said of her, referring to the words of the psalmist, that "she trod the valley of weeping and made it a place of springs" (Ps. 84:6,). "She did not let her aching heart become bitter, sour, sullen; she learned to turn sorrow into a symphony of service. In her heart, suffering became a song." [6]

In such lives we find demonstrated the words of the psalmist: "Weeping may endure for a night, but joy cometh in the morning" (Ps. 30:5). "They that sow in tears shall reap in joy" (Ps. 126:5). In them also we discover the message of the Cross. Indeed, it has been said that the only problem of suffering in which Jesus was interested was the practical problem of how to meet it and how to win out of it what good there may be in it. "Upon his high, triumphant cross, Jesus solved the mystery of sorrow; He turned a question into a conquest." And so may we turn sorrow into a transfiguring sacrament of healing and service. As Pearl Buck put it: "There is an alchemy in sorrow. It can be transmuted into wisdom which, if it does not bring joy, can yet bring happiness." [7] But more than that, the sorrowed heart has discovered the deeper dimensions of life which can minister in a special way to the needs of others. Such a one can be as Isaiah's description: "A man shall be as an hiding place from the wind, and a covert from the tempest; as rivers of water in a dry place, as the shadow of a great rock in a weary land" (Isa. 32:2).

It has been popular with some people to say that all death is the will of God. This is not true. Some sorrow comes because of ignorance, human accidents, germs, sin, unaccountable tragedies, and human carelessness. It is folly to blame God for this. Nor can it be said that God sends death to our loved ones to save us or to teach us a lesson. These are crude misrepresentations of the way of God with his children. But it is true, nonetheless, that when sorrow does come it may be used of God to open to us lives of greater depth and power than ever. For, as the Revised Standard Version puts a familiar word of Paul: "We know that in everything God works for good with those who love him" (Rom. 8:28). So it is that some of history's choicest spirits and some of man's noblest works have been cradled in grief hallowed by faith.

Modern psychologists are telling us that differences in the way people see things are the keys to their personalities. That is, a person is what he sees. The most famous test in this field is known as the Rorschach test. In it the person tested is asked to look at a series of inkblots in jagged shapes and tell the tester what he sees in them. Two people, for instance, will look at the same inkblot. One may see a sunrise. The other will see a storm cloud. Neither is "right," but the personalities thus projected are entirely different.[8]

In some such way God tests us all by the ragged shapes and blots which sorrow makes. It is the way we react that counts. Men of faith see in them not meaningless blotches or some frightening act of God but new shapes and forms with challenge and opportunity to enrich life and glorify God. In the good providence of God sorrow has its own ministry. What we see in it makes us what we are. "He hath sent me . . . to comfort all that mourn . . . to give unto them beauty for ashes, the oil of joy for mourning, the garment of praise for the spirit of heaviness" (Isa. 61:1–3). These words of God's messenger were spoken to the burdened people of Israel. But the same idea has a message for us all when Jesus used the same words to describe his own mission to men and women of every name and sign (Luke 4:17–19).

Additional biblical references: Ps. 23; John 14; I Cor. 15; Rev. 21.

Am I willing to admit the true cause of my unhappiness?
What are the guideposts to happiness?
What does it mean to be happy?

15 WHEN WE ARE JUST PLAIN UNHAPPY

SOMEONE HAS DEFINED happiness as a state of mind which is caused by the release of tension. Therefore, unhappiness is caused when our tensions are not released enough. This means that the number of unhappy people is legion. It also means that many people try to find short cuts to happiness by relaxing tensions by some temporary or artificial means. Drinking alcohol is one way. Taking a trip sometimes helps. An exciting movie will do it for a few hours, or losing oneself in an absorbing novel. These, of course, do not last. Then there is the dangerous habit of taking barbiturates. So widespread has this become that Dr. Thomas Parran, former Surgeon General, declares that sleeping pill addiction has become one of the country's major health problems. And Dr. Harris Isbell, a narcotic expert, says that the barbiturate habit is more dangerous than the morphine habit. The true nature of these drugs is seen in the nicknames the users give them: yellow jackets, red devils, blue heaven, thrill pills, goof balls, and idiot pills.[1]

But a case of chronic unhappiness calls for more basic treatment than a shot of bourbon or a dose of goof balls. We must probe the causes and find cures. Our unhappiness may have many causes. Illness, lack of acceptance by some group, being trapped in an undesirable but unchangeable situation, and financial failure are among them. But whatever be the cause, there is always a way out if we are honest enough to find it and earnest enough to take it.

An old English saying has it that the secret of happiness is to learn to accept the impossible, to do without the indispensable, and to bear the intolerable. Like many other pat formulas, this is good counsel. But how to do these things? It is just here that the Bible gives us solid help. It offers no simple short cuts on how to be happy. But it does suggest some underlying attitudes of life by which our tensions are relieved and from which happiness comes. Moreover, it tells us that joy is a normal state for the child of God. Religion is not a depressing, glum affair. "Rejoice in the Lord alway: and again I say, Rejoice" (Phil. 4:4). The Bible offers no support to those who see religion only as a grim business. Or who say Christians should not be happy in days of world crisis. Jesus amazed the people of his time to whom religion had become a burden by giving as his mission: "I am come that they might have life, and that they might have it more abundantly" (John 10:10).

Most of our pictures of Jesus see him as a "man of sorrows." But the gospel records show him to be a person possessed of a deep inner joy that was evident both in his influence on others and in his own actions and teaching. The scribes and Pharisees did not like the fact that he enjoyed eating and attending the parties of his friends who were not on the approved list. Jesus admitted that they called him a "gluttonous man, and a winebibber, a friend of publicans and sinners" (Luke 5:27–34; 7:31–35). They thought that he and his disciples should do more fasting and praying. But Jesus did not like the religion of those who fasted twice a week and went around with mournful faces. His religion was a thrilling, adventurous way to true and lasting happiness. This is a note that often is missing in our modern faith. The early Christians confounded the pagans by the joy with which they faced death and endured persecution. It is an important weapon of the spirit for anyone, anytime.

When we are unhappy we need to make peace with ourselves.

Much of our unhappiness comes because we are not unified inside. That is, we often live double lives, at cross-purposes with ourselves. Our ambition outruns our abilities. We are both good and bad and we know it. Our ideals fight our desires. We want to be loyal to more than one interest or person. And these loyalties often divide us. We want to do things our health will not permit. In other words, our lives become battlegrounds with contending forces doing constant battle. These things keep us mixed up and uncertain. They cause inner disunity and conflict. We live on the fence, and this makes us unhappy. And unhappiness makes for sour dispositions and personal inefficiency. These, in turn, only increase our discontent.

This is a very real problem for many people. Dr. Ralph T. Collins of the American Psychiatric Association said that the study of interpersonal relations is the number one job of psychiatrists and social scientists. "We need to help people to understand themselves," he declared. "Better adjustment to themselves and their environment will lead us to the will to work and to job satisfaction." [2]

Bible writers recognized this problem and prescribed for it long before modern psychiatry. The Bible states that the divided heart is a basic cause of chronic unhappiness. "Keep thy heart with all diligence; for out of it are the issues of life" (Prov. 4:23). The Bible stresses the importance of a unified personality as the basis of well-being. "The light of the body is the eye: if therefore thine eye be single [or sound], thy whole body shall be full of light" (Matt. 6:22). The Bible gives us the one sure prescription for attaining this unity. It is the simple need of salvation: "Ye must be born again" (John 3:7). Both the Old and New Testaments contain the one great unifying principle by which men may find unity of spirit, mind, heart, and purpose: "Thou shalt love the Lord thy God with all thy heart . . . and thy neighbor as thyself" (Luke 10:27). And in Jesus Christ this principle becomes a person in whose cleansing and re-creating power men become saved and are made whole and therefore happy. Salvation literally means wholeness. And out of a unity of center and purpose comes joy. Said Jesus: "These things have I spoken unto you, that my joy might remain in you, and that your joy might be full" (John 15:11). The unified person is the happy person.

There is nothing particularly mysterious about all this. It simply means that our happiness depends upon ourselves and not on any outward circumstances. Dr. Martin Gumpert, in his book *The Anatomy of Happiness*, says that the unhappy individual is one who is "haunted by anxiety and guilt, clinging to illusions, afraid or negligent of death, working without enjoyment, ignorant or lazy, unaware of his reserves or his limitations, stingy and unwilling to offer and to give, burdened with suspicions and secrets." [3] No one else can remove these causes of unhappiness. But we can! We can make peace with our anxiety and guilt and our fear of death as we make peace with God and accept his forgiveness and trust his care. We can learn to live with things as they are if we can not change them. We can school ourselves to accept and use our limitations. We can trust and serve and forgive our fellow men and live before all men a life that is an open book. What we need, in other words, is not a new set of rules but a new life in Christ. We do not need a new set of circumstances. We can find happiness right where we are.

This is exactly why so many of us are unhappy. We are always looking for happiness somewhere else except in our own hearts and in our own jobs and in our own environment. We are like the old prospector, Alex Heffern, who spent years looking for gold in northern Ontario. Then, being broke, he went to work for a mine in another part of Canada, digging asbestos. One day he asked a fellow worker when they would come to the asbestos. His neighbor said they were digging in it all the time. Alex was dumfounded. "I've been knee deep in that kind of rock for years." It turned out that all the years he had been looking for gold in northern Ontario, he had been walking over vast asbestos deposits not knowing what it was or that it was valuable. Alex led company geologists to this remote spot. It proved to be the second largest deposit of asbestos in the Western world and became the basis of a multimillion dollar mining corporation.[4]

It is so with us. "Thou hast put gladness in my heart" (Ps. 4:7). God has put it in every heart. The trouble is we do not recognize it or know its value. We insist on prospecting afar for things that glitter like gold when, if we only knew it, we are knee deep in the plain stuff of happiness all the while. It is strictly up to us! We do not dare blame our unhappiness on somebody or something else. If we take the trouble to look, we will find that the Kingdom of joy is in the midst of us all the time.

Coincidentally in two companion passages Paul speaks about contentment. He says that in spite of all the ups and downs that came to him, he had learned "in whatsoever state I am, therewith to be content" (Phil. 4:11, 12). He was a happy man whether free or in prison, whether he had plenty or was hungry. Then to the Thessalonians Paul urges three things that make for our well-being: quietness, minding your own business, and work (I Thess. 4:11, 12). Thus he himself was an example of his own teaching. It is good counsel for unhappy moderns.

When we are unhappy we should come to terms with the little things.

The little things are often more important than the big things in the cause and cure of unhappiness. James L. Mursell in his book *How to Make and Break Habits* gives an interesting example of this. He tells of a group of factory workers who were very upset and unhappy. The pay was good, the hours were not unduly long, the working conditions were excellent. The workers admitted all this. Yet they seethed with discontent. The management was baffled and worried. They finally called in an industrial psychologist. He studied the situation. He found that the trouble was in the men's shoes. The workers had to stand for long periods on a hard floor. Their feet and legs got very tired because standard-type shoes did not give them proper support. The fatigue that started in their feet spread to their nerves. And soon every molehill was a mountain. The company had special shoes made and the discontent disappeared.[5]

It is so many times with many of us. The smaller things affect us no end. One bad day spoils a week. One unkind word cancels a friendship. One bad habit ruins a character. One little worry starts a train of worries. One little ache or pain can become enlarged in our minds until it becomes a deadly disease. A dripping faucet can get on our nerves. A misfit shoe can upset a factory. Indeed, most of us are experts at making mountains out of molehills.

Immanuel Kant was one of the greatest thinkers of history. He made profound contributions to philosophy. He wrote nobly of the imperative place of duty in life. His *Critique of Pure Reason* is one of the landmarks of thought. Yet Kant was unable to keep from eating sweet, sticky little cakes of which he was very fond. They were bad for him and made him sick. But he ate them anyway. Of what use the categorical imperative when there were sweet, sticky little cakes around?[6]

We are like that. We hold to high principles and give assent to noble ideals. These do not make us unhappy and sick of mind and soul. It is the little grudges we bear, the little regrets that haunt us, the secret greed or prejudice or lust we harbor, the little frustrations that block our plans, the little hates we hide, the little misunderstandings we brood over. These undo our happiness. They fester and multiply and fasten themselves upon us. We must come to terms with them or we are doomed to chronic unhappiness. If we are not careful, our love for sweet, sticky cakes will keep us in hot water in spite of our best intentions.

The Bible would have us come to terms with these things by being bigger than they are. It would have us offset their appeal by living lives tall of soul, generous of judgment, forgiving of heart, clean of mind, broad of sympathy, loving of spirit, patient of disposition, slow to anger.

Dr. Karl B. Pace, of Greenville, North Carolina, was chosen as the "family doctor of 1954." He said that nerves and tension are our worst maladies today. For them he gave this prescription: "Live each day as it comes—don't worry about next week. . . . Learn to live instead of trying to get rich. . . . Never stay mad. . . . Start out by liking everyone you meet. . . . Take a rest after lunch to help you relax." [7] It is a prescription not only for health but for happiness as well. For the joyous spirit is the spacious spirit detached from worry about things not worth worrying about.

We can live like that when we live daily as in the presence of God. No one can be truly dedicated and petty at the same time. When we set our "affections on things above" the nagging little things can not take hold of us. "Glory and honor are in his presence; strength and gladness are in his place" (I Chron. 16:27). "In thy presence is fullness of joy; at thy right hand there are pleasures for evermore" (Ps. 16:11). It is as we live in active relationship with God that we can live above and beyond the power of the superficial hurts, slights, injustices, disappointments, and annoyances that often cloud our spirits and make us unhappy. Only then can we realize the actual unimportance of much that we feel to be important.

When we are unhappy we must learn to find our satisfactions in the things that can satisfy.

Americans have more things, creature comforts, and luxuries than ever before. Yet the psychiatrists and mental clinics are busier than ever. Why? Simply because we have not yet learned that our happiness does not lie in the extent of our possessions. John Steinbeck put the plight of many of us in his book *Sweet Thursday*. "Where does discontent start?" he asks. "You are warm enough, but you shiver. You are fed, yet hunger gnaws you. You have been loved, but your yearning wanders in new fields." [8] This is so because true happiness is a spiritual quality. It can not be bought.

Yet most of us try to take a short cut to happiness—and with very little luck. We are like Uncle Jim who set out to trap some wild turkeys. He rigged up a big box as a trap. A string was tied to the pole that held up the side of the box. Uncle Jim hid in a clump of bushes nearby with the other end of the string to spring the trap. With some corn as bait, several turkeys showed up. In fact, eleven of them walked under the box. But one was still outside. So Uncle Jim waited a bit in order to get all twelve. But while he waited, three of the eleven under the box walked out. He wished he had taken the eleven. But now he thought he would wait until at least one of the three went back in. But instead, five more walked out. That left only three inside. Uncle Jim was not going to be satisfied with just three when he might have had eleven. So he waited until one or two would go back in. But just then two of the three wandered out, leaving only one under the trap. And as Uncle Jim was trying to decide what to do, that one stalked out also and all twelve turkeys went their way unharmed. And they left Uncle Jim very unhappy! [9]

This is all too typical. We want to beat the law of averages. We try too hard. We press our luck. We scheme schemes. We want to make a killing. We are never satisfied. We lie in wait for the big deal. We think that happiness lies in trapping a dozen turkeys. But the fact is we so often miss the objective that way. The greedy heart is never the happy heart. Happiness does not depend on the number of turkeys we catch. The Bible warns us against the deceitfulness of riches as a bringer of happiness. "Better is little with the fear of the Lord, than great treasure and trouble therewith" (Prov. 15:16). "Lay not up for yourselves treasures upon earth, where moth and rust doth corrupt, and where thieves break through and steal" (Matt. 6:19). In other words, happiness runs out on those who try to trap it in the wrong places. More people become unhappy in trying to accumulate more and more things than in any other way. The Bible tells us that the true basis of our joy lies in the things of the spirit. If our happiness is geared to gold, we are doomed to disappointment. Its source is God himself.

Happiness is available to all because of what God has given to all men the gifts of life, love, beauty, and of a friendly universe. "The

Lord hath done great things for us; whereof we are glad" (Ps. 126:3). The Bible wants us to know that goodness and godliness are also conditions of happiness. "The kingdom of God is not meat and drink; but righteousness, and peace, and joy in the Holy Ghost" (Rom. 14:17). And happy or "blessed is the man that walketh not in the counsel of the ungodly, nor standeth in the way of sinners, nor sitteth in the seat of the scornful. But his delight is in the law of the Lord" (Ps. 1:1, 2). The Bible shows us that if our spirits are rooted in the infinite God we can maintain a serenity that cannot be upset by the upsets of life. "The Lord is my strength and my shield; my heart trusted in him, and I am helped: therefore, my heart greatly rejoiceth; and with my song will I praise him" (Ps. 28:7). The Bible also makes it plain that self-love and self-worship are enemies of happiness. Most of us are too selfish to be really happy. We are unhappy as long as we think only of ourselves. We will find our deepest satisfactions only as we keep busy at useful and worth-while tasks. For the Master declared that the happy people are those who are meek, gentle in spirit, merciful, pure in heart, and makers of peace. "Whosoever will save his life shall lose it; but whosoever shall lose his life for my sake and the gospel's, the same shall save it" (Mark 8:35).

When are we happy? In a word, when we learn to trust a loving God and enjoy the beauty and wonder of his world; when we have faith in ourselves as his children; when we love and serve our brother men; when we possess a pure mind and clear conscience. Then happiness finds us; we do not have to look for it. For it is then that we can feel secure in our world and our tensions can be relaxed. God has made us for himself and we are restless and unhappy until we find him. Our hearts will never be satisfied until he is at the center. To be sure, this is no easy, clever formula. But it is a timeless and priceless prescription for our discontent.

Additional biblical references: Job 38–40; Pss. 103, 104; Isa. 40.

What must I do to be saved?
What does salvation mean?
Why do I need God?

16 WHEN WE LOSE THE WAY

ONE EVENING A few years ago, a man was making his weary way home outside a little village in Lebanon. It was dusk and he had been working all day in the vineyards. His name was Raji. He was walking slowly along a lonely path. Suddenly he stumbled over something in the shadows. Raji found to his great surprise that it was a book which someone must have dropped. He could read a little so he hurried homeward to take a look at his find. For books were scarce. After a simple meal, Raji sat down and opened the volume. His family went off to bed. But he continued to read as best he could. The next morning when his family came into the kitchen they found Raji fast asleep with his head on the book. The lamp by his side had burned itself out. In reply to questions about the book, Raji said: "It is the Tow rahk, the Christian Bible. It is wonderful! I'll hurry home this evening and read some of it to you." And for weeks Raji read the Bible in the evenings to his family and friends. For he had told many about the wonderful book. As time went on Raji knew he believed the truths he had found in the book. He went to the Christian mission in Beirut where he was given instruction and baptized. And he brought back Bibles for his friends. He then began to teach them the way of life he himself had found from a book he had stumbled upon in the darkness.[1]

This true story has a great meaning for modern man in any setting. Most of us have no end of books to read. Yet there are many who walk a weary way along a gloomy path. We are fretful and sinful and unhappy. We have stifled something fine within us and have gone down an attractive but misleading road. We have missed the way and we know it. If this be so, the Bible is the one book we need. For it finds us where we are and leads us to the way everlasting.

The Bible shows us our need of God.

Evangelist Billy Graham, addressing an audience in the Waldorf-Astoria Hotel, New York, said: "The problem of the world is not the hydrogen bomb, or even communism. The problem is depraved human nature. . . . There is no difference in the nature of a savage walking a jungle trail with a spear in his hand, and an educated, cultured American flying a bomber overhead." [2] It is a strong word which goes to the heart of things. It does not matter whether or not we believe that man's nature is sinful from the beginning. The plain fact is that sin blights life and human society. And when men leave God out, human nature becomes depraved, bestial, and dangerous.

This is nothing new. Billy Graham was but echoing the words of many ancient voices from the Scriptures. Israel's woes were part of a universal guilt which brings suffering to all who rebel against God. "All we like sheep have gone astray; we have turned every one to his own way" (Isa. 53:6). Daniel's penitent prayer for his people might well include us all: "We have sinned, and have committed iniquity, and have done wickedly, and have rebelled, even by departing from thy precepts and from thy judgments" (Dan. 9:5). Paul gives a simple reason for the plain fact that man is not as God intended him to be: "For all have sinned, and come short of the glory of God" (Rom. 3:23).

Not one of us but who has felt, with St. Paul, the endless contest between good and evil that goes on within us. The good things we would do, we do not. Things we ought not do, we do (Rom. 7:19). We have all felt what Augustine felt: "How often have I lashed at my will, and cried 'Leap now! Leap now!' And as I said it, crouched for the leap, and it all but leapt: and yet it did not leap. And the life to which I was accustomed held me more than the life for which I really yearned!" [3]

It is this disobedient will that gets us into trouble. We resist the call of the upward trail. We never bring ourselves to make the next commitment. Our very freedom of will, which is the gift of God, gets us into real trouble. We turn away from God. We think we know better. We want to have our own way. We follow after our own selfish interests and passions. Like the lost sheep or the prodigal son, we carelessly wander down some inviting path until we are lost.

Lost in that soul sickness that is compounded of pride, self-will, sensuality, and cynicism.

Most of us will find plenty of evidence of this soul sickness when we look within our own hearts. We are lonely in the midst of crowds. We are fearful although physically secure. We are hungry while surrounded by plenty. We are at odds with ourselves and our world even though it makes us miserable. We are plagued by an uneasy conscience and inward turmoil in spite of our outward calm. We are at heart greedy and lustful and hateful and all the while we present a respectable front. We are sinners trying to act like saints. And it will not work!

In trying to get relief from this basic illness of the soul, we are willing to try almost any convenient pill. But most of these pills are self-prescribed *placebos*. A placebo is an inactive medicine, like a sugar pill. It is sometimes given by doctors merely to satisfy a patient. It has no medicinal value. But the sick person has the satisfaction of thinking that he is taking a healing potion. In medical circles the placebo is known as the "humble humbug." [4]

How modern man likes to humbug himself with placebos! These take all forms from pseudo-psychiatry to psychic phenomena and from sex license to sleeping pills. We worship the golden calf until we get ulcers. Then we worship the ulcers. We try rest cures until we get more restless than ever. We run the gamut from alcoholism to atheism, including all the isms in between. But there is no cure in them! They are attractive and easy to take. But we are only fooling ourselves. They are placebos. They have no medical power to cure the aches of the heart and the scars of the soul. When will we learn that we cannot save ourselves?

An actress was found in a hotel room in a coma with her dead baby in her arms. A note read: "Bury us both in the same box. . . . I can't make it for her no matter how hard I try." [5] Of course we cannot make it by ourselves! No one can! No matter how hard we try!

There is only one cure. We do not make the rules. We are not our own judges. We are accountable to God. When we have lost the way we need God. And we are unhappy until we find him. The Bible tells us every man stands before the judgment of God and will find his mercy in penitence and humility. "With the Lord there is mercy, and with him is plenteous redemption" (Ps. 130:7). "The Father . . . without respect of persons judgeth according to every man's work" (I Pet. 1:17). "A broken and a contrite heart, O God, thou wilt not despise" (Ps. 51:17). Here the Bible is our greatest aid. For in the Bible we are assured that man is in the hands of a loving, merciful, saving God who redeems us from our sin and our waywardness and shows us the way of life everlasting. "Let the wicked forsake his way, and the unrighteous man his thoughts: and let him return unto the LORD, and he will have mercy upon him; and to our God, for he will abundantly pardon" (Isa. 55:7). "By grace are ye saved through faith; and that not of yourselves: it is the gift of God" (Eph. 2:8). If we have lost the way we first need to know our need of God, and to pray, with the psalmist: "Show us thy mercy, O LORD, and grant us thy salvation" (85:7). We need not be afraid of God. We can trust "the Judge of all the earth to do right" (Gen. 18:25) because "who is a God like unto thee, that pardoneth iniquity, and passeth by the transgression of the remnant of his heritage? he retaineth not his anger for ever, because he delighteth in mercy" (Mic. 7:18).

When the Hebrew exiles returned to Jerusalem the former glory was gone. The successor to Solomon's Temple was a very poor affair compared to what it had been. The people were discouraged. Some of them felt that God had indeed deserted them. In this situation the prophet Haggai voiced the faith that God was still with them and that they could yet come back with his help. Indeed, he said that their future would be greater even than their past. It was in this vein that he encouraged them to look to God for their salvation. "Be strong, all ye people of the land, saith the LORD, and work: for I am with you, saith the LORD of hosts" (2:4). The theme of this little story runs all through the Old Testament, and, of course, the New. The men of God always kept the hope before the people that they would recover from their sins and their neglect of God if they would but turn to him. Indeed, centuries later Paul echoes Haggai when he suggests that we must co-operate with God in helping to work out our own salvation (Phil. 2:12, 13).

The Bible assures us of the forgiveness and peace of God when we turn to him in penitence and humility.

"Hide thy face from my sins, and blot out all mine iniquities. Create in me a clean heart, O God; and renew a right spirit within me" (Ps. 51:9, 10). This is a golden note that is sounded throughout the Bible. It declares that man does not lift himself by the bootstraps of his own nature. It holds that our salvation is in God and from God and with God. In fact, divine forgiveness is the only route to biblical salvation. That is, forgiveness is the only way by which a sinner may find his way back to the fellowship of God. We are, therefore, not doomed to defeat and despair.

In Acts 26:12–19 Paul recounts the story of his conversion before King Agrippa. He said that when the voice spoke to him on the Damascus road he heard these words: "Saul, Saul, why persecuteth thou me? it is hard for thee to kick against the pricks." This is an Oriental expression referring to the goad which the donkey driver used to help along his beast. Sometimes the donkey kicked back, but only to hurt himself more. The point is that we only hurt ourselves when we defy the laws and guidance of God. When we have lost the way God still seeks us out and we must come to terms with him. When God calls to us we will be miserable until we like Paul are "not disobedient unto the heavenly vision."

The psalmist glories in God's forgiveness: "Thou, Lord, art good, and ready to forgive; and plenteous in mercy unto all them that call upon thee" (86:5; see also Ps. 34:18). It rings out clear and strong in Isaiah: "Incline your ear, and come unto me: hear and your soul shall live" (55:3; see also Isa. 59). Joel echoes the idea in these words quoted later in Acts: "And it shall come to pass, that whosoever shall call upon the name of the Lord shall be delivered" (Joel 2:32). But it is in the New Testament that the song of deliverance comes to full chorus. In Matthew the Master himself makes the meaning plain: "Except ye be converted, and become as little children, ye shall not enter into the kingdom of Heaven" (18:3); "This is my blood of the new testament, which is shed for many for the remission of sins" (26:28). In Acts the melody returns as the theme song of the early church: "Repent ye therefore and be converted, that your sins may be blotted out" (3:19). And Paul makes the refrain the key to his dynamic ministry. "Be ye reconciled to God" (II Cor. 5:20); "Christ died for our sins" (I Cor. 15:3); "Whosoever shall call upon the name of the Lord shall be saved" (Rom. 10:13). In I John it is in simple words: "If we confess our sins, he is faithful and just to forgive us our sins, and to cleanse us from all unrighteousness" (I John 1:9).

So it is that we do have a real cure for the sin and soul-sickness of life. It is in God! The message of salvation of the Bible has been a lifeline to sinful men through all the centuries. At its direction cynics and murderers, thieves and alcoholics, liars and sensualists, have turned their backs on their sins and have been made whole again. Under its divine guidance countless men have had their hearts washed clean of the grime and ill will that choke the soul. They have been released from the deadening grip of the self and of the senses. Salvation is the gift of God, but it has conditions and imposes responsibilities.

The classic biblical story of those who have lost the way and found it again is the immortal tale of the prodigal son. Willfully he turns his back on his father and goes down an alluring but wayward path. Finally he comes to his senses and penitently turns back. And he finds a glad welcome home from his father (Luke 15:11–32). It is a story that has numberless counterparts throughout the years. In them all is one key human necessity. Men must recognize their own weakness and they must make the definite decision to turn away from their sins and to make their way to God. God takes the initiative in forgiving us. But we are not saved against our wills. And neither are our wills enough to save us. (See Chapter 9).

Dostoevski was for years a chronic gambler. He sank lower and lower through this vice which he seemed unable to control. He struggled helplessly against it. Good resolutions did no good. He was heartsick and ashamed. Yet the disgrace went on for years. And suddenly one day it ended. He knew it had ended. He was a new man. He continued to live above a gambling den and had to pass the door daily. But he never again went in. The sin that had bullied him for years never returned—not even once. In some such way God can change human nature and give us new lives for old.

Men and women who have sinned and who are desperate before the naked issues of life and death need more than a kindly philosophy, or economic security, or friends, or success. They need to surrender themselves to God. And they find him in the gospel of salvation of the Bible. Henry Sloan Coffin told of two Christian women who visited a murderer in his death cell. He was totally unresponsive to their appeals. They left him a copy of the New Testament. What happened was not discovered until after his execution.

Among his effects was this note: "I put the New Testament on the shelf. . . . When I was tired of doing nothing, I took down the book again and began to read. This time I saw how Jesus was handed over to Pilate and tried unjustly and put to death by crucifixion. As I read I began to think. I went on and my attention was next taken with these words: 'Father, forgive them, for they know not what they do.' I stopped. I was stabbed to the heart as if pierced by a five-inch nail. What did the verse reveal to me? Shall I call it the love of the heart of Christ? Shall I call it his compassion? I do not know what to call it. I only know that with an unspeakably grateful heart I believed." [6]

Few of us will ever await execution in a murderer's cell—nor be the victim of gambling mania. But we are all sinners of the spirit. In our pride and covetousness and self-will and vanity and hatred and jealousy and envy and deceit and arrogance and impure minds and love of the world, we have all just as surely broken the moral laws of God and have shut ourselves away from his presence. These things eat out the inner supports of life and make us unhappy and unhealthy persons. Most of us learn the hard and bitter way that "No man can serve two masters: for either he will hate the one, and love the other; or else he will hold to the one, and despise the other. Ye cannot serve God and mammon" (Matt. 6:24). In those days a master had complete control. It must be so in every person. We need a master. And when we are mastered by worldliness we shut God out. Thus, when the world gets the best of us we need the peace and forgiveness of God. And we find it when we are humble enough to turn and come to God with the admission of our mistakes, even as a child comes to its father. For he lifts the burden, cleanses the stain, and makes us free and happy again. "Though your sins be as scarlet, they shall be as white as snow; though they be red like crimson, they shall be as wool" (Isa. 1:18).

The Bible points us to Jesus Christ as the one true way of life.

"I am the way, the truth, and the life: no man cometh unto the Father, but by me" (John 14:6). We find this forgiveness of God best through Jesus Christ who revealed him to be a loving heavenly Father. So it is that the saving power of Jesus Christ becomes the climax and centerpiece of the Bible. Explain it as we will, the fact remains that the preaching of the death and resurrection of Jesus for the salvation of men became the spearhead of the vitality of the early church. "For the preaching of the cross is to them that perish, foolishness; but unto us which are saved, it is the power of God" (I Cor. 1:18). Thus Paul faced the challenge of pagan Rome with his own challenge: "I am not ashamed of the gospel of Christ: for it is the power of God unto salvation to everyone that believeth" (Rom. 1:16). Even in prison Paul and Silas bore witness to this redemption. The age-old question was posed by the jailer himself: "What must I do to be saved?" And the answer is given in words that have themselves challenged men across the centuries: "Believe on the Lord Jesus Christ, and thou shalt be saved, and thy house." (Acts 16:25–32). It was this message of salvation that established the Christian faith in those early years and that has been the key to its power ever since.

Jesus Christ is not only the centerpiece of the Bible. He is the centerpiece of history. And, for those who would find the true and eternal way, he is the centerpiece of our lives and hearts. For in Christ is the way to a new life that is free, clean, healthy, whole, joyous, strong, and everlasting. No other saviour has done so much for so many. In Christ, God breaks through our resistance and redeems us from our sins.

Yet many modern minds overlook this simple truth. We are so broad-minded we want to include Christ as one among many and like to think of all religions as of equal value. Arnold Toynbee tries to do this in his litany of the saints in which he expresses his own personal religion. He links Christ with many pagan religious leaders and philosophers, stating: "Christ Tammuz, Christ Adonis, Christ Osiris, Christ Balder, hear us, by whatsoever name we bless Thee for suffering death for our salvation. . . . Buddha Gautama, show us the path that will lead us out of our afflictions. . . . Mithras, fight at our side in our battle of Light against Darkness. . . . Valiant Zarathustra, breathe thy spirit into the Church Militant here on earth. . . . Blessed mo-ti, disciple of Christ . . . transmit thou too the message of love. . . ." [7]

Let us grant the valued insights of many seers. But when we try to worship all the gods there are, we find none. And life is empty and we miss the way. No wonder, therefore, the Bible boldly proclaims:

"Neither is there any salvation in any other: for there is none other name under heaven given among men, whereby we must be saved" (Acts 4:12). Christianity contains the best in all religions. But a synthetic religion that adopts only a part of Christianity with other faiths is an insipid and powerless philosophy. "Thou shalt call his name JESUS: for he shall save his people from their sins" (Matt. 1:21). Christianity is unique because it has Christ!

Irving Stone wrote a novel about the artist Vincent van Gogh. It is called *Lust for Life*. In it the author tells how for the first time Van Gogh saw at an art exhibition, shortly after coming to Paris, the pictures of the Impressionist School: the brilliant and colorful paintings of Degas, Monet, Manet, and others. These bright pictures were a revelation to him. They were fresh, vivid, living with color. Says Irving Stone: "From the age of twelve he had been used to seeing dark and sombre paintings . . . flat colors shaded slowly into each other. . . . The paintings that laughed at him merrily from [these] walls [in Paris] were like nothing he had ever seen or dreamed of. Gone were the flat, thin surfaces. Gone was the sentimental sobriety. Gone was the brown gravy in which Europe had been bathing its pictures for centuries." [8]

So it is that the beauty and light and life of Christ stand out in appealing contrast against the dull and somber tones of all others who would paint for us the picture of God. Christianity is not a brown-gravy religion like many others. The Christ way is not a flat, forbidding way. It is the way of infinite peace, of boundless joy, and of triumphant power. And those who find it know that their search is over. "If any man be in Christ, he is a new creature: old things are passed away; behold, all things are become new" (II Cor. 5:17). "Thanks be to God, which giveth us the victory through our Lord Jesus Christ" (I Cor. 15:57).

Additional biblical references: Ps. 51; Isa. 53; John 3:1–21; I John 1.

How important is it that I believe in God?
Can an educated man believe in the unseen?
What can we believe?

17 WHEN DOUBT DISTURBS THE MIND

THE *New Humanist* carried this frank statement of modern skepticism: "We regard the universe as self-existing and not created. We believe that man is a part of nature and that he has emerged as the result of a continuous process. We reject the traditional dualism of mind and body. We assert that modern science makes unacceptable any supernatural or cosmic guarantees of human values. . . . We are convinced that the time has passed for theism, deism and modernism." [1]

This piece was signed, among others, by John Dewey, generally considered the most influential figure in modern American education. In his own book, *What I Believe*, Dewey made his position clearer still when he said: "Faith in the divine author and authority in which Western civilization confided . . . [has] been made impossible for the cultivated mind of the Western world." [2]

Such lofty attitudes of unbelief have come to be accepted, often unwittingly, by many people. Doubt and skepticism seem to come easily to modern man. We have enjoyed our cynicism as if it were something new and desirable and terribly respectable.

But many of us on the other hand are recovering from the pleasant luxury of living with question marks. We are up against it! And we are beginning to see that the end of unbelief is chaos for man and for his society.

It is like that in our personal lives, too. We can get along without believing in much while times are pleasant. But when a crisis comes we need something bigger than we are to stand by us and steady us. The Bible helps us at this point. It is not a book of unwavering faith.

In its pages is also recorded the black despair that sometimes comes to good men. There is Job, for instance, wrestling with the eternal question of why good men suffer. And there is the agony of Jesus on the Cross when he felt that God had forsaken him. Then there is the story of the man who came to Jesus with a son possessed of an evil spirit. "Jesus said unto him, If thou canst believe, all things are possible to him that believeth. And straightway the father of the child cried out, and said with tears, Lord, I believe; help thou mine unbelief" (Mark 9:23, 24).

This is a common cry of us all. We like to think we are believers. Then doubts and circumstances come and leave our hearts barren. "We are strange mixtures of belief and unbelief." And when doubt does disturb the mind, the Bible is here to help.

The Bible reminds us of the necessity of belief.

"Let not the wise man glory in his wisdom, neither let the mighty man glory in his might, let not the rich man glory in his riches: but let him that glorieth glory in this, that he understandeth and knoweth me, that I am the Lord which exercise loving kindness, judgment and righteousness, in the earth" (Jer. 9:23, 24). But that is just our trouble. We have gloried in our wisdom, our might, and our riches. And we have left our faith in God, the most important thing of all. Thus when these things fail us we are left desolate. We are like doubting Thomas who said he would not believe unless he could touch the nail prints in the hands of Jesus. We like to think we can believe only in the things we can touch and measure and see. We need the reminder of Jesus to Thomas that to believe what we cannot see is more important still (John 20:26–29). It is the fool, said the psalmist, that "hath said in his heart, There is no God" (14.1).

"For therein is the righteousness of God revealed from faith to faith: as it is written, The just shall live by faith" (Rom. 1:17). Paul here is declaring that belief can lead to the divine transforming and saving power. It involves the acceptance of God and trust in him. God's infinite resources and saving power are ours. There is nothing too mystical or theological about this. It is a simple statement of the kind of belief that has transformed countless lives and shaped history. He is saying that it is the intangibles of belief that make the difference between inadequate living and triumphant living. This was the great text that ended Martin Luther's search for truth and peace. As such it sparked the Protestant Reformation. And even today it sums up one of the moving forces of life.

The necessity of belief is underscored in many ways by modern science. The late Waldemar Kaempffert told about the machines that have been devised to substitute for the heart, lungs, kidneys, and liver when these are diseased. Such instruments are marvelous inventions, But, said Mr. Kaempffert, "the brain is the one organ of the body that cannot be isolated." [3] We can live with artificial lungs and hearts. But we cannot live without the brain! And it is the brain that is the basic instrument of belief. So it is! We can do without many things we once thought necessary. But we cannot live without the function of belief. And there is no substitute for it.

Even some psychiatrists are at long last recognizing this as a necessity of human life. Dr. Viktor Frankl, president of the Austrian Society of Medical Psychotherapy, is one. He said: "To deny the spiritual side of one's nature does it great violence. . . . Men and women are driven not only by sex and ambition, but also by an overriding need for God. They must overcome the modern-day notion that religion and God are not real needs." [4]

To be sure, we are earthly creatures and we depend on things of the earth for our physical survival. But we do not live by bread alone (Matt. 4:4)! Neither can we live by negations alone. Nor neutrality. Nor relativity. Nor open-mindedness. Nor nihilism. And yet this is what modern man has tried to do. We like to pride ourselves on our tolerance. We say that everything is relative, that one man's opinion is as good as another. We see so many sides to all questions we are afraid to have any convictions of our own. We like to affect skepticism as a mark of the smart, modern temper. We seem to think that we are dated if our faith is showing. Yet, today as always, "The fear of the LORD is the beginning of knowledge: but fools despise wisdom and instruction" (Prov. 1:7).

A cartoon in *The Saturday Review* showed the officers of a national opinion service reading the results of a certain poll. The caption read: "The figures . . . are as follows: For, 9 . . . Against, 11 . . . Don't know, 17,344,692." [5] Why is it, in matters of moral values and spiritual reality, so few of us want to declare ourselves and so many are willing to be counted among those who do not know and do not care?

The Bible faces us squarely with man's basic need of faith. It is a book about faith and assumes man's need to believe. It infers that we were born to believe. It declares that we are the children of God and are bereft without him. "The fear of the Lord is the beginning of wisdom: a good understanding have all they that do his commandments" (Ps. 111:10). "Trust in the Lord with all thine heart; and lean not unto thine own understanding" (Prov. 3:5). And Paul put faith high on the list of the most valuable possessions of man: "Above all, taking the shield of faith" (Eph. 6:16). This is the way of life and light. When Jesus gave the great commandment about loving God he repeated its Old Testament form except that he added the word "mind" (Matt. 22:37).

Said Gilbert K. Chesterton: "The purpose of an open mind, like that of an open mouth, is to close it on something solid." So be it. We cannot hold in suspension forever the claims of the spirit. Man must believe something, or he will die inside! The Bible would have us be numbered among the believers, no matter how weak or unsure our faith! Thank God we do not have to know all the answers in order to live by our faith in the reality of God.

One of the questions that bother us is the existence of evil. "Why dost thou look on faithless men, and art silent when the wicked swallows up the man more righteous than he?" (Hab. 1:13, RSV). In the midst of one of Judah's crises the prophet here voices the question that has been on the lips of millions of men since that time: "Why doesn't God do something?" Habakkuk wanted to believe in God but he was discouraged when he saw the good people taken in by evil men. However, the questions are not all on one side. The doubter still has many things to account for. He cannot explain the goodness that does exist. And in his doubting he finds no explanation for the suffering and injustice of life. As Roy L. Smith puts it: "The tragedy is that he has no faith in anything which will come to his rescue." [6] Habakkuk addressed his question direct to God. And God made reply to him: "The righteous shall live by his faith" (2:4).

The Bible proclaims the reality of the unseen world.

The Bible shows us that we are citizens of two universes, physical and spiritual. But it insists that the unseen is as real as the seen. In spite of our modern skepticism, this idea is as old as the race—and as up to date as today. But still there are those who think it smart to live only for the things that are solid and visible.

The ancient Chinese philosopher, Lao Tzu, once tried to teach his pupils the value of the nonexistent. He said: "Thirty spokes unite in a wheel; but the utility of the cart depends on the hollow center [of the wheel] in which the axle turns. Clay is molded into a vessel; the utility of the vessel depends on its hollow interior. Doors and windows are cut in order to make a house; the utility of the house depends on the empty spaces in it." [7]

If the nonexistent is important for earthy uses, how much more so is the invisible presence of the spirit of the eternal God. The Bible records its reality as the dynamic, creative center of the wheel of human history, the reality of the vessel that is the physical world, and the heart of the human house that is the body. It is the Eternal Mind that brought the world into being. The Bible declares that in the beginning there was not chaos or nothingness—but God! Human beings are not composed wholly of clay or animal tissue; they have the breath of life in them! Nations rise and fall not of their own strength but as they obey the divine will and law. The wonder and beauty and intricacy of the universe itself bear mute witness to the handiwork and glory of the Eternal Spirit. "All thy works shall praise thee, O Lord" (Ps. 145:10). The great advances of the race toward freedom and enlightenment are not accidental. They come by faith in unseen values. "By faith Abraham . . . looked for a city which hath foundations, whose builder and maker is God" (Heb. 11:8, 10). The one continuing, stable, and permanent thing in the midst of universal change, decay, and death is the unseen. "We look not at the things which are seen, but at the things which are not seen: for the things which are seen are temporal; but the things which are not seen are eternal" (II Cor. 4:18).

Is all of this an old wives' tale? Is our universe nothing but mud and matter? Is history but the dismal record of blundering men driven helplessly before the sex urge and the hunger drive? Is the human being merely a bundle of cell tissue and blood? The modern intellectual who likes to think so is wrong! He is like the woman in the jury box reported in *The New Yorker*. She turned to the woman next to her during the course of a trial and said: "I don't listen to the evidence. I like to make up my own mind." [8]

For the evidence in this case shows unmistakably that the structure of the world and all that is in it is not fixed, inert, and material. It is alive with forces and powers and spirit. Those in the know, know this to be true. Said A. Cressy Morrison, former president of the New York Academy of Science: "We are still in the dawn of the scientific age and every increase of light reveals more brightly the handiwork of an intelligent Creator. . . . With a spirit of scientific humility and of faith grounded in knowledge we are approaching ever nearer to an awareness of God." [9]

The writer to the Hebrews preceded Dr. Morrison by some nineteen hundred years. But he said the same thing: "By faith we understand that the worlds have been framed by the word of God, so that what is seen hath not been made out of things which appear" (11:3, ARV).

The act of belief is not a matter of witchcraft, sentimentality, magic, or superstition. The unseen world is not a figment of imagination. The very fact that men venture to continue to dream and hope and love is evidence itself of the unseen. For ideals and faiths and moral values are the most real things in the world today. It is the believer who is in tune with the infinite. The skeptic is lost and powerless in his own materialism. The most wretched persons among us are those who refuse to believe anything they cannot see or measure or handle with their hands. They are the victims of their own stupidity and become bogged down in their own bitter disillusionment. When will we ever learn, as Paul said, to "walk by faith, not by sight" (II Cor. 5:7)? In fact, believing what we cannot prove is as essential to scientific method as it is to religion. When tests show that the application of a scientific principle leads to useful conclusions, we accept it. And when faith in God brings satisfying results we are led to the acceptance of the existence of God.

The Bible gives us something significant to believe in.

The reason our faith seems to waver is that so often it is attached to temporary and inadequate things. Our capacity for belief is tested by the size of the things we believe in. When we are content to believe only in little things our faith is shriveled and weak.

Tennessee Williams said one time that his own creed as a playwright is fairly close to that expressed by the painter in Shaw's play,

The Doctor's Dilemma: "I believe in Michelangelo, Velásquez and Rembrandt; in the might of design, the mystery of color, the redemption of all things by beauty everlasting and the message of art that has made these hands blessed. Amen." [10] This sounds nice. But it is not big enough! The cults of sweetness and light are not strong enough to sustain life and keep it going. We need something vaster than color and someone more significant than Rembrandt to believe in.

Nor is the philosophy of defeatism big enough for the soul of man to live by and grow on. It is found in the novelists and playwrights who make a fetish of violence, hopelessness, and human degeneracy. It attracted the morbid and the psychotic in the theories of the French Existentialists. They tried to make a religion out of nothingness. They held that man is an animal, that he is responsible only to himself, and that his complete doom is certain. It appealed to the unstable and the sensualist. It is a cult that has failed because man cannot long believe only in himself and only in the gratification of his own desires.

Likewise, the faith of modern man in his own knowledge is as pathetic as it is insufficient. The scientist, J. Arthur Thomson, put it well when he said: "Scientific knowledge is indispensable, but it is, as schoolmen said, 'evening knowledge' . . . cold, grey and shadowy: religious knowledge is 'morning knowledge' . . . where all is seen in the growing light of a new day. So we come back to the God of our fathers, whose name Jehovah was said to mean, 'I am that I am.' " [11]

Why do we seek so hungrily in this place and in that for something big enough to believe in—something to which we can give all our worship and from which we can get peace and order and purpose and strength for life? It is because God has set eternity in our hearts. He wants us and waits for us. We are never satisfied until we find him.

The Bible is both source book and guide book to eternal values and faiths that are significant enough to satisfy and sustain us. It reveals to us the one and only everlasting, righteous, and loving God who is the giver of life and the strong rock of refuge and defense for the human soul against all its enemies. It shows us the work among men of the Holy Spirit of God which is available always for human guidance and support. The Bible tells us of Jesus Christ, who saves us from our sins and sets our feet on the road to life everlasting. The Bible declares that there is eternal sanction for the right and eternal punishment for the willful wrong. It lets us know that this world belongs to God and that we are the children of God. The Bible assures us of the supreme worth of the human soul and that life is worth living and can be lived victoriously. It holds before us the high and holy moral and spiritual laws that govern life and the universe. It charges us to lift our eyes from the picayune and inconsequential and to catch a vision of the sweep and wonder of life with God. "Now the God of hope fill you with all joy and peace in believing, that ye may abound in hope, through the power of the Holy Ghost" (Rom. 15:13).

When doubt disturbs the mind, it is at these springs that we renew our faith. Here are things worthy of our undying devotion! These alone are the things that make life livable and great. We can believe in them with our minds as well as our hearts, because they have divine foundations. "Let us hear the conclusion of the whole matter: Fear God, and keep his commandments: for this is the whole duty of man" (Eccles. 12:13).

If these commitments are too much for us, we can at least humbly but confidently take our position on the side of that great host who venture, in spite of apparently contrary evidence, to assert with the writer of Hebrews: "Now faith is the assurance of things hoped for, the conviction of things not seen" (Heb. 11:1, RSV). And, with Moses, to endure, "as seeing him who is invisible" (Heb. 11:27). It is this that makes modern men of God invincible, even in an age of science and persistent evil.

Additional biblical references: Pss. 37, 73, 103; Matt. 10; Heb. 11, 12.

What are the measures of a successful life?
Is it wrong to want to achieve?
How may I stretch my abilities?

18 WHEN WE WANT TO AMOUNT TO SOMETHING

SOME YEARS AGO football coach Harvey John Harmon picked an all-biblical football team. This was his line-up: Abner, left end; Job, left tackle; Peter, left guard; Samson, center; Moses, right guard; Jacob, right tackle; Gideon, right end; David, quarterback and captain; Daniel, left half; Joshua, right half; John the Baptist, fullback. By way of explanation Harmon said, "For center Samson—he could take out all seven of the opposing linemen at once. For guards, Peter the rock and Moses—Moses was so strong and able to take the gaff that I'd not only make him a guard but put him on the rules committee, too. For half-backs—Joshua, of whom the Bible says that he 'passed through,' and Daniel, who was resolute and stuck to the right. I'd put Daniel in charge of the training table, too: he showed that he knew his simple fare was better than the pyorrhea-giving diet of the Babylonians. For fullback, John the Baptist—he'd prepare the way." [1]

This imaginative use of the Bible may be a bit far-fetched, but it does serve a purpose. It reminds us that Bible characters were real people; not just names in a book. And it suggests in a dramatic way that the qualities of life and spirit demonstrated by men of God in Bible times are quite as important today if we are to amount to something. The kind of faith and character the Bible talks about is not a rarefied, otherworldly thing. It is a rugged and down-to-earth and useful quality. It comes to life in persons. And most of all, in the life of Jesus.

Studies at the University of California have found four basic qualities of a good athlete. These are, according to Dr. Anna Espenschade: A strong grip. A good sense of aim or direction. An unwavering sense of balance. A sense of force.[2] It is interesting to know that the Bible a long time ago set forth the same factors as necessary to make life count for something in any field.

The Bible warns us to stand up straight.

A strong physical grip is a must for the superior athlete. In the tests it was found to be the single best measure of one's over-all physical condition. So also, a strong grip on the basic moral virtues is absolutely necessary for anyone who is to amount to anything anywhere. Gaylord A. Freeman, Jr., a Chicago banker, summed up the thinking of a group of business leaders in a paper on the subject, "The Selection, Training and Development of Tomorrow's Executives." The number one requirement that he listed for a good executive was Integrity!

Personal integrity is made up of moral principle, self-restraint, dedendable honesty, and unquestioned honor. It is a rock-bottom foundation for successful living. Not every honorable person is materially a success. But no one makes anything worth while of his life who tries to build it on the convenient use of cheating, lying, broken promises, and unethical dealings. This vital role of integrity was proclaimed by biblical writers some twenty-five hundred years before banker Freeman. "Till I die I will not remove mine integrity from me" (Job 27:5). "Judge me, O LORD, according to my righteousness, and according to mine integrity" (Ps. 7:8). "No good thing will he withhold from them that walk uprightly" (Ps. 84:11). "He that walketh uprightly walketh surely" (Prov. 10:9). "He that walketh righteously, and speaketh uprightly. . . . He shall dwell on high" (Isa. 33:15, 16). "Herein do I exercise myself, to have always a conscience void of offense toward God, and toward men" (Acts 24:16).

There is evidence, however, that self-indulgence is weakening this central phase of integrity in the make-up of many youth. Psychiatrist E. J. Kelleher has said that modern American young people have been so pampered that they are becoming soft morally. He said, "The character trait of truthfulness is disappearing. Many young people feel it is all right to lie if they can get away with it. They feel they should be permitted to do what they wish, without social restriction." [3] This must not be so! For it builds habits that can only lead to personal failure and disaster.

The Great Wall of China was built to keep out the Mongol army.

It was high as a hill and broad enough for six horses to ride abreast along the top. For many years it kept out the northern barbarians. Behind it the Chinese felt secure. Even the mighty Genghis Khan could not breach it by force. But this crafty warrior one time sent word in secret to one of the gatekeepers that he, the gatekeeper, would have gold and high position if he would open the gate. Tempted by this offer, the gatekeeper opened the gate from within and the armies of the enemy poured in. Legend says that the first act of the conqueror Genghis Khan was to order the treacherous gatekeeper beheaded.

It is a parable of life. We present bold fronts to the world. We feel secure behind our protective walls of education and culture, position and money. But our real weakness is inside our own minds and hearts. We are tempted to surrender our own inner integrity by some false lure or bribe. But when we do open the door to sin and evil, we succeed only in destroying ourselves in the end.

Whatever importance we may put on other things, the Bible warns us to build on the solid rock of the moral laws of God if we want to make life count for something. The shifting sands of expediency and hypocrisy will support no worthy personal structure in time of crisis.

"Therefore whosoever heareth these sayings of mine, and doeth them, I will liken him unto a wise man, which built his house upon a rock: And the rains descended, and the floods came, and the winds blew, and beat upon that house; and it fell not: for it was founded upon a rock. And everyone that heareth these sayings of mine, and doeth them not, shall be likened unto a foolish man, which built his house upon the sand: And the rain descended, and the floods came, and the winds blew, and beat upon that house; and it fell: and great was the fall of it" (Matt. 7:24–27). This is the well-known parable of the rock and the sand with which Jesus closes the Sermon on the Mount. The foolish man ignores the laws of God and of the spirit in claiming the right to do as he pleases in his search for success. But the wise man knows that he can really amount to something only as he builds his life on the rock of faith, truth, and service which Jesus has outlined in the preceding discourse. It is a strange thing that, whereas men try to use God's laws in the fields of science, engineering, medicine, and the arts, man is presumptuous enough to defy them in the field of human character and human relations. But God's moral and spiritual laws are as exact as his physical laws. And when we defy them we die. Many an able and clever man has cracked up because he tried to build a career or a home on the sands of greed, deception, and lust. But when we obey God's laws and use them we have a chance to amount to something.

The Bible directs us to aim high.

In the University of California studies of athletic skills, students were blindfolded and asked to throw sandbags onto a target on the gym floor. The good marksmen were always the good athletes. And none of the poor ones excelled in any sport.

It is so in life. Without a goal, life comes apart. We get nowhere unless we are going somewhere. Without a sense of direction we get lost. We never count for much unless we first take a good aim at something worth shooting at.

It is at this point that the Bible gives wise counsel. For it tells us to make our aim high and to keep on trying to reach it. If we never reach it we will get further than if we had no goal at all or an unworthy one. And if we make mistakes we can get back on the track and keep on going. "Forgetting those things which are behind . . . I press toward the mark for the prize of the high calling of God in Christ Jesus." (Phil. 3:14). This "high calling of God" is the goal of life the Bible holds before us. We are called to live as the children of God! We are to honor him in our thinking, our ambitions, our homes, our relations with others, and the work of our hands. "Set your affections on things above" (Col. 3:2). "Lift up your eyes on high" (Isa. 40:26). The Bible repeats the challenge over and over. No aim in life could be higher and finer than this.

And no goal can be more demanding of our best talents and our most persistent efforts. For this is a lifelong undertaking. The parable of the talents emphasizes the divine sanction that is upon the intelligent and earnest investment of what we have as a trust from God. Mme. K. C. Wu, wife of the former governor of Formosa, is an expert in the fragile and dainty art forms of China. It takes a steady, sure hand to paint in the Chinese tradition. The hand must be trained over long years to sweep delicate patterns unerringly onto fabric or paper, for a brush stroke cannot be erased. Said Dr. Wu himself, "The saying goes in China that it takes at least three years to learn to paint a landscape, nine years to learn to paint a bamboo shoot, and ten years to learn to paint an orchid." [4] No wonder Mme. Wu has been learning to master the art since the age of seven!

So it is. Some simple goals can be reached quickly. In fact, most of us, with a bit of practice, could learn to hit a target with a sandbag. And many people settle for that or its equivalent. But the "high calling of God" takes time and patience and sacrifice and endless devotion. We need to begin early and keep at it. If we are to "covet earnestly the best gifts," it means that we have to give up the lesser and cheaper things. Said the Master: "My meat is to do the will of him that sent me" (John 4:34). When we are possessed of this ambition, the minor hopes and pleasures of life do not seem so important after all. The Bible challenges us to set the direction of life toward God. This is to be our aim and purpose however imperfect our achievement. "Not as though I had already attained, either were already perfect: but I follow after . . ." (Phil. 3:12). To this end we set our faces like flint and never turn back!

"Blessed is the man that walketh not in the counsel of the ungodly, nor standeth in the way of sinners, nor sitteth in the seat of the scornful. But his delight is in the law of the LORD; and in his law doth he meditate day and night. And he shall be like a tree planted by the rivers of water, that bringeth forth his fruit in his season; his leaf also shall not wither; and whatsoever he doeth shall prosper. The ungodly are not so: but are like the chaff which the wind driveth away. Therefore the ungodly shall not stand in the judgment, nor sinners in the congregation of the righteous. For the LORD knoweth the way of the righteous: but the way of the ungodly shall perish" (Ps. 1).

The Bible counsels us to serve well.

The California tests also disclosed a true sense of balance as another mark of a good athlete. Students were required to try to walk a straight line while blindfolded. The best athletes were always those who wabbled and swayed the least in their walk. The same idea holds in the matter of a career. Here, too, a sense of balance is important, and one of the most valuable things we can learn is to balance self-interest with useful service. The completely selfish person is lopsided. He sways and wabbles and goes in circles. He has nothing outside to balance himself with and to keep him steady and surefooted. If we are to make life count for something we must invest it in something big beyond the area of our own interests. "If a man think himself to be something, when he is nothing, he deceiveth himself . . ." (Gal. 6:3). Jesus tells us to beware the objective of laying up treasures on earth. These are perishable. He wants us to look more to our spiritual assets. "For where your treasure is, there will your heart be also" (Matt. 6:19–21). The trouble with the rich young ruler was that he failed to balance an otherwise good life with the service ideal (Mark 10:17–22).

When God wants a job done, most of us tell him to get somebody else. We cannot be bothered. We are too interested in our own affairs. We need more of the spirit of Isaiah of old who replied to such a call, "Here am I, Lord, send me" (Isa. 6:8). There are many Kingdom tasks in our troubled world awaiting that kind of an answer from us. We will never make life count for much until we are willing to serve. And the reason is plain. "If any man desire to be first," said Jesus, "the same shall be last of all, and servant of all" (Mark 9:35). "Whosoever will be great among you, let him be your minister" (Matt. 20:26). "Bear ye one another's burdens, and so fulfil the law of Christ" (Gal. 6:2). This is hard to understand. Yet it is a law of life itself. Self-fulfillment comes through self-sacrifice and service. If we try to save our lives, we will lose them. If we give them away, we will save them. This is no musty thought from an old book. It is as up to date as today's newspaper.

In fact, it was demonstrated in a story that began when a drifter in Australia saw an advertisement in a year-old American newspaper he found in a desert. Tom Ellis was his name. The ad was about a correspondence course in electricity. He had no money to pay for the course. But the need of the man appealed to the chief engineer of the school, Fenton L. Howard. So, without payment or hope of return, Mr. Howard taught the Australian bum, Tom Ellis, all he could in a correspondence between America and Australia that lasted over several years. Seventeen years later, during World War II, the teacher, Fenton Howard, was a naval electrician aboard a United States ship in the Pacific. A generator flew apart and he was critically injured. An S.O.S. was sent out. An Australian ship answered the call. Its ship electrician installed a D.C. motor and the American vessel limped home in time to save Howard's life. The Australian ship's electrician was Tom Ellis! He was the bum who learned to be an electrician by mail. Thus the life of the generous teacher was saved by the man whom he had taught years before and across thousands of miles.[5]

"Give, and it shall be given unto you; good measure, pressed down, and shaken together, and running over, shall men give into your bosom. For with the same measure that ye mete, withal it shall be measured to you again" (Luke 6:38). Few of us will ever have such a dramatic demonstration of the operation of this principle. But it holds just the same in the routine and commonplace affairs of a workaday world. The tragedy is that so few of us discover this tremendous secret by which we may make life count. The richest and happiest people are not those who make the most. They are those who give the most of themselves, their time, their money, and their influence for the Kingdom of God. One big reason our religion does not make us happier is simply that we are not giving enough to it.

The Book of Esther seems almost out of place in the Bible. It never mentions the word God, nor does it speak of the Holy Land—the only book in the Old Testament to make such omissions. There is also much immorality in the book. However, it records the story of a woman who, even in an Oriental harem, risked her life for a great cause. Esther amounted to something, rating a place in the Scriptures, because she took a stand for a principle in the face of great odds. A wicked courtier named Haman had decreed that all the Jews should be killed. Mordecai asked Esther, who was a Jewess but a favorite of the king, to get the king to save the people. "Who knoweth, he said, but that thou art come to the kingdom for such an hour as this?" Esther knew the risk she took, for none was allowed to approach the king on the affairs of state. But she made reply: "And so I will go in unto the king, which is not according to the law: and if I perish, I perish" (Esther 4:16). She made a plea for her people and she prevailed. In fact, in the process Haman was himself hanged on the gallows he had prepared for Mordecai. The crafty schemer was caught in his own trap. It is a tale of intrigue, but in all the trappings of an ancient court we find a beautiful woman willing to risk everything she had in the interest of justice. God uses many people of many backgrounds to further his kingdom. Even men and women of wealth and social position can amount to something in times of crisis by taking an unpopular position in the interest of a great moral cause.

The Bible offers us a divine leader.

In the California studies the fourth mark of a superior athlete was a sense of force. Without this it was found that a basketball player could not pass well. And a golfer would either overdrive or underdrive. So it is in any field of activity. We all need this sense of force or drive or power. And we find it in Jesus Christ. From Jesus we get the drive to do but not to overdo. Under his direction we have the power to become the sons of God. "Follow me and I will make you . . ." (Matt. 4:19). This was Jesus' challenge to those he wanted for disciples. Make you fishers of men! Make you strong, appealing, joyous persons whose lives count for something! "Whatsoever ye do in word or deed, do all in the name of the Lord Jesus" (Col. 3:17). When we do that we find that a power not our own comes to our aid. It is the power of God channeled through the spirit of Christ. "But as many as received him, to them gave he power to become the sons of God" (John 1:12). It was this that made an ordinary man into the greatest personality of his generation. We hear him now as Paul said, "I can do all things through Christ which strengtheneth me" (Phil. 4:13). Such a power can make us what we ought to be! Certainly it can make us much finer persons than we are.

John A. Reed tells of the time as a boy when his father let him plow his first furrow on their farm. His dad lined up the team of horses and told him to drive them straight for a certain fence post across the field. John said he started off well. But in a few minutes he turned around to see how he was getting along. In doing so he twisted the reins and the horses turned off course. When John looked ahead again he could not tell which fence post he was supposed to be going to! [6] It is just that way if we want to accomplish anything worth while. For Jesus himself said that if anyone put his hands to the plow and looked back he was not fit for the kingdom (Luke 9:62). We will plow a straight furrow so long as we keep Jesus in the center of our devotion. For he is our guide, our teacher, our leader, and our Master. He will never fail us.

Jesus is a demanding leader. He expects much of us. The way of love over which he takes us is often a costly way. It takes us through narrow gates, and down roads lined with crosses. It calls for a strong and dynamic faith. "If ye have faith as a grain of mustard seed, ye shall say unto this mountain, Remove hence to yonder place; and it shall remove: and nothing shall be impossible unto you" (Matt. 17:20). When Christ is our leader self-examination and self-understanding are required. "I say, through the grace given unto me, to every man that is among you, not to think of himself more highly than he ought to think; but to think soberly, according as God hath dealt to every man the measure of faith" (Rom. 12:3). But the leadership of Christ enriches personality with invaluable qualities. "The fruit of the spirit is love, joy, peace, longsuffering, gentleness, goodness, faith, meekness, temperance" (Gal. 5:22, 23). And in the end our devotion to him proves an asset of tremendous saving power. "For he that soweth to his flesh shall of the flesh reap corruption; but he that soweth to the Spirit shall of the Spirit reap life everlasting" (Gal. 6:8). All of this follows when "one is your Master, even Christ" (Matt. 23:8). Here is a driving force that can make something of anyone.

Additional biblical references: Josh. 1; Matt. 6; Luke 19.

Is prayer possible?
What are the elements of true prayer?
Does God answer my prayers?

19 WHEN WE WANT TO LEARN HOW TO PRAY

WE ARE TOLD that we can live forty days without food. We can live a few days without water. But we cannot live longer than seven minutes without air. Our very life depends on air! It is for this reason that the earth is likely the only planet with human beings. Saturn, for instance, has a temperature of 243 degrees below zero. It is surrounded with ammonia—frozen into tiny crystals. And Venus has a daily change in temperature from 122 degrees above zero to 22 degrees below zero. Scientists have found no trace of oxygen in the atmosphere of Venus.[1]

It is air that makes our own planet habitable. It keeps us from broiling in the daytime and freezing at night. It is the means of distributing water vapor and rain, so necessary to life. And, of course, its cleansing action in the human body makes it possible for us to stay alive.

Something like this is certainly true also of the life of the spirit. For the soul of man needs purification and sustenance if it is to stay alive and be strong. And the Creator God has surrounded us with a spiritual atmosphere in the presence of his own divine spirit. It is available to any and all. Yet so few ever know it or find it. The key to its discovery and use is prayer. Prayer is to the life of the spirit what breathing is to physical life. And the reason so many of us so often find our spirits at low ebb, or something inert and dead, is because we do not avail ourselves of this life-giving factor.

Most of us believe vaguely in prayer as a good thing. But in practice we neglect it because we do not know how to pray. The disciples felt this. Therefore, they asked the Master to teach them to pray (Luke 11:1). And the prayer the Lord taught them has been a model of the simplicity and reality of prayer through the centuries. The Bible gives other valuable helps to guide us in the adventure of prayer. In the history of the Jewish people we find the priests offering sacrifices on the altar for the whole nation. But we find also, notably in Jeremiah, that prayer can be a personal thing, communion between an individual and God. Every man could pray to God without benefit of priest or ritual. "For I desired mercy, and not sacrifice; and the knowledge of God more than burnt offerings" (Hos. 6:6).

Also, in many Old Testament writings we find men praying unashamedly for God's protection over them and for the destruction of their enemies. And we find men asking God what he wanted them to do, and seeking strength and courage to carry out his purposes even in the face of danger and death. An example is found in Jeremiah. He undertook a difficult task because, in talking with God (which is the heart of prayer), he was convinced that God wanted him to do it and that God would support him in it. In a conversation with the Eternal Jeremiah protested that he was too young for the job. But God assured him that he would prevail: "For I am with thee, saith the LORD, to deliver thee" (Jer. 1:6–8, 18, 19). A similar example may be found in the case of Elijah as found in I Kings 19:13–16, 18.

The Bible tells us to pray honestly.

Many of our prayers are dishonest. This is so because we try to impose our will on the will of God. We try to get him to do something we want done. Our motives are often selfish. Our true desires are hidden behind a false front. Such prayers are both foolish and futile. To be sure, we are to seek God's help and guidance in our personal needs. But all these must be subject to the over-all will and purpose of God for our lives.

The Lord's Prayer asks God to "give us this day our daily bread" (Matt. 6:11). But the sentence just before that asks that God's will be done. And in his Gethsemane prayer, Jesus himself, in the face of a desperate crisis was driven to pray: "Father, all things are possible unto thee; take away this cup from me: nevertheless not what I will, but what thou wilt" (Mark 14:36).

This is the central core of prayer. For prayer is fellowship with

God. And unless we are basically committed to his will for us, that fellowship is only marginal. We will never learn how to pray until we are honest enough with ourselves to surrender ourselves to him without reservation. This is the word of God from Jeremiah to John: "Ye shall seek me, and find me, *when ye search for me with all your heart* . . ." (Jer. 29:13). "*If ye abide in me, and my words abide in you*, ye shall ask what ye will, and it shall be done unto you" (John 15:7). We are great ones to ask. But we forget first to abide. We will find the will of God when we are willing to search for it with all our heart.

A new sport and hobby has been developed by the Swedish people in Scandinavia. It is called "Orienteering." It means to find one's way through unknown territory by the use of map and compass. Its devotees spend days and weeks in dense forests or rugged mountains finding their way to an objective by these means alone without outside help. It has become very popular. There are fifteen hundred clubs in the Swedish Orienteering Association. It has a great appeal to the hardy and adventurous.[2]

In a very real sense, prayer is spiritual "orienteering." For prayer is the map and compass by which we make our way through rough and unfamiliar ways. It gives divine direction to life. It leads us upward and onward to God. That is its purpose and use. To abuse it is to be dishonest with ourselves and with God. Real prayer demands utter sincerity. It requires many an inward struggle. It is for hardy and adventurous spirits.

All this means that superficial prayers do not amount to much. The mumbling of petitions by rote or the counting of beads on a string become quite beside the point. That is why Jesus condemned the Pharisee for his much public praying, and why he told his followers to go into an inner chamber to pray to God in a personal, intimate, honest way (Matt. 6:5–6). It is there that the deep issues of life are met. It is in the privacy of the soul before God that we find the trail through the underbrush and up the mountainside. On the one hand, this passage, which is a prelude to the Lord's Prayer, is a warning against the futility of cant and form, as such, in our worship. On the other hand, it is a charge that prayer becomes true and real only as we strip ourselves of every pretense, disguise, and crutch, and stand alone in the eternal presence.

The Bible urges us to pray affirmatively.

That is to say, we are to pray for things that we can back up with our lives and labors. Prayer is a reaching out for something above and beyond. We are not to pray for protection from harm so much as for the power to do good. We are not to pray to get rid of some unwanted burden but to have the strength to carry it. We are not to pray for easy ways but for courage and faith to do a job for God. We are not to pray for forgiveness for ourselves until we first forgive others. "Forgive us our debts, as we forgive our debtors" (Matt. 6:12). "When ye stand praying, forgive, if ye have aught against any: that your Father also which is in heaven may forgive you your trespasses" (Mark 11:25).

Our prayers are not to be hesitant or timid. We do not need to be afraid to pray, if our prayers are honest. God seems unreal to us in prayer when we think of him as distant and elusive. But God is ever ready and willing to meet with us in the fellowship of prayer. We do not have to seek him afar off. We do not have to go through special motions or ceremonies to attract his attention. His presence surrounds us. He wants nothing but good for us. We can trust him completely. All this we need to accept. Our doubts and questionings keep him at a distance. But when we open our hearts to him he is there. He is "OUR Father which art in Heaven" (Matt. 6:9). OUR Father! What a tremendous thing that is!

God is waiting for us to open the channel of communication, Therefore, says Isaiah, "seek ye the LORD while he may be found, call ye upon him while he is near" (55:6). The writer of Hebrews put it this way: "Let us therefore come boldly unto the throne of grace, that we may obtain mercy, and find grace to help in time of need" (4:16). And Paul urges us to state our case plainly before God: "By prayer and supplication with thanksgiving let your requests be made known unto God" (Phil. 4:6). We need to know, therefore, that God is already on our side. Our need is to get on his side.

Our prayers, then, are to be affirmative prayers. That is, in prayer we declare our faith in God. We acknowledge him as the supreme Ruler of the universe and of our lives. As his children we are, in prayer, claiming his cleansing support and power to make of life what it ought to be and can be. In prayer we call the divine, secret, infinite forces of the universe to our aid. Not that we may retreat from life, but that we may live it up with enthusiasm and joy.

"The effectual fervent prayer of a righteous man availeth much" (James 5:16). This is so because he is then fortified with resources from above that are not his own. This sets our hands to many tasks of service. This revises our standard of values and helps us to see what things are really worth working for. This leads us to have confidence in ourselves and to expect great things from God. This opens the way to positive, vital, triumphant living. It changes us from cringing, fearful beings into serene and responsible children of God. "The same Lord over all is rich unto all that call upon him" (Rom. 10:12).

The Bible wants us to pray realistically.

Paul uttered one of the most important statements about prayer when he said, "I will pray with the spirit, and I will pray with the understanding also" (I Cor. 14:15). To pray with the understanding! It means, of course, to pray with the *mind*, as the Revised Standard Version translates the word. The thing Paul was talking against was the custom of many to speak and pray in unknown tongues. But Paul's deeper meaning is that we should honor God by using our intelligence and good sense in our prayers. Jesus put it this way: "And in praying do not heap up empty phrases" (Matt. 6:7, RSV). Prayer is not a matter of magic. And yet many modern prayers are much like the rites and incantations of the ancients. They might as well be in unknown tongues. God gave us our good common sense and he wants us to use it in our prayers. Yet it is amazing how many of us think brains and prayer do not mix.

Prayer is not a matter of reaching into a heavenly grab bag to get us anything we want. To be sure, Jesus said, in speaking of moving mountains into the sea, "What things soever ye desire, when ye pray, believe that ye receive them, and ye shall have them" (Mark 11:24). This is an example of the dramatic speech which Jesus used sometimes to awaken the minds of his hearers to a great truth—in this case, the desire and will of God to meet our deepest needs. Another example is the passage "Ask . . . Seek . . . Knock . . ." (Matt. 7:7). In these passages Jesus was challenging the people with the unexplored power of prayer! It is a power that can do wonderful things when those things are within the scope of the law and will of God. But to expect prayer to change the laws and order of the universe is pure fantasy. For a world in chaos would be the result.

Jesus did not pray for impossible things. The Lord's Prayer carries no petition that we be made prosperous or avoid suffering, or that the laws of the universe be set aside for our benefit. It does, on the other hand, express reverence for God and the desire for the Kingdom of God and our place in it. The prayer of prayers also speaks of our trust in the goodness and forgiveness of God and of our wish to be like him in deed and spirit. When we pray for these things we may be sure that it is within the will of God to give them to us.

The example of Jesus in prayer illustrated his teaching. It stressed importunity (Luke 11:5–13); a right attitude toward men (Mark 11:25); and directness and simplicity (Mark 12:40).

The point is that prayer has limits and boundaries. These are the nature of God and of his universe, and must be taken into account. Said the writer of James: "Ye ask, and receive not, because ye ask amiss" (James 4:3).

This, however, is not to limit the true power of prayer. For God has surprising things in store for those who pray earnestly with the spirit and the mind. In Jeremiah is this word of God: "Call unto me, and I will answer thee, and show thee great and mighty things, which thou knowest not" (Jer. 33:3). Cried the psalmist in words that have been echoed in a multitude of faithful souls: "In the day of my trouble I will call upon thee: for thou wilt answer me" (Ps. 86:7). Jesus prayed what seems to us an unbelievable prayer for those who crucified him: "Father, forgive them; for they know not what they do" (Luke 23:34).

Prayers for trust and faith and fortitude lead to surprising results, as did the prayers of Louis Martin, a Negro laborer making forty dollars a week. He put his twelve children through college. The secret was a prayer closet in his little home where through the years Louis Martin found divine support in his unequal struggle. "If any man be a worshipper of God, and doeth his will, him he heareth" (John 9:31).

The realistic prayer is the genuine prayer. It comes from the heart. It need follow no set pattern. Indeed, the Bible records many varieties of prayer. It may be simple communion (Mark 1:35); petition

(Ps. 25); a "wrestling" (Gen. 32:22–32); confession (Ps. 51); the utterance of vows (Gen. 28:18–22); praise and thanksgiving (Luke 1:46–55, 67–79); unspoken "desire in the heart" (I Sam. 1:12–15); mere ejaculation (Matt. 8:25); or a prolonged utterance (John 17).

The Bible suggests that we pray regularly.

Our heavenly Father surely wants us to come to him at any time and in any emergency. However, in a time of crisis most of us turn to prayer as a last resort. Or we use prayer as a quick pick-up for the spirit; a shot-in-the-arm for the soul. This is like the oxygen treatments given in a new beauty salon for men. Quick sniffs of pure oxygen are helpful in cases of physical exhaustion or hangovers. This particular shop has installed several oxygen machines under expert operators, charging eight dollars and fifty cents for five- to ten-minute sniffs!

Like oxygen for the body, prayer does revive and vitalize the mind and heart of man. But to take only occasional "sniffs" of prayer to recover from a spiritual hangover is to misuse prayer and to miss the point. And that point is that oxygen in the atmosphere is necessary *at all times* if life is to be sustained. Seven minutes without it and we are dead! In like manner, our spirits become weary and die unless they are regularly supplied with spiritual nourishment in prayer. "Wait on the LORD: be of good courage, and he shall strengthen thine heart: wait, I say, on the Lord" (Ps. 27:14).

The Bible emphasizes the place of prayer as an established and continuing part of the personal program of the child of God. In I Chronicles we read, "Seek the Lord and his strength, seek his face continually" (16:11). And centuries later we hear Paul saying the same thing in I Thessalonians: "Pray without ceasing" (5:17). This should not be surprising to us. Most real achievements come slowly. It took God, even with the help of the DuPont scientists and twenty million dollars, all of twenty years to produce nylon. It took thirty years to create the Diesel engine.[3] It takes a lifetime of prayer to establish a life of godliness.

The reason is simple and the meaning is clear. Prayer is fellowship with God. And if that fellowship is to be real, intimate, and effective, it must be on an established and permanent basis. If we are not well acquainted with God, it is hardly becoming to run to him only when things get out of hand. The great men of the Bible were men of prayer. Daniel and David and Peter and Paul and a host of others. Likewise, of course, the prayer life of Jesus was one secret of his poise and power. Otherwise the disciples would not have asked him to teach them to pray. They sensed that here was a spiritual weapon of genuine value. In more than one of his parables Jesus taught the value of persistence in prayer. He introduced the parables of the unjust judge with these words: "And he spake a parable unto them to this end, that men ought always to pray, and not to faint" (Luke 18:1).

The occupations of men have a way of leaving telltale marks. The boxer shows his cauliflower ears. The finger ends of the bricklayer are worn smooth by handling rough bricks. The house painter has flecks of paint on his hands and face and callous spots on his shins from bracing against ladders. The trumpet player has enlarged lips. So also the avocations of men leave their marks. As Christians, not many of us have calloused knees to show for a lifetime of prayer. But all of us should have the visible marks of those who live with God in prayer. These are: faces lighted with faith from above, spirits serene and steadfast, characters rooted in the moral laws of God, and attitudes of forgiveness, love, and service. This is what prayer is for and this is what the Bible says unceasing prayer can do for all men. "O come, let us worship and bow down: let us kneel before the Lord our maker" (Ps. 95:6).

Additional biblical references: I Kings 8; Ps. 42; Matt. 18:19; Luke 11:1–13; Luke 18:10–14; John 17; Eph. 3.

What can I do about it?
Does God need me in his business?
How can one person make a difference?

20 WHEN WE WONDER WHAT ONLY ONE PERSON CAN DO

ALL OF US have been overexposed to radio and television commercials. In fact, one of the most overworked sentences in the language appears to be "But first a word from our sponsor!" We all get tired of much of this. Yet it does sell goods. Why? One reason was uncovered in a survey made by the *American Peoples' Encyclopedia 1954 Yearbook.* A study was made of 300 commercials. It was found that the word "you" was used a total of 2400 times, far more than any other word. "Wonderful" was a poor second, used 187 times. An average of eight times in each commercial the sponsor singled out the individual listener. He declared that he had *your* interest at heart! *You* were the key to the whole matter! He wanted to get *you* to do something about something!

In a very real way this is what the Bible does. It is the record of how God singled out individuals. "The LORD God called unto Adam, and said unto him, Where art thou?" (Gen. 3:9). Adama could not hide from God, even in the Garden of Eden! He also called to Abraham and to Noah, to Joseph and to Moses, to Amos, to Gideon, and to Isaiah and to David, to Jesus and to Paul and to many others. "*You,*" he said, "I want *you.*" But this call of God in the Bible is by no means in the past tense. The Bible speaks to the individual in every generation. It speaks to us. It speaks to YOU. It tries to catch YOUR attention. It says that God has a job for YOU to do. It wants YOU to do something about something—about God and the Kingdom of God. "You are the light of the world" (Matt. 5:14, RSV).

The trouble is that we always want somebody else to do the something that needs to be done. More than that, we like to think that no one person can do much of anything. The call of God in the Bible has a hard time getting through the static and interference of our selfishness and our alibis. We excuse ourselves by saying that our world is too big and too complicated. What good can one person do anyway?

The Bible shows the importance of the individual person in action.

"And I heard the voice of the Lord, saying, Whom shall I send, and who will go for us? Then I said, Here am I, send me" (Isa. 6:8). This call to Isaiah and his response is typical. The Bible is not a formal statement of religious codes and social movements. In the main it tells how God depends on individuals to get his work done. This great fact was evident even in the tribal solidarity of the Hebrew people. A hundred years after Isaiah, the prophet Jeremiah spoke out strongly for moral individualism. And Jeremiah became one of the prophets of personal spiritual religion. Then there was Amos who dared to break with the religious conventions of his day. He declared that the moral claims of God were upon all men and not for the nation Israel only. Centuries later God laid his hands on Saul. He became Paul the missionary, thrusting the gospel across the known world. And the record tells of many lesser people who were led of God to do mighty things for him.

The Bible makes it clear that God does not depend on social action, conventions, group dynamics, or committee meetings. Someone has said that "Holy Writ is a record of what the prophets and not what the Sanhedrin had to say." The supreme message of the Bible in this connection is, of course, the birth, person, and work of Jesus himself. God in his infinite wisdom chose to save the world through one person, his Son, our Saviour. No one at the time ever dreamed that this one man, who was largely overlooked by the busy whirl about him, would be more important for history and for humankind than all the greatness, armies, gold, and might of the Roman Empire. To say nothing of the vast authority and entrenched power of the priests and temples of his time. But this is the way God works. And Jesus himself taught it. In the little parables of the mustard seed and the leaven he indicated the dependence of the larger growth of the Kingdom on small beginnings (Matt. 13:31–33). That is to say, God's work is done as one plain man or one ordinary woman is stirred to respond to the challenge of Christ: "Let your light so shine before men, that they may see your good works, and glorify your Father which is in heaven" (Matt. 5:16). This is the key to the dynamic story of the gospel in history. And it is more important today than ever.

It is so important because the individual is likely to think that he does not amount to anything in a world of grave and far-reaching issues. He therefore does nothing. He remains silent. He goes along without bothering. He turns his own destiny over to the state or to the corporation or to the labor union or to the political boss. His own initiative is smothered by a sense of personal helplessness.

E. T. Leech, editor of the *Pittsburgh Press,* put his finger on a vital point when he spoke of one difference between Communists and the average American citizen. He said: "Get a Communist into a club or or a union or an office or a school or a fraternal society, and he'll go right to work. His first job is to convert some other member of the group to his viewpoint. Then there'll be two of them—and their next job is to try to convert two others—thus making four. . . . They are past masters as evangelists. . . . As for the average loyal American, he enjoys the greatest privilege—but also the most dangerous one—which democracy can offer . . . the privilege of complete indifference. And he enjoys it overtime. . . . Americans belong to all sorts of things—but they just belong. They don't work; they don't meet; they don't vote." [1]

It is here, said Mr. Leech, where "the individual American citizen can aswer the question, 'What can I do?' . . . He, too, can be a missionary."

It is an idea straight from the Bible. For Jesus, living in a society plagued with social evils, poverty, and war, chose to spend a great deal of time ministering person to person with ordinary individuals. Not only that; he sent his disciples out two by two to win others. He rested the success of his cause, not upon organizations, but upon individuals. This is our challenge and our opportunity.

This idea was dramatized in the awarding of the Nobel Prize for 1947 to the American Friends Service Committee. Why? Because, according to Quaker leaders, "in an age when increasingly the state was held to be supreme and the individual only a tool, the prize had gone, in a basic sense, to that way of life which holds each individual to be a child of God and therefore of supreme value." But behind this official explanation was the real story of the Friends Service Committee. Thousands of nameless individuals ministered to other nameless individuals. There was the nameless New Jersey woman who made over one thousand dresses by hand for her unknown sisters in need. There was the nameless woman in Iowa who darned more than five hundred pairs of stockings for those who had none. There were the nameless students who went without meals to feed other students.[2] Of such is the Kingdom of God on earth.

What can I do? There is not a person anywhere who cannot bring to bear on some life or situation the redeeming witness of the love and righteousness of God. "Therefore, my beloved brethren, be ye steadfast, unmoveable, always abounding in the work of the Lord, forasmuch as ye know that your labor is not in vain in the Lord" (I Cor. 15:58).

The Bible stresses the need for individual moral conviction.

"I had rather be a doorkeeper in the house of my God, than to dwell in the tents of wickedness" (Ps. 84:10). This emphasis upon the power of the individual to stand for God and goodness in spite of all opposition is one of the strong messages of the Bible. If Moses had listened to men instead of God, there would have been a minority report to the Ten Commandments. We see this idea come to life in Joshua's farewell address, although it is actually addressed to the people as a whole: "If it seem evil unto you to serve Jehovah, choose you this day whom ye will serve; whether the gods which your fathers served that were beyond the River, or the gods of the Amorites, in whose land ye dwell: but as for me and my house, we will serve Jehovah" (Josh. 24:15, ARV). We see it in young David's putting to rout the Philistines by bravely and alone killing Goliath their leader with a slingshot. "Let no man's heart fail because of him," said David. "Thy servant will go and fight with this Philistine" (I Sam. 17:32). We see it in Daniel's praying before his open window as his enemies persuade the King to throw him into the lions' den, from which he escaped unhurt (Dan. 6:10). We see it in Nehemiah's classic answer to those who threatened him with death unless he quit doing his sacred duty. To these he said simply: "Should such a man as I flee?" (Neh. 6:11). We see it supremely, of course, in Jesus' hanging on the cross rather than following the course of appeasement to save himself.

The Bible, therefore, challenges men of God in any time to be bold and fearless in standing by their righteous and godly convictions. This any one person can do. And in so doing he will find that God is with him and that he will be invincible. For one person and God are a majority in any situation. It is an unbeatable combination. The devil is not afraid of a whole company of halfhearted people. But let one man get on fire for God and the devil takes off. "If so be the LORD will be with me," said Joshua, "then I shall be able to drive them out" (14:12).

In the midst of a wild Brazilian jungle is a pleasant little paradise spot called Canal Torto. The road to it is one of the roughest in Brazil. Giant virgin forests serve as hiding places for fugitives from justice. Land and lives are cheap. In the dirty little villages along the road live rough, vicious people. Long knives and pistols hang from men's belts. Fights and killings result from too much Brazilian hard liquor called *cachaca*. But it is a different story when one gets to the valley called Canal Torto. Here are clean homes, flower beds, fruit trees, and carefully tended fields. There is a store and a school and a beautiful white-steepled church. The difference is due to one man, Jaco Benitti. He moved to the valley with his wife and seventeen children. They were Methodists and they built their lives upon their faith. There was no preacher for two hundred miles so they built their own church. For more than thirty years the valley has prospered. There is no alcohol or gambling allowed. The people carry no guns or knives. Services are held every Sunday and people come from miles around. In the middle of a pagan environment Jaco Benitti and his family had plenty of opportunity to turn from their simple, strict faith. But it served them well and they remained steadfast. The primitive jungle people all around could serve what gods they would. As for Jaco, he and his house were going to serve the Lord God and Jesus Christ his Son. This conviction will make a paradise in the midst of any modern jungle.[3] "Let the redeemed of the Lord say so" (Ps. 107:2). And there are many ways to say it.

It is a far cry from Canal Torto, Brazil, to Minneapolis, Minnesota. Several years ago a young advertising man set up a small company in that city. His name was Fran Faber. He was an active Christian layman. He laid down the policy that his business was to be conducted on strictly Christian principles. One of these was that no liquor would ever be served to customers or prospective clients. An old-time advertising man told Mr. Faber no company could do business that way today. He predicted they would fold in six months. The company lost some clients but gained others. After six years and six months, Fran Faber moved his rapidly growing business into its own building. Instead of a cocktail hour at the opening he had a dedication service. It closed with this prayer: "To the advancement of the ideals of honesty and integrity in business, applying the Golden Rule in all our dealings, we dedicate this building in the name of the Master Builder, even Jesus Christ, the cornerstone of our lives." [4] Whatever else we can do, we can maintain our own integrity! We have plenty of precedence for this in the Bible. "As for me, I will walk in mine integrity" (Ps. 26:11).

This carries its own influence. Take salt, for instance. Salt was very valuable in ancient times. In the climate of Palestine it was vital in the preservation of food. And it likewise gave zest to the dishes on the table. This was the function of a Christian, said Jesus: "Ye are the salt of the earth" (Matt. 5:13); that is, to add sparkle and vitality to the common life of men and to keep it free from the corruption of dangerous and unclean elements of society. The point is that just a pinch of salt is enough to have the desired effect on food. It is so in society. Only one devoted and godly person is needed to purify a home or office or business or social group. The amazing, contagious power of righteousness needs to be experimented with in our modern world. When evil men take over it is only because someone has defaulted in the trust God gives to each of his children to represent him on earth. "Better is the poor that walketh in his integrity, than he that is perverse in his lips, and is a fool" (Prov. 19:1).

The Bible points to the wide influence possible from one dedicated life.

Far too many Christians are intimidated by the evil around them. Most of us have never tested the power of our convictions. We find it easier to conform. But there is not an evil practice in business or an ugly spot in society that cannot be corrected by the determined moral conviction of one man. The sensualists, crooks, racketeers, and gangsters, in high places and low, need to be challenged by men of God with the courage of their convictions. Albert Schweitzer has a vital word for us: "The activities and aims of our time are penetrated by a kind of obsession that if only we could succeed in perfecting or reforming the institutions of our public and social life, the progress demanded by civilization would begin of itself. But civilization can only revive when there shall come into being in a number of individuals a new tone of mind, independent of the prevalent one among the crowd, and in opposition to it . . . a tone of mind which will gradually win over the collective one and in the end determine its character. Only an ethical movement can rescue us from barbarism, and the ethical comes into existence only in individuals." [5]

The tremendous influence of Schweitzer gives authority to his words. He is a modern counterpart of many men in the Bible. And his words are an echo from its pages: "If ye have faith as a grain of mustard seed . . . nothing shall be impossible unto you" (Matt. 17:20). "If thou canst believe, all things are possible to him that believeth" (Mark 9:23). "A little leaven leaveneth the whole lump" (I Cor. 5:6).

It is a fact that is writ large in history. Every upward movement among men is associated with the name of one man or one woman. It was St. Paul who led in the establishment of the early Christian church. It was Robert Raikes who began the Sunday Schools. It was Florence Nightingale who made nursing an honored profession and a noble ministry. It was Abraham Lincoln who freed the slaves and united a nation. It was John Howard who was responsible for more humane treatment of prisoners in the jails of the country. It was John Marshall who gave the Supreme Court of the United States dignity, authority, and power. And not a one but who faced opposition and discouraging obstacles.

But most of us like to excuse ourselves for our spiritual laziness because we say we are not in positions of large influence. We forget that the dedication comes first. Then the influence. And this can operate on a small scale as well as a large one. It always begins with one person.

There was Dorothy Dix, at the age of thirty-three a schoolteacher in Cambridge, Massachusetts. She saw something of the terrible conditions of insane persons in the House of Correction. She decided to do something about it. It was 1840 and the insane were regarded as brutes and treated as beasts. She quietly gathered data on conditions. Her presentation to the state legislature shocked the people into action. Her work was opposed by those who profited in human misery. But she kept at it all across the country. Miss Dix lived to be eighty-seven and saw more than one hundred and ten mental institutions built to care properly for the mentally ill.

There was Willie Lee Buffington, a twenty-one-year-old textile mill worker in Edgefield, South Carolina. Willie wanted to help a new school for Negro children that had just been built. But he had only ten cents and no means of raising more. It was 1931 and times were woefully hard. He decided to do something anyway. In an old church magazine Willie took the names and addresses of five preachers who had contributed to that issue. He wrote them each a letter asking for books for the new school. With his ten cents he bought five two cent stamps for the letters. Four did not reply. But one did. Dr. L. H. King, of St. Mark's Methodist Church in New York, sent one thousand books to start the library for the little school! [6]

There is Leo Axlrod, who owns a furniture factory in Florida. He had a concern for crippled people, since his own son was handicapped. So he employs only handicapped people in his plant, and has thus given a new lease on life to thousands.[7]

There is Samuel H. Marcus of St. Louis. His home is a sixteen-room house in an older, fashionable section of town. The area was rezoned and a Negro family moved into the block. "For Sale" signs went up on many houses. Then Mr. Marcus put up a sign: "This house is not for sale. We like our fine neighbors. Your race, religion and politics are not our concern. All who take pride in their homes are welcome on this street." After that, every "For Sale" sign came down! [8]

It is an endless story and a glorious one. There are many jobs that God wants done today. They will never be done until some one dedicated person strikes out on his own and says, "Here am I, send me." God appoints each of us a committee of one to do his work. Everyone has some influence somewhere. If we do not speak up for God our silence gives aid and comfort to the enemy. For, as Paul put it, "none of us liveth to himself, and no man dieth to himself" (Rom. 14:7). We make our mark, for good or ill, whether we like it or not. And we will surprise ourselves when we venture to speak up for God and stand for the things we know are right and good. For "no good thing will he withhold from them that walk uprightly" (Ps. 84:11).

God puts high store on the power of one dedicated life. He has great tasks for those who are ready for them. One good man could save a city. It is never lack of opportunity for service that keeps the individual from doing a job for God and humanity. It is always the lack of the one person who is devoted enough to measure up to the opportunities that are all about us. The fields are white but the laborers are few. In any city or situation one unselfish, good, and willing person can multiply his influence manyfold.

Additional biblical reference: I Sam. 3; Jer. 1:4–12; Matt. 17:20; Luke 8:27; Rom. 12:1–2.

Does death end it all?
How can I dare believe in life after death?
What is it like in the world beyond?
Why should I be afraid to die?

21 WHEN WE WONDER WHAT HAPPENS AFTER DEATH

A MODERN NOVEL, called *All Men Are Mortal,* tells the story of a man who could not die. His name is Fosca. Back in the fourteenth century, Fosca drank a mysterious potion which made him forever secure against death. He was doomed to live forever. He travels back and forth from one country to another and through one century into another. It is the story of a meaningless existence described as follows: "Nothing is good, nothing is evil; nothing commendable, nothing shameful, nothing important. To be alive—to exist—is the hideous, imminent fact; to die is the only release. 'Everything is useless.' So much for God, man, history, spiders and turtles." [1] It is a story that rejects all religion, all ethics, all standards. The story of Fosca rejects humanity itself and is the frightful tale of those who know nothing but negation, anguish, and despair.

Here is nihilism at its bitter depth. To have a chance to live forever and to find that life is not worth living! To long for the release of death which never comes! Is this the nature and end of human existence? That it is entirely without meaning? That living is futile and dying is oblivion? That personality is an empty, worthless thing? That the universe is a hollow void?

There are those who see it so. But it is a ghastly caricature possible only to those who first reject God. For when we see life and death in their true Godlike dimensions and from the perspective of the New Testament we see that life is not an end in itself. We find then that life is good but that it is only a prelude and a foreshadowing of a still greater life that begins when death opens the door. "As we have borne the image of the earthy, we shall also bear the image of the heavenly" (I Cor. 15:49). "If a man keep my saying, he shall never see death" (John 8:51). That is to say, death is but one event in the total life of man. And it is here that the Bible gives us insights that make life rich and full, no matter how long or short, and that make death a triumphant experience. The Old Testament, of course, is concerned in the main with Israel. Therefore, the idea of personal immortality does not come into true focus until after the coming of Christ. Thus across the centuries the Jewish idea of immortality went from that of a vague existence in Sheol to the resurrection of the body.

After death we are still in God's care and keeping.

Human life seems so small and insignificant when measured by the immensities of the universe. But it is so only when we leave God out, or when we think of God only in human terms. The God who created us is a far greater God than most of us think. The Bible declares that he is "from everlasting to everlasting." His wisdom is beyond our wisdom. For instance, we are told that the entire amount of stuff we call life is only one billionth of the weight of the planet upon which it lives. All life if put together would appear, when placed next to the earth, as a mosquito appears in relation to a melon. Yet this fragile film of life has clung to the surface of the earth for hundreds of millions of years. The seemingly permanent mountains have lifetimes that are insignificant in comparison.[2] This is no cosmic accident, and no human mind could have ordered it. It is so because there is a great and wise God who planned it so and who keeps it so.

It is our limited idea of God that gets us in trouble when we think of the mystery of life and death. "Then shall the dust return to the earth as it was: and the spirit shall return unto God who gave it" (Eccles. 12:7). Our spirits belong to God. And death only restores to the owner what was his all the time. We think of eternity as beginning with death. But eternity is all of one piece. It has no beginning. We are in eternity now. We always will be. Nothing can shut us off from God. Not even death. "Whether we live, we live unto the Lord; and whether we die, we die unto the Lord: whether we live, therefore, or die, we are the Lord's" (Rom. 14:8).

An analogy here may help. Thomas A. Edison one time urged Roger Babson to discover something that would shut off the force of gravity. Years later Mr. Babson set up what has been called the most useless scientific project of the twentieth century. It is called the Gravity Research Foundation. Its main purpose is to find some type of "gravity screen," a substance that will cut off gravity in the same way a sheet of steel cuts off a light beam. This is no new notion. It was a favorite idea of early science fiction writers. And in H. G. Wells' fantasy, *The First Men in the Moon,* a spaceship operates by means of such a substance called *cavorite.* Since Einstein, however, this dream of a gravity screen has vanished. According to Einstein, gravity is not a force which pulls objects to the earth. Rather, gravity is a "warping of the space-time continuum." This warping causes an apple to fall. But a screen between apple and earth would have no effect because there is no force to be screened off.[3]

In some like manner, men with clever but small minds have tried to "screen off" God from man. But the skepticism of scientific and so-called "practical" minds is a screen that has no effect. And completely useless also is the idea of a materialist that death is the complete end of everything. Death is no screen to shut us off from God! It can have no effect upon our relationship to God, for the simple reason that we are his now and forever. And nothing can come between us. According to the Bible, that is the way the universe is built. "For I am persuaded, that neither death, nor life, nor angels, nor principalities, nor powers, nor things present, nor things to come, Nor height, nor depth, nor any other creature, shall be able to separate us from the love of God, which is in Christ Jesus our Lord" (Rom. 8:38, 39). That is, we can not screen off God any more than we can screen off gravity!

This is one of the great affirmations of the Scriptures. "God will redeem my soul from the power of the grave: for he shall receive me" (Ps. 49:15). This shout of triumph of the psalmist is heard in ascending tones through the Bible. It is no hypothesis, no theory, no argument, no mere wistful hope. It is a plain statement of the glorious reality and truth of God. "Now unto him that is able to guard you from stumbling, and to set you before the presence of his glory without blemish in exceeding joy, to the only God our Saviour, through Jesus Christ our Lord, be glory, majesty, dominion and power, before all time, and now, and forevermore" (Jude 1:24, 25, ARV).

Why should it be so hard to accept? God cares for his creatures in ways that are marvelous to behold and difficult to understand. The bobolink summers in southern Canada and winters in Paraguay. It makes 5,000 miles of travel each way. The Arctic tern breeds in the far north and winters in the far south. Its winter and summer homes are 11,000 miles apart. Yet it makes the 22,000 mile trip unerringly and on schedule.[4] Why should we doubt, then, that God should make provision for us and guide us on the long journey from our earthly home to the one on high? "Thou shalt guide me with thy counsel, and afterward receive me to glory" (Ps. 73:24).

After death we are still alive.

Those who say that the grave is the end usually base their disbelief in immortality on the lack of factual evidence for it. They contend that there is no proof of life after death; that the idea is based solely on belief and faith. This may be true. But so is the idea that death brings oblivion and nothingness. There is no proof for that, either! So that the notion of *nonexistence* after death is really only a belief, also! Nonexistence has to be taken on faith, too! In other words, there is no actual reason to assume that life beyond the grave is impossible.

On the other hand, there is abundant reason to believe that life is a continuing experience and that death only changes its form. Indeed, it is inconceivable on the face of it that, in a world of marvelous law and order, the highest and fairest creation of all, human personality, should be the one "mad and meaningless thing."

There are suggestions of immortality in the Old Testament. We find it in some of the Psalms: "God will redeem my soul from the power of the grave" (49:15). And Isaiah said, "He will swallow up death in victory; and the Lord God will wipe away tears from off all faces" (25:8). "And many of them that sleep in the dust of the earth shall awake, some to everlasting life, and some to shame and everlasting contempt" (Dan. 12:2). In the New Testament immortality is assumed and taken for granted. "He shall receive . . . in the world to come eternal life" (Mark 10:30). "For God so loved the world that he gave his only begotten son, that whosoever believeth in him should not perish, but have everlasting life" (John 3:16). "The gift of God is eternal life through Jesus Christ our Lord" (Rom. 6:23). "This mortal must put on immortality" (I Cor. 15:53).

The Old Testament men wanted to live a long time to see how

God was going to work things out. But the men of the New Testament seem to think of time and mortality as the unreal things. We usually think of death as sleep. But the man of faith thinks of death as an awakening. "We shall find when we die," said Richter, "that we have not lost our dreams, but that we have only lost our sleep." Our sleep and all the error, the passions, the accidents, and the defects to which the flesh is heir. These, too, we lose as the spirit comes into its true and rightful existence.

Botanists have known for some time of the existence in the long ago of the Dawn Redwood tree. Through eons of time its lovely leaves have been preserved as fossils imbedded deep in rocks. Scientists said the tree had been extinct for sixty million years. Then, not long ago, the Chinese found one sprouting on a riverbank. It had come from a seed of these Dawn Redwood trees—trees on which dinosaurs had lived in the dim past. Shoots were taken and have lived to grow. So for the first time may be seen the real color and beauty of the leaves which up to now had been only dimly outlined in the rocks. A tree dead for unnumbered centuries was found to be still alive! [5]

How could such a surprising thing happen? No one knows. But do we have to know how it happened to accept it as a fact? There is so much that is mysterious in life and in the universe. There is so little that we really know finally and fully. Those who pride themselves on believing only those things which they can verify by the physical senses or by the processes of reason are poor and blind and cannot see. To demand physical proof of life after death is only to expose their own ignorance of the nature of life itself.

The simplest form of life is the cell. Take it apart and what does it contain? Nitrogen, oxygen, carbon, hydrogen, a little chlorine, phosphorus, sulphur, sodium, calcium, silicon, iron, manganese, iodine, magnesium, and fluorine. But mix these things together in the right proportion in the laboratory and what do you have? Only a "laboratory mudpie," as someone has called it.[6]

Life is more than its chemical and physical parts! It answers to higher laws than those discoverable by scientific analysis. And God who made it has ordained that its true beauty will be known only when it escapes the skeleton and fossil and is viewed from a timeless perspective. What form and body does it take after death? We can leave that mystery with God. We do not know, any more than we know the mysterious relationship that exists between the human mind and the handful of gray matter we call the brain. We dare not disbelieve just because we cannot comprehend. For we do not require that of ourselves in life as it is. The Bible tells us that what we can know for sure is this: "For now we see through a glass, darkly; but then face to face: now I know in part; but then shall I know even as also I am known" (I Cor. 13:12).

After death we still have the kind of life we are prepared to understand and appreciate.

Endless existence alone is hardly the full nature of life after death. If all human life is immortal anyway, why do Christians share the belief of Jesus when he said, "I am the resurrection, and the life: he that believeth in me, though he were dead, yet shall he live." (John 11:25)? The answer is that life after death, whatever else it may be, is life with God. And Jesus shows us more clearly than any other the true nature of God. Therefore, if we are to live creatively with God after death, we must know him as he is. "This is life eternal, that they might know thee the only true God" (John 17:3). "It doth not yet appear what we shall be: but we know . . . we shall be like him; for we shall see him as he is" (I John 3:2).

This should not be hard to understand. It is so in our life on the earth. The quality of our lives is measured by the quality of the things we can appreciate. We are saved here as we find in Christ that the true measure of life is of the spirit. It is only as we love and serve and live by the things of God that we can know God. It is the pure in heart that see God in death or in life. The sensualist, the materialist, and the skeptic cannot know him as he is. This is why the Bible warns us against the death of the soul. Paul said that flesh and blood cannot inherit the Kingdom (I Cor. 15:50). Said Jesus: "Fear not them which kill the body, but are not able to kill the soul" (Matt. 10:28). In other words, to know God and to love him is life which death cannot touch. It is life which finds its final growth and fulfillment in the house not made with hands, eternal in the heavens. But its roots and beginnings are now. For eternal life begins on earth. When we find in Christ the kind of life that is free and clean and loving and Godlike, we may be sure that our development will not stop just because our bodies decay and die. "He that soweth to his flesh shall of the flesh reap corruption; but he that soweth to the Spirit shall of the Spirit reap life everlasting" (Gal. 6:8).

The idea of life after death did not originate with Christianity. It is a hope common to most religions and existed long before Jesus. But Christ rescued it from the shadowy uncertainty of the Hebrew Sheol, and made it a living, personal, triumphant reality. There is no suggestion with Jesus that future existence is a merging of personal identity with the infinite, such as the Nirvana of Buddhism. The details of the future dwelling place and state of being we may leave with God. Paul suggests that we will have a "spiritual body." But we do ourselves an injustice if we are so worldly wise as to demand blueprints of heaven. For, "Eye hath not seen, nor ear heard, neither have entered into the heart of man, the things which God hath prepared for them that love him" (I Cor. 2:9).

How shall we who are sinful and so limited in our understanding share in this wondrous thing? Certainly not in our own nature can we hope to enjoy the presence of God for eternity. It is the death and resurrection of Jesus that guarantees our hope. The Risen Christ has broken the power of sin over human life. It is in him and with him that we dare walk into the light with hearts unafraid and banners flying. "Because I live, ye shall live also" (John 14:19b). "Thanks be to God which giveth us the victory through our Lord Jesus Christ" (I Cor. 15:57). Here is our cause for joy and our assurance for things to come.

"But some one will ask, 'How are the dead raised? With what kind of body do they come?' You foolish man! What you sow does not come to life unless it dies. And what you sow is not the body which is to be, but a bare kernel, perhaps of wheat or some other grain. But God gives it a body as he has chosen, and to each kind of seed its own body. For not all flesh is alike, but there is one kind for men, another for animals, another for birds, and another for fish. There are celestial bodies and there are terrestrial bodies; but the glory of the celestial is one, and the glory of the terrestrial is another. There is one glory of the sun, and another glory of the moon, and another glory of the stars; for star differs from star in glory. So is it with the resurrection of the dead. What is sown is perishable, what is raised is imperishable. It is sown in dishonor, it is raised in glory. It is sown in weakness, it is raised in power. It is sown a physical body, it is raised a spiritual body. If there is a physical body, there is also a spiritual body. . . . For this perishable nature must put on the imperishable, and this mortal nature must put on immortality. When the perishable puts on the imperishable, and the mortal puts on immortality, then shall come to pass the saying that is written: 'Death is swallowed up in victory.' 'O death, where is thy victory? O death, where is thy sting?' The sting of death is sin, and the power of sin is the law. But thanks be to God, who gives us the victory through our Lord Jesus Christ." (I Cor. 15:35–44, 53–57 RSV).

Additional biblical reference: John 11, 17, 20; II Cor. 4, 5; Rev. 7:9–17; 21:1–5.

22 IS THE BIBLE OUT OF DATE?

When archeologists in northwest India dug down through the sand they found a complete ancient city, Mohenjodaro, in the valley of the Indus River. Many of the homes were intact and filled with household possessions. Mohenjodaro drew its water from the Indus by means of irrigation canals. These filled with silt through the years and had to be abandoned. In the course of the centuries the city was completely covered and forgotten.

A similar fate came to the once beautiful city of Petra in the Arabian desert. It lived off the agriculture of the neighboring hillsides. This agriculture was made possible by an elaborate system of terraces. Invading nomads conquered the city. They were ignorant of the part the terraces played and let them fall into decay. And the city came to an end. Many places in Palestine suffered a like fate. Invaders came. Not understanding the vital role of the irrigation and terracing systems, they allowed them to fall into disuse. That was the beginning of the end! [1]

There is a parable here for our modern world. Our Western civilization, with all its limitations and defects, is the fairest in history. The source of its life and vitality is the Bible. From the ideas and truths of Scripture come the terraces and irrigation canals that make possible a good and free society. But invaders have come which either ignore religion or would write a new Bible of materialism and humanism.

Is the Bible really out of date? In our fast-moving and fast-changing world we are likely to let its terraces decay and its canals fill up with silt. This must not be so.

The Bible is the historical charter of man's enlightenment and liberties.

Augustine—who was later to become the first Archbishop of Canterbury—and his little band of missionaries came to England from Rome in the seventh century. There they found a pagan people steeped in witchcraft. But the missionaries brought to England a force far more powerful than witchcraft. This was a handful of nine Latin books, sometimes called England's first library. They were: a two-volume Bible, two copies of the Psalms, two of the Four Gospels, a copy of *Lives of the Apostles*, a copy of *Lives of the Saints*, and an *Exposition of the Gospels and Epistles*. This Bible-centered library before long completely changed the character and dominated the culture of England. Eight hundred years after its arrival in England, the Bible was translated into the English tongue by Wycliffe. When the printing press came in the fifteenth century, the Bible became the book of the common people. And then nothing could stop its powerful upward thrust to the human mind and its cleansing influence in human society.

The Bible was central likewise in the days of the Reformation. It was while reading the Book of Romans that Luther came to his great convictions which led to the breakup of medievalism and the coming of the Renaissance. And Luther's translation of the Bible was the motive power behind the movement of enlightenment throughout Europe that marked the end of the middle ages.

Two centuries after the Reformation a Church of England preacher was listening to the reading of Luther's "Preface to the Epistle to the Romans." He felt his heart strangely warmed. His name was John Wesley. And that event sent him forth to purify English society and change the course of English history.

The divine right of kings was doomed when the common man began to read the precious handwritten pages of Wycliffe's translation of the Bible. It was this, too, that later led to the birth of America in freedom. And the foundations of American life cannot rightly be understood apart from one great fact. That fact is, for five generations, one hundred and fifty years, beginning at Jamestown and Plymouth Rock, the children of the colonial schools took the Bible daily as the basic textbook of their study.

The importance of the Bible for today may be measured by its place in history. Whenever the Bible has been in the language and hands of the people it has lighted the minds of men and has made for human progress. Whenever it has been neglected or banned or interpreted only by a totalitarian church, the way has been opened for tyranny, superstition, and social decay. As the writer of Proverbs put it: "When the righteous are in authority, the people rejoice: but when the wicked beareth rule, the people mourn" (29:2).

The Bible is the supreme directive for man's victory over himself.

These was an earlier Augustine than the missionary, whose experience also has meaning for us today. This Augustine was born in 354 into a Christian home and possessed a brilliant mind. But in his earlier years he became both a sensualist and a skeptic. His good mind and his bad morals led him to follow first this ism and then that. For nine years he was a believer of the Manichaean heresy, which taught that there were two Christs, one a bad man and the other a divine deliverer. His distrust of this teaching led him into the skeptical philosophy of the New Academy. Still later he switched to Neoplatonism. But his mind remained restless and his heart found no satisfaction in his moral dissipation. He felt sharply the basic conflict between his philosophical idealism and his personal conduct.

In the summer of 386, Augustine was reading the 13th chapter of Romans. This verse changed the course of his life: "Not in rioting and drunkenness, not in chambering and wantonness, not in strife and envying: But put ye on the Lord Jesus Christ, and make not provision for the flesh, to fulfil the lusts thereof" (13:13, 14). From that moment on Augustine's soul was at peace. In his *Confessions* he states that never after that did he lack the divine power to overcome the sins that had beset him up to that time.

Following this conversion Augustine lived to become the most influential Christian since Paul. In fact, he was to be the forerunner of the Reformation. In the words of Francis Carr Stifler: "Through the Bible God had spoken directly to Augustine's soul and in him had raised up one who should set men's feet thereafter more firmly in the direction of the truth." [2] So it is that men shape history!

Modern man is caught in the same trap as Augustine. In our sophisticated minds we think we have outgrown the Bible with its redemptive message of the forgiving love of God in Jesus Christ. And at the same time in our lives we have sinned against God and are unhappy in our sin. We go in for many attractive isms and cults just as did Augustine. But, like him, we find no peace or satisfaction in them. In spite of our best intellectual efforts, we will find that there is no name given by which we may be saved except that of Jesus Christ, the Son of God, revealed in the Bible.

This redemptive power of the Bible, as we have seen, which comes to focus in the life and teaching of Jesus, makes it a key book for modern life. For behind the economic and political problems of today is the ugly fact of human sin and moral decay. We have tried to put the blame for our troubles on an economic interpretation of history or on a view of man as merely a biological organism. But actually modern man, just like men of every generation, needs the moral and spiritual redemption that come from the forgiving and renewing power of Almighty God. "If my people, which are called by my name . . . shall humble themselves, and pray, and seek my face, and turn from their wicked ways; then will I hear from heaven, and will forgive their sin, and will heal their land." (II Chron. 7:14).

Modern man can never master his world unless he wins first a spiritual and moral victory over himself. To this end the Word of God speaks to our day its greatest challenge: "Let the wicked forsake his way, and the unrighteous man his thoughts: and let him return unto the LORD" (Isa. 55:7).

The Bible is the basic promise of a better world.

The threat of total destruction by the hydrogen bomb casts a pall of fear over the whole world. The aggressive threat of world communism makes free men wonder if a better and peaceful world is possible at all. Pessimism and defeatism have a demonic appeal to many modern minds. In such a situation the Bible declares that this is God's world; that he is in charge of things; and that he is greater than the powers of darkness. The Bible says that even the wrath of men shall be made to praise God. It assures us that God's world is not fixed or doomed, but that in it are always the seeds of rebirth and renewal. In Genesis is this word: "Shall not the Judge of all the earth do right?" (Gen. 18:25). Said the Psalmist: "I have seen the wicked in great power, and spreading himself like a green bay tree.

Yet he passed away, and, lo, he was not: yea, I sought him, but he could not be found" (Ps. 37:35). And this great climax in Revelation: "I heard as it were the voice of a great multitude, and as the voice of many waters, and as the voice of mighty thunderings, saying, Alleluia: for the Lord God omnipotent reigneth" (Rev. 19:6).

These great truths of Scripture have been verified over and over again in human experience. When Jesus was crucified people were sure that the end had come to the Christian movement. Then God laid his spirit on Paul and a new force appeared in the ancient world. In the fifteenth century many people said the end of the world had come, so dark and hopeless seemed the times. In fact, on July 12, 1493, the Nuremberg *Chronicle* published a prediction that the world would pass soon into the seventh and final age of man. There were six blank pages in the paper on which were to be recorded the last terrible events which were sure to transpire before the day of judgment. The editors said that only the wicked would prosper again and that there would no longer be any faith, law, truth, or decency. Yet almost the very same year Christopher Columbus opened up a new world that set fresher and larger horizons before the minds of men.[3]

It is easy to see in our kind of world how those who think the Bible is out of date are the victims of despair and futility. They need to know something of the inexhaustible vitality and life-giving power that resides in the Book and its message. It may be banned and burned and outlawed but it cannot be obliterated. Empires and dictators may rise against it but the Bible will outlive them all. It speaks to us today as the perennial source of hope for humankind.

Adolf Hitler built a huge stadium in Berlin for the Olympic Games of 1936. In it he often harangued crowds of hundreds of thousands of his hysterical followers. His position and power seemed supreme forever. Just a few years ago a meeting of Christians was held in the same stadium. Three hundred thousand people had come to Berlin from East and West Germany. A huge cross had been erected where the swastika once stood. And where once the dictator's hoarse voice shouted its curses, the loudspeakers now carried the triumphant hymns and prayers of the Christian multitudes.[4] "The perverseness of transgressors shall destroy them" (Prov. 11:3).

To be sure, no man knows what the future will hold. When mighty forces struggle for power, what can the individual Christian do? The answer of the Bible is simple. "Denying ungodliness and worldly lust, we should live soberly, righteously, and godly, in this present world" (Titus 2:12). It was the same answer that St. Francis of Assisi gave one time. He was hoeing in his garden. Someone asked him what he would do if God told him he would die that night. Said St. Francis: "Keep on hoeing in the garden." It is an answer of wisdom and faith. For we who believe in the God and in the gospel of the Bible can well afford to leave ultimate answers with him. It is our part to be faithful to the trusts of life and the challenge of truth. If this be so we know that every advance in science and industry and human affairs only underscores the place and need of the Bible in the life of today.

REFERENCES

CHAPTER ONE. GETTING HELP FROM THE BIBLE

1. J. Carter Swaim, *Right and Wrong Ways to Use the Bible*, Westminster, 1953, p. 166.
2. From *Varsity*, Cambridge University, England.
3. Roger Butterfield, "How Well Do You Know the Bible?" *Saturday Evening Post*, April 21, 1951, p. 127.
4. J. Richard Green, *Short History of the English People*, American Book Co., 1916, p. 460.
5. Reported in *Time*.
6. From an article in *The Christian World*.
7. Bernhard W. Anderson, *Rediscovering the Bible*, Association Press, 1951, chap. 1.

CHAPTER TWO. WHEN WE WONDER WHERE GOD IS

1. Harrison Brown, *The Challenge of Man's Future*, Viking Press, 1954, pp. 217, 218.
2. Ruth Moore, *Man, Time and Fossils*, Alfred A. Knopf, 1953 p. 150.
3. Edward Wagenknecht, *A Preface to Literature*, Henry Holt & Co., 1954, p. 96.
4. From an address by E. F. McDonald, Jr., president of the Zenith Radio Corporation, 1954.
5. Lillian Lauferty, *God Keeps an Open House*, Bobbs-Merrill, 1952, p. 17.

CHAPTER THREE. WHEN LIFE BECOMES ORDINARY

1. Arthur Mayer, *Merely Colossal*, Simon and Schuster, 1953, p. 132.
2. Quoted by Joseph Wood Krutch in an article in the *Saturday Review*.
3. *New York Times*, April 15, 1953.
4. *Saturday Review*, July 17, 1954, p. 32.
5. *Time*, July 12, 1954, p. 72.
6. *Words to Live By*, quoted by Wilfred Funk, Oct. 2, 1954.

CHAPTER FOUR. WHEN FEAR HAUNTS OUR DAYS

1. Edwin Way Teale, *The Wilderness World of John Muir*, Houghton, Mifflin, 1954, p. xiii.
2. Jack Roth in *New York Times Magazine*.
3. Lincoln Barnett, *The World We Live In*, Simon & Schuster, 1955, p. 244.
4. *Through the Looking Glass*, The Lewis Carroll Book, Dial, 1934, p. 261.
5. Richard W. Husband, *The Psychology of Successful Selling*, Harper, 1953, p. 76.
6. Quoted in *The Pulpit*, Christian Century Foundation.
7. Jacqueline Cochrane, *The Stars at Noon*, Little, Brown, 1954, p. 21.

8. Reported in *Your Life*.
9. *New York Herald Tribune*, Oct. 17, 1947.

CHAPTER FIVE. WHEN WE NEED TO GET RID OF THE DEVIL

1. Walter Bromberg, M.D., *Man above Humanity*, J. B. Lippincott, 1954, p. 53.
2. Lt. James Devery, head of the bureau of identification. Chicago, Ill.
3. Lillian Roth, *I'll Cry Tomorrow*, Fell, 1954, pp. 208, 209.
4. Edward Spencer Cowles, M.D., *Conquest of Fatigue and Fear*, Henry Holt, 1954, p. 187.
5. Elsie King Moreland, "The Big Blame," *Coronet*, Sept. 1953, p. 23.
6. From an address by Judge Miner privately printed.

CHAPTER SIX. WHEN THE YEARS GO SWIFTLY BY

1. Reported in *This Week*, Aug. 23, 1953, p. 11.
2. Annual Report of the Smithsonian Institution, 1953.
3. Reported by Associated Press, Aug. 25, 1954.
4. Rudolph Flesch, *How to Make Sense*, Harper, 1954, p. 62.
5. Amoam Scheinfeld, *The New You and Heredity*, J. B. Lippincott, 1950.
6. Reported in *The Christian Century*.
7. Steven M. Spencer, *Wonders of Modern Medicine*, McGraw-Hill, 1953, p. xxii.
8. Abraham S. Wolf Rosenbach, *Books and Bidders*, Little, Brown, 1927, p. 269.

CHAPTER SEVEN. WHEN WE ARE SICK IN MIND AND BODY

1. Martin Gumpert, M.D., *The Anatomy of Happiness*, McGraw-Hill, 1951, p. 277.
2. Glenn Clark, *How To Find Health through Prayer*, Harper, 1940, p. 68.
3. Reported in *Time*, March 30, 1953, p. 78.
4. *Life*, Feb. 19, 1954.
5. E. Stanley Jones, *Abundant Living*, Abingdon-Cokesbury, 1943, p. 175.
6. Leslie Weatherhead, *Psychology, Religion and Healing*, Abingdon, 1951, p. 432.
7. From an article in *P. E. O. Record*, August, 1953, p. 7.
8. William S. Sadler, *Modern Psychiatry*. C. V. Mosby, publ.
9. B. H. Streeter, *The Spirit*, Macmillan, 1935, p. 110.

CHAPTER EIGHT. WHEN WE NEED INNER QUIETNESS

1. Bruce Bliven, *Preview for Tomorrow*, Knopf, 1953, p. 186.
2. E. S. Turner, *The Shocking History of Advertising*, Dutton, 1953, p. 277.
3. *Ibid.*, pp. 52, 53.
4. From a privately printed article.
5. Bennett Cerf, *Encyclopedia of Modern American Humor*, Doubleday, 1954.

6. Lincoln Barnett, *The World We Live In*, Simon & Schuster, 1955, p. 150.
7. Jacob Rosin and Max Eastman, *The Road to Abundance*, McGraw-Hill, 1953, pp. 99, 100.

CHAPTER NINE. WHEN WE LOSE FAITH IN OURSELVES

1. Charles A. Lindbergh, *The Spirit of St. Louis*, Scribner's, 1953, chap. 6.
2. Story by Thomas Morrow in *Chicago Daily Tribune*, Sept. 9, 1954, Part 3, p. 1.
3. D. D. Williams, *God's Grace and Man's Hope*, Harper, 1949, p. 185.
4. Quoted in *Time*, Aug. 2, 1954, p. 76.
5. Dale Carnegie, *How To Stop Worrying and Start Living*, Simon and Schuster, 1948, p. 94.
6. *This Week*, July 18, 1954, p. 2.
7. T. S. Eliot, *Collected Poems, 1909–1935*, copyright, 1936, by Harcourt, Brace and Company, Inc. and reprinted with their permission.

CHAPTER TEN. WHEN WE WONDER WHAT GOD IS LIKE

1. Reported in *Evangelical Press*.
2. Thomas Heywood, *Hierarchie of the Blessed Angles*, in Luccock and Brentano, *The Questing Spirit*, Coward-McCann, 1947, p. 271.
3. Reported in *Time*, June 14, 1954, p. 88.
4. *The Interpreter's Bible*, Abingdon-Cokesbury, 1952, vol. 8, p. 510.
5. James Keller, *Careers That Change Your World*, Doubleday, 1951, p. 114.
6. *Chicago Daily News*, Oct. 18, 1954.
7. Reported in *Time*, Aug. 9, 1954.

CHAPTER ELEVEN. WHEN THE ODDS SEEM STACKED AGAINST US

1. *Chicago Daily Tribune*, Aug. 22, 1956.
2. Reported in *Time*, June 28, 1954.
3. Jacqueline Cochrane, *The Stars at Noon*, Little, Brown, 1954.
4. From a lecture at University of Louisville.
5. Cynthia Pearl Maus, *Christ and the Fine Arts*, Harper, 1938, p. 668.
6. Jacob Rosin and Max Eastman, *The Road to Abundance*, McGraw-Hill, 1953, p. 79.
7. W. P. Knowles, "Breathe Easier," *American Mercury*, August, 1954, p. 97.
8. Glenn Clark, *How To Find Health Through Prayer*, Harper, 1940, p. 104.

CHAPTER TWELVE. WHEN THE FUTURE LOOKS FORBIDDING

1. *Time*, Oct., 1954.
2. James Keller, *Three Minutes a Day*, Doubleday, 1949, p. 29.
3. Julian Huxley, *Evolution in Action*, Harper, 1953.
4. Steven M. Spencer, *Wonders of Modern Medicine*, McGraw-Hill, 1953.
5. Jacob Rosin & Max Eastman, *The Road to Abundance*, McGraw-Hill, 1953, p. 108.
6. Report to National Association of Manufacturers, annual convention 1954.

7. *The Christian Science Monitor*, July 19, 1954.
8. Kenneth Scott Latourette, *A History of Christianity*, Harper, 1953, p. xxv.

CHAPTER THIRTEEN. WHEN WE FIND IT HARD TO GET ALONG WITH PEOPLE

1. *The New Yorker*, Sept. 11, 1954.
2. Harrison Brown, *The Challenge of Man's Future*, Viking, 1954, p. 68.
3. G. M. Smith, *More Power to Your Mind*, Harper, 1952, p. 59.
4. From the book, *What Happens to Communists?* Quoted in *London Times*, *Quote* Vol. 27, No. 23, p. 8.
5. Shakespeare, *The Merchant of Venice*, Act IV, sc. 1.
6. Phyllis Goslin Lynip, *Great Ideas of the Bible*, Harper, 1954, Vol. 1, p. 48.
7. Stuart Chase, *Roads to Agreement*, Harper, 1951, p. 8.
8. Ordway Tead, *Good Business*, *Quote*, Vol. 28, No. 10, p. 3.
9. In *This Week* magazine.
10. From *Voice of Youth*, Slovene National Benefit Society.

CHAPTER FOURTEEN. WHEN SORROW SHADOWS THE SOUL

1. James Gordon Gilkey, *When Life Gets Hard*, Macmillan, 1945, p. 103.
2. Paul E. Irion, *The Funeral and the Mourners*, Abingdon-Cokesbury, 1954, p. 35.
3. William M. Elliott, Jr., *For the Living of These Days*, John Knox Press, 1946, p. 108.
4. *Life*, Dec. 27, 1954, p. 18.
5. Herbert Merrill in *The Saturday Evening Post*, July 26, 1952. Reprinted with permission of the author.
6. Joseph Fort Newton, *Living Up to Life*, Harper, 1941, p. 208.
7. In Alexander Klein (3rd), *Courage is the Key*, Twayne Publisher, 1953, p. 131.
8. Rudolph Flesch, *How to Make Sense*, Harper, 1954, p. 101.

CHAPTER FIFTEEN. WHEN WE ARE JUST PLAIN UNHAPPY

1. Mort Weisenger, *Sleeping Pills are Worse than Dope*, *Coronet*, Jan., 1955, p. 51.
2. In an address before the 44th annual meeting of the Illinois Society for Mental Health, April 7, 1954.
3. Martin Gumpert M.D., *The Anatomy of Happiness*, McGraw-Hill, 1951, p. 5.
4. Anne Fromer, "Canada's Asbestos Capital," *Coronet*, Jan., 1955, p. 107.
5. James L. Mursell, *How to Make and Break Habits*, Lippincott, 1953, p. 182.
6. Arthur John Gossip, *Experience Worketh Hope*, Scribner's, 1945, p. 48.
7. Reported by Associated Press, Nov. 29, 1954.
8. John Steinbeck, *Sweet Thursday*, Viking, 1954, p. 22.
9. In *Life*, Jan. 3, 1955, p. 66.

CHAPTER SIXTEEN. WHEN WE LOSE THE WAY

1. Reported in *Christian World Facts*, Division of Foreign Missions of the National Council of the Churches of Christ in America, 1951, p. 73.
2. Reported by *Associated Press*, in *Quote*, Dec. 26, 1954.
3. Arthur John Gossip, *Experience Worketh Hope*, Scribner's, 1945, p. 50.
4. From an article in *Lancet*, London, reported in *Time*, Aug. 26, 1955.
5. *Chicago Daily News*, Feb. 26, 1955.
6. Henry Sloan Coffin, *God Confronts Man in History*, Scribner's, 1947, p. 78.
7. Arnold Toynbee, *A Study of History*, Oxford University Press, 1947.
8. Rudolph Flesch, *How to Make Sense*, Harper, 1954, p. 172.

CHAPTER SEVENTEEN. WHEN DOUBT DISTURBS THE MIND

1. *New Humanist*, May-June, 1933.
2. John Dewey, "What I Believe," *New York Times*, April 8, 1928.
3. Waldemar Kaempffert, *Explorations in Science*, Viking, 1953, p. 46.
4. Vicktor Frankl, "A Psychiatrist Discovers God," *Woman's Home Companion*, April, 1954.
5. *Saturday Review*, July 31, 1954, p. 23.
6. Roy L. Smith, *New Light from Old Lamps*, Abingdon, 1953, p. 120.
7. Lionel Giles (tr.), *The Sayings of Lao Tzu*, Dutton, 1910, p. 43.
8. *The New Yorker*, Sept. 11, 1954.
9. A. Cressy Morrison, *Man Does Not Stand Alone*, Revell, 1944.
10. George Bernard Shaw, *The Doctor's Dilemma*, Act. 4, Brentano's, 1923, p. 100.
11. Quoted in Arthur John Gossip, *Experience Worketh Hope*, Scribner's, 1945, Preface.

CHAPTER EIGHTEEN. WHEN WE WANT TO AMOUNT TO SOMETHING

1. J. Carter Swaim, *Right and Wrong Ways to Use the Bible*, Westminster, 1953, p. 26.
2. Lester David in *Bluebook*.
3. Reported in *Chicago Daily News*, Dec. 4, 1954.
4. Reported in *Chicago Daily Tribune*, Aug. 31, 1954.
5. Reported in *Chicago Daily Tribune*, Dec. 12, 1953.
6. From a sermon in *Successful Fund Raising Sermons*, edited by Julius King, Funk & Wagnalls, 1953, p. 173.

CHAPTER NINETEEN. WHEN WE WANT TO LEARN HOW TO PRAY

1. Wallace Capel, "The Air You Breathe," *Coronet*, April, 1955.
2. W. J. Bank, "Orienteering," *The Rotarian*, Jan., 1955, p. 38.
3. Thomas H. Grainger, "The Emergency in Basic Science," *The Saturday Review*, July 16, 1955, p. 11.

CHAPTER TWENTY. WHEN WE WONDER WHAT ONLY ONE PERSON CAN DO

1. James Keller, *You Can Change the World*, H. Wolff, 1948, p. 335.
2. Clarence E. Pickett, *For More than Bread*, Little, Brown, 1954.
3. Eugene L. Smith, *They Gird the Earth for Christ*, The Advance, 1952, p. 7.
4. From an article in *The Minneapolis Times.*
5. Quoted in Arthur John Gossip, *Experience Worketh Hope*, Scribner's, 1945, p. 62.
6. Alfred Stefferud (ed.), *The Wonderful World of Books*, Houghton-Mifflin, 1953, p. 217.
7. *The Christian Advocate*, Mar. 18, 1954, p. 9.
8. *The Christian Century*, Feb. 2, 1955, p. 133.

CHAPTER TWENTY-ONE. WHEN WE WONDER WHAT HAPPENS AFTER DEATH

1. Simone de Beauvoir, *All Men Are Mortal*, World, 1954. Review by Richard Sullivan, *Chicago Sunday Tribune*, Magazine of Books, Jan. 30, 1955, p. 3.
2. Harrison Brown, *The Challenge of Man's Future*, Viking, 1954, p. 3.
3. Martin Gardner, *In the Name of Science*, Putnam, 1952, p. 92.
4. William T. Hornaday, *The Mind and Manners of Wild Animals*, Scribner's, 1922.
5. From *The Manchester Guardian Weekly*, quoted in *Saturday Review*, Sept. 19, 1953, p. 9.
6. Waldemar Kaempffert, *Explorations in Science*, Viking, 1953, p 93.

CHAPTER TWENTY-TWO. IS THE BIBLE OUT OF DATE?

1. Bruce Bliven, *Preview for Tomorrow*, Knopf, 1953, pp. 78, 79.
2. Francis Carr Stifler, *Take Read*, American Bible Society, 1955, p. 3.
3. From a privately published article by J. Wallace Hamilton.
4. From an article by Bishop Hanns Lilje of Hanover, in *Life*, May 10, 1954.

HELPS IN READING THE BIBLE

WHERE TO FIND IT IN THE BIBLE

The account of Creation: Gen. 1–2:4a.
The account of the Flood: Gen. 6:5–9:19.
The Ten Commandments: Exod. 20:1–17; Deut. 5:1–21.
The Shepherd Psalm: Ps. 23.
The account of the birth of Jesus: Matt. 1:18–25, 2:1–12; Luke 2:1–20.
The account of the temptation of Jesus: Matt. 4:1–11; Mark 1:12, 13.
The Beatitudes: Luke 4:1–13; Matt. 5:3–12; Luke 6:20–23.
The Sermon on the Mount: Matt. 6:9–13; Luke 11:1–4.
The account of the last days of Jesus: Matt. 26:3–27:66; Mark 14:1–15:47; Luke 22:47–23:56; John 18:1–19:42.
The account of the Last Supper: Matt. 26:17–30; Mark 14:22–26; Luke 22:14–23.
The account of Gethsemane: Matt. 26:36–46; Mark 14:32–42; Luke 22:39–46.
The account of the Resurrection: Matt. 28:1–20; Mark 16:1–8; Luke 24:1–53; John 20:1–21:25.
The Magnificat: Luke 1:46–55.
The Benedictus: Luke 1:68–79.
The Nunc dimittis: Luke 2:29–32.
The Transfiguration: Mark 9:2–8; Luke 9:28–36.
The Great Commandments: Matt. 22:34–40.
The Great Commission: Matt. 28:16–20.
The Parable of the Good Samaritan: Luke 10.
The Parable of the Prodigal Son: Luke 15.
The Parable of the Sower: Matt. 13; Mark 4; Luke 8.
The Last Judgment: Matt. 25.
The outpouring of the Holy Spirit: Acts 2.
The Golden Rule: Matt. 7:12; Luke 6:31.

SOME FAVORITE CHAPTERS OF THE BIBLE

Five thousand members of the Chicago Bible Society selected these as the fifteen most-loved chapters of the Bible:

Isa. 55	Ps. 121	Ps. 91
Ps. 23	Matt. 5	I Cor. 13
Luke 2	Matt. 6	John 3
Luke 15	Matt. 7	John 14
Isa. 53	Rom. 8	John 17

The following chapters were runners-up in this poll:

Gen. 1	Ps. 27	Acts 2
Gen. 2	Ps. 103	Rom. 12
Gen. 3	Isa. 40	I Cor. 15
Exod. 20	Matt. 25	Heb. 11
Josh. 1	John 10	Heb. 12
Ps. 50	John 15	Rev. 21
Ps. 19		Rev. 22

SOME GREAT TEXTS OF THE OLD TESTAMENT

The Lord watch between me and thee, when we are absent one from another. GEN. 31:49.

I . . . am a jealous God, visiting the iniquity of the fathers upon the children unto the third and fourth generation. EXOD. 20:5.

And thou shalt love the Lord thy God with all thine heart, and with all thy soul, and with all thy might. DEUT. 6:5.

And if it seem evil unto you to serve the Lord, choose you this day whom ye will serve . . . but as for me and my house, we will serve the LORD. JOSH. 24:15.

Though he slay me, yet will I trust in him. JOB 13:15.

Blessed is the man that walketh not in the counsel of the ungodly, nor standeth in the way of sinners, nor sitteth in the seat of the scornful. PS. 1:1.

What is man, that thou art mindful of him? and the son of man, that thou visitest him? For thou hast made him a little lower than the angels, and hast crowned him with glory and honor. PS. 8:4, 5.

Let the words of my mouth, and the meditation of my heart, be acceptable in thy sight, O LORD, my strength, and my redeemer. PS. 19:14.

The Lord is my light and my salvation; whom shall I fear? the Lord is the strength of my life; of whom shall I be afraid? PS. 27:1.

Search me, O God, and know my heart: try me and know my thoughts: and see if there be any wicked way in me, and lead me in the way everlasting. PS. 139:23, 24.

The fear of the Lord is the beginning of knowledge. PROV. 1:7.

And he shall judge among the nations, and shall rebuke many people: and they shall beat their swords into plowshares, and their spears into pruning hooks: nation shall not lift up sword against nation, neither shall they learn war any more. ISA. 2:4.

They that wait upon the LORD shall renew their strength; they shall mount up with wings as eagles; they shall run, and not be weary; and they shall walk, and not faint. ISA. 40:31.

Seek ye the Lord while he may be found, call ye upon him while he is near: Let the wicked forsake his way, and the unrighteous man his thoughts: and let him return unto the LORD, and he will have mercy upon him; and to our God, for he will abundantly pardon. ISA. 55:6, 7.

The fathers have eaten a sour grape, and the children's teeth are set on edge. JER. 31:29.

For they have sown the wind, and they shall reap the whirlwind. HOS. 8:7.

Let judgment run down as waters, and righteousness as a mighty stream. AMOS 5:24.

He hath shewed thee, O man, what is good; and what doth the LORD require of thee, but to do justly, and to love mercy, and to walk humbly with thy God? MIC. 6:8.

SOME GREAT TEXTS OF THE NEW TESTAMENT

Blessed are the pure in heart for they shall see God. MATT. 5:8.

Let your light so shine before men, that they may see your good works, and glorify your Father which is in heaven. MATT. 5:16.

Seek ye first the kingdom of God, and his righteousness; and all these things shall be added unto you. MATT. 6:33.

Therefore all things whatsoever ye would that men should do to you, do ye even so to them. MATT. 7:12.

I say also unto thee, That thou art Peter, and upon this rock I will build my church; and the gates of hell shall not prevail against it. MATT. 16:18.

Whosoever will be great among you, let him be your minister. MATT. 20:26.

Thy faith hath made thee whole. MARK 5:34.

Whosoever will come after me, let him deny himself, and take up his cross, and follow me. MARK 8:34.

What therefore God hath joined together, let not man put asunder. MARK 10:9.

For God so loved the world, that he gave his only begotten Son, that whosoever believeth in him should not perish, but have everlasting life. JOHN 3:16.

Jesus said unto her, I am the resurrection, and the life: he that believeth in me, though he were dead, yet shall he live: And whosoever liveth and believeth in me shall never die. JOHN 11:25, 26.

Sirs, what must I do to be saved? And they said, Believe on the Lord Jesus Christ, and thou shalt be saved. ACTS 16:30b, 31.

Remember the words of the Lord Jesus, how he said, it is more blessed to give than to receive. ACTS 20:35.

We know that in everything God works for good with those who love him, who are called according to his purpose. ROM. 8:28 (RSV).

Now the God of hope fill you with all joy and peace in believing, that ye may abound in hope, through the power of the Holy Ghost. ROM. 15:13.

And now abideth these three, and the greatest of these is love. I COR. 13:13 (RSV).

Be not deceived; God is not mocked: for whatsoever a man soweth, that shall he also reap. GAL. 6:7.

In nothing be anxious; but in everything by prayer and supplication with thanksgiving let your requests be made known unto God. And the peace of God, which passeth all understanding, shall guide your hearts and your thoughts in Christ Jesus. PHIL. 4:6–7. (ARV.)

Whatsoever things are true . . . honest . . . just . . . pure . . . lovely . . . of good report . . . think on these things. PHIL. 4:8.

I have learned, in whatsoever state I am, therewith to be content. PHIL. 4:11.

Now faith is the substance of things hoped for, the evidence of things not seen. HEB. 11:1.

So that with good courage we say, The Lord is my helper; I will not fear: What shall man do unto me? HEB. 13:6 (ARV).

WHAT THE BIBLE SAYS ABOUT SOCIAL ISSUES

(Arranged by the American Bible Society)

Economic Justice

Exod. 5:1–9, 21:23–25, 22:25–27, 23:1–8; Lev. 19:1–15, 33–37; Deut. 8:1–10, 10:17–22, 15:7–18, 16:18–20, 24:14–22, 25:13–16; I Kings 21:1–14; Neh. 9:32–38; Ps. 72:1–20, 82:1–8, 104:24–28; Prov. 4:18, 11:1, 16:8–13; Isa. 11:1–5, 41: 1–7; Ezek. 45:9–12; Joel 2:26; Amos 5:6–24, 8:4–11; Matt. 5:23–26, 20:1–16, 25:1–13; Luke 6:38, 12:29–32; John 10:10; I Tim. 6:3–10; II Tim. 2:1–7.

Property

Exod. 20:17, 22:1–15; Lev. 19:9, 10, 20, 24:17–22, 25:23; Deut. 1:16, 17, 6:4–12, 19:14, 22:1–4; II Sam. 12:1–9; Ps. 15:1–5, 24:1; Isa. 5:8, 61:1–4; Jer. 23:5, 6; Mic. 6:1–8; Matt. 5:38–48, 7:1–5, 20; 26–28; Luke 12:13–15, 48; 16:19–31, 23:39–43; Acts 4:31–37, 11:27–30; I Cor. 4:1, 2; II Cor. 9:1–9; Phil. 4:8–19; Rev. 3:14–22.

Poverty

Gen. 1:9–13; Lev. 19:9–18, 25:35–37; Deut. 8:11–20, 24:12–21; Ps. 37:1–16, 41:1–13, 50:9–12; 62:8–12; Prov. 19:1–8, 17–22, 24–30–34, 30:7–9; Isa. 40:1–8; Hag. 2:4–8; Matt. 6:24–34, 7:7–14, 25:31–46; Mark 12:38–44, 14:3–9; Luke 11:9–13, 12:16–21, 14:25–35, 16:9–15; Acts 20:28–36; I Cor. 16:1–3; II Cor. 6:1–10, 8:1–9, 9:10–15, 16:1–3; Heb. 13:5, 6; James 2:2–26; I John 3:16–19; Rev. 7:13–17.

Labor

Gen. 1:26–31, 3:19, 14:1–13; Exod. 20:8–11; Neh. 4:6–21; Ps. 104:14–23; 128: 1–6; Prov. 4:5–8, 6:6–11, 10:1–16, 12:11–14, 14:23–35, 20:12, 13, 21:2–5, 10, 21, 27:23–27, Isa. 65:17–25; Mal. 3:7–12; Matt. 5:13–16, 9:36–38, 20:1–15, 25:1–13, 14–29; Luke 5:1–11, 10:1–9; John 4:31–38, 5:10–17, 6:27–29; Acts 6:1–6; Rom. 8:26–39, 12:9–21; I Cor. 3:7–23, 12:4–31, 15:58; Eph. 4:23–32; Col. 3:12–17; I Thess. 4:9–12; II Thess. 3:6–12; I Tim. 5:1–18, 6:1–8.

Personal Rights and Responsibility

Gen. 1:25–29, 18:23–33; Lev. 19:15–18; Deut. 6:4–7, 10:12–22, 22:1–4; II Sam. 12:1–10; I Kings 21:1–29; II Kings 6:8–23; Ps. 10:10–18, 62:1–12, 103:1–6; Prov. 1:29–33; Isa. 41:10–13; Lam. 3:22–36; Ezek. 3:4–11, 18:1–30; Matt. 5:43–48, 12:11, 12; Luke 10:25–37, 38–42, 13:6–9; John 8:28–32; Acts 4:5–21, 20:28–35; I Cor. 8:1–13; Eph. 2:13–22, 6:5–9; Phil. 2:3–13, 4:11–13; Col. 2:6–10, 3:8–15; I Thess. 3:11–13; I Tim. 6:17–21; II Tim. 2:15–19; Philem. 1–25; James 4:10–17; I John 3:11–18.

Protection and Security

Deut. 6:1–7, 8:5–20, 28; 1–14; II Sam. 22:29–37; I Kings 19:8–12; Ps. 1:1–3, 23:1–6, 46:1–11, 73:23–28, 91:1–16, 119:161–168, 121:1–8, 139:1–10; Prov. 3:5–26; Isa. 30:15–18, 41:10–13; Ezek. 34:11–16; Hag. 1:5–7; Matt. 6:24–34, 11:25–30; Luke 13:1–5; John 9:1–5, 14:23–31; Rom. 8:28–39; Eph. 6:10–20; II Tim. 2:14–26, 3:12–17.

Civic Duty

Ps. 24:1–6; Prov. 2:1–11; Isa. 55:1, 2, 58:6–12; Jer. 9:23, 24; Dan. 6:4–17; Matt. 4:1–11, 6:1–6, 19–34, 18:23–35, 19:16–30, 20:20–23; Mark 4:14–20, 8: 34–36, 10:23–27, 11:15–19, 17:24–27, 22:17–21; Luke 12:13–21, 14:7–14, 16: 19–31, 18:18–30; John 10:9–11; Acts 4:32–37, 20:32–35; Gal. 5:1–14, 6:7–10; Phil. 4:5–9; James 4:1–10; I John 2:15–17.

Politics and Government

Exod. 18:13–27, 20:2–17; Deut. 4:1–8; II Sam. 23:1–4; II Kings 22:1–20, 23:1–37; Job 34:12–28; Ps. 8:1–9, 33:10–22, 72:1–14, 111:1–10; Prov. 14:26–35; Ezek. 5:4–9; Isa. 2:2–5, 32:1–20; Dan. 5:18–28; Zech. 8:9–17; Matt. 6:10, 17:24–27, 22:35–40, 27:23–27; Mark 9:38–50; Luke 17:20–22; John 18:33–28, 19:8–12; Acts 5:29–32; Rom. 12:1–8, 13:1–10; I Cor. 12:4–14; Eph. 4:4–16; James 1:1–8; I Pet. 2:9–17; Rev. 11:15, 21:1–4.

Race and Brotherhood

Gen. 4:8–13, 9:1–7; Num. 15:1–16; Ps. 133:1; Matt. 5:14–16, 43–38, 8:5–13, 22:37–40; Mark 11:15–19; Luke 10:25–37, 15:1–10; John 3:1–17, 17:7–11; Acts 2:1–11, 7:22–33, 8:26–40, 10:1–35; Rom. 3:22–30, 10:5–13, 12:3–14, 13:7–14, 15:1–11; I Cor. 12:11–31, 13:1–13; Gal. 3:23–29, 5:13–26; Eph. 4:1–6, 23–32; Col. 3:1–15.

Nationalism

Gen. 11:1–9; Deut. 7:6–11; Ruth 1:1–18; Ps. 22:1–5, 22–31, 33:1–12; Isa. 5:20–30, 49:7–13; Mic. 4:1–3; Matt. 7:1–6, 15:21–28, 28:16–20; Luke 9:51–62, 13:22–30, 24:44–53; John 4:20–24; Acts 1:1–8, 14:15–17, 17:22–31; Rom. 1:18–32, 2:1–13; Phil. 3:17–21; Heb. 13:17; Rev. 7:9–12, 11:15.

Peace

Gen. 13:1–12; Exod. 18:13–23; Judg. 3:7–12; Ps. 46:8–11; Prov. 15–16–18, 17:1–14; Isa. 2:1–5, 9:6, 7, 11:6–9, 26:1–12; Jer. 6:9–14, 8:6–15; Ezek. 12:16; Hos. 2:18–20; Mic. 4:1–4; Zech. 8:18–23; Matt. 5:1–12, 10:21–36, 24:4–14; Luke 1:67–79, 2:8–14, 9:49–56, 22:47–51; Rom. 12:17–21, 13:1–4; Eph. 2:13–22, 6:10–16; I Thess. 5:11–15; I Tim. 6:11–17; II Tim. 2:1–4, 4:1–8; James 4:1–8; I Pet. 2:9–14, 3:8–14; Rev. 12:7–12, 19:11–18.

Family Relationships

Gen. 2:18–24; Deut. 5:6–21, 6:4–18; Josh. 23:14–22; Judg. 14:1–20, 16:1–20; Ruth 2:1–13; Ps. 78:1–8; Prov. 3:11, 12, 22:1–6, 31:10–31; Song of Sol. 2:1–17; Zech. 8:1–5; Matt. 5:27–32, 12:46–50, 18:1–11, 20, 19:3–15, 22:23–33; Mark 10:1–12; Luke 2:41–52, 10:38–42, 14:25–35, 15:11–32; Acts 16:25–34; I Cor. 6:12–20, 7:24–40, 11:1–12; II Cor. 6:14–18, 12:9–21; Gal. 6:1–18; Eph. 5:18–33, 6:1–4; Col. 3:18–21; I Tim. 5:1–16; Titus 2:1–8.

BIBLIOGRAPHY FOR FURTHER STUDY

ANDERSON, BERNHARD W., *Rediscovering the Bible*, Association Press, 1951.

BLAIR, EDWARD P., *The Bible and You*, Abingdon-Cokesbury, 1953.

BLAIR, EDWARD P., *Getting to Know the Bible*, Abingdon, 1956.

BOWIE, WALTER RUSSELL, *The Bible*, Association Press, 1940.

BUTTRICK, GEORGE A. (ed.), *The Interpreter's Bible*, Abingdon, 1951–57.

BROWN, CHARLES REYNOLDS, *Ten Short Stories from the Bible*, Century, 1925.

BURROWS, MILLAR, *Bible Religion*, Abingdon-Cokesbury, 1938.

CHASE, MARY ELLEN, *The Bible and the Common Reader*, Macmillan, 1952.

FOSDICK, HARRY EMERSON, *A Guide to Understanding the Bible*, Harper, 1938.

GOODSPEED, EDGAR J., *How to Read the Bible*, John C. Winston, 1946.

HARKNESS, GEORGIA, *Toward Understanding the Bible*, Abingdon, 1952.

KITTEL, GERHARD, *Bible Key Words*, Harper, 1951.

KLEMME, HUBER F., *The Bible and Our Common Life*, The Christian Education Press, 1953.

KOPPLIN, DOROTHEA S., *Scripture to Live By*, Hanover House, 1955.

LOVE, JULIAN PRICE, *How to Read the Bible*, Macmillan, 1951.

LYNIP, RYLLIS GOSLIN, *Great Ideas of the Bible*, Vols. I and II, Harper, 1954–55.

MILLER, M. S. and J. L., *Harper's Bible Dictionary*, Harper, 1952.

PATTERSON, JOHN, *The Book That is Alive*, Scribner's, 1954.

POLING and THOMAS (eds.), *The Glory and Wonder of the Bible*, Crowell, 1954.

SMITH, ROY L., *New Light from Old Lamps*, Abingdon-Cokesbury, 1953.

SWAIM, J. CARTER, *Understanding the Bible*, Westminster, 1954.

SWAIM, J. CARTER, *Right and Wrong Ways to Use the Bible*, Westminster, 1953.

WALKER, E. JERRY, *Five Minute Stories from the Bible*, Abingdon-Cokesbury, 1948.

WILLIAMS, ALBERT N., *The Book By My Side*, Duell, Sloan & Pearce, 1951.

WILLIAMS, ALBERT N., *Key Words of the Bible*, Duell, Sloan & Pearce.

WISE, CARROLL A., *Psychiatry and the Bible*, Harper, 1956.

[illegible] Word [illegible] Association Press, [illegible]

[illegible]
[illegible] Getting to Know the Bible, Westminster [illegible]
[illegible]
[illegible] The [illegible]

[illegible] Indian from [illegible]

[illegible]
[illegible] Book of [illegible]

[illegible] A Guide to Understanding the Bible [illegible]

[illegible] How to Read the Bible [illegible]
[illegible] the Bible [illegible]
[illegible] Harper, 1951 [illegible]
[illegible] Life [illegible]
[illegible]
[illegible] Hanover House, 195[illegible]
[illegible] How to Read the Bible, Macmillan, 1951
[illegible] Great Ideas of the Bible, Vols. I and II, Harper, [illegible]

Miller, M. S. and J. L., Harper's Bible Dictionary, Harper, 1952
[illegible] The Book that is Alive, [illegible]
[illegible]

[illegible] Abingdon-Cokesbury, 195[illegible]
[illegible] Understanding the Bible, Westminster [illegible]
[illegible] Use the Bible, [illegible]

[illegible] Stories from the Bible, Macmillan, [illegible]
[illegible] The Bible [illegible] Duell, Sloan & Pearce, [illegible]

[illegible] of the Bible, Duell, Sloan & Pearce, [illegible]
[illegible] and the Bible, Harper, 195[illegible]